EMBODYING GRACE

*Proclaiming Justification
in the Real World*

Andrea Bieler and Hans-Martin Gutmann

Linda M. Maloney, Translator

Fortress Press
Minneapolis

Cover image: Thomas D. McAvoy
Cover design: Laurie Ingram
Book design: PerfecType, Nashville, Tenn.

Library of Congress Cataloging-in-Publication Data
Bieler, Andrea, 1963-
[Rechtfertigung der "Überflüssigen." English]
Embodying grace : proclaiming justification in the real world / by Andrea Bieler and Hans-Martin Gutmann ; translated by Linda M. Maloney.
p. cm.
Includes bibliographical references (p. 203) and index.
ISBN 978-0-8006-6346-9 (alk. paper)
1. Justification (Christian theology) 2. Poverty—Religious aspects—Christianity. 3. Preaching.
4. Justification (Christian theology)—Sermons. 5. Poverty—Religious aspects—Christianity—Sermons. 6. Sermons, German—Translations into English. I. Gutmann, Hans-Martin. II. Title.
BT764.3B5413 2010
234'.7086'942—dc22
                              2009048547

EMBODYING GRACE

CONTENTS

PREFACE TO THE
AMERICAN EDITION

SINCE THE GERMAN EDITION of this book came out in 2007, a global economic crisis has erupted, with tremendous impact on local economies around the world. In the wake of crashing financial markets, tumultuous stock prices, and faltering banks, numerous people in the United States lost their jobs, had their homes foreclosed on, and saw their retirement funds shrink. Both the U.S. automobile industry and huge investment banks received bailout money from the federal government. Other economic sectors as well as private households benefited from various stimulus packages designed to stabilize the situation. For a while, it seemed that the civil religious belief in the omnipotence of the market as divine force which reigns over our lives was stumbling. In the wake of these events, some have challenged the religion the market produces, such as a belief in limitless economic growth and the accumulation of capital as a source of life that provides future and security.

Our book seeks to highlight the question of what it means to witness to divine grace poured out abundantly into the world amid economic situations in which many people are made superfluous in relation to the market and in their access to economic and social resources. What does it mean to preach justification in an unjust world in which the labor, creativity, and social contribution of so many are considered to be expendable? While we focus in this volume on the development of a homiletic that takes these questions seriously, we are certainly aware that the issues touched upon here have an impact on many more arenas of religious life.

We wish to express our gratitude to Linda Maloney, who provided a splendid translation of this volume. We are also indebted to Wade Mayer and Jessica Oya, who did a careful reading of this text, and to David Kangas, who helped with the translation. Our special thanks go to Michael West and Neil Elliott, who made the publication with Fortress Press possible, and to our editors, David Lott and Sheila Anderson, who tremendously enhanced the final version of the manuscript.

PREFACE TO THE GERMAN EDITION

SOMETIMES THE ART OF preaching reveals surprising and disturbing connections by which the lived experiences of faith, the socioeconomic conditions with which we are struggling, and the narrative thread of Scripture are so interwoven that divine grace can unfold and finds an embodied expression. Our work is indebted to this art of preaching.

As teachers of practical theology at the University of Hamburg and the Pacific School of Religion in Berkeley, California, we frame our aesthetic, phenomenological, and theological questions in individual, existential, and social terms. We seek ways to ask our questions while facing urgent social conflicts. Accordingly, we have been tracing the correspondences between economic processes and bodily experiences, liturgical resonances and unemployment, the prophet Jonah and the embodiment of grace in the preaching on the justification of the "expendables." The complex theme of economic injustice is a prime topic for us. Therefore, we locate the homiletical reflections that follow on the margins of the market society.

We are grateful to a variety of people and institutions who have contributed to the flourishing of this project: the Pacific School of Religion granted Andrea Bieler a sabbatical that enabled her to work on the manuscript with Hans-Martin Gutmann in Germany. Both colleagues and students in the department of Evangelische Theologie at the University of Hamburg have, despite constant buffets of "university reform" and the "Bologna process," maintained an atmosphere of common and mutual effort within which Hans-Martin Gutmann has been able to continue his creative work.

We thank Pastor Ossai Okeke and his wife, Christina Okeke, Pastor Glenda Hope, and Father River Sims, as well as Professor Hans van der Geest, who have made available to us their previously unpublished reflections, sermons, and liturgical texts. With the chosen examples, we strive for a more global perspective as an attempt to broaden and productively challenge our own homiletical reflections, owing to the particular character of our theme.

We are grateful to the Gütersloher Verlag for accepting this volume into its publishing program. Diedrich Steen has aided us, once again, in outstanding fashion. We are also grateful to Tanja Scheifele, who coordinated our communications and a great deal more. Our heartfelt thanks go also to Frau Sharma, who gave us excellent assistance in the production of the manuscript, and to Till Karnstädt for making the index.

Rudolf Bohren introduced his instruction on preaching in 1971 with an ecstatic shout: "There are four things in which I take passionate pleasure: Watercolor painting, cross-country skiing, felling trees, and preaching."[1] In our case, other passions would take their places in this list, but preaching would be just as present there, along with writing a book together about preaching. There is almost nothing that has given us so much pleasure in the months past. Writing a book together as an act of deeper listening, batting ideas and texts back and forth until we almost come to an agreement (and sometimes also being astonished, disturbed, and again and again excited at the other's ideas), provided us joy in the midst of labor.

1
EMBODYING GRACE
Preaching Justification in the Context
of Economic Injustice

In the Beginning: A Multitude of Voices

"The only thing in that service that felt real to me was the alcohol fumes from the person next to me," a friend of mine snorted harshly after going to church in a small town in North Hesse. "I don't know what the pastor's sermon was supposed to say to my everyday life. Since I've been unemployed I have a hard time listening to this abstract talk about God's love being for all of us. When I look around me and think about what is happening in the lives of the people near me in the pews, I ask myself whether what goes on in church really has anything to do with our daily lives."

✺

"I just can't stand it any more, to have to swallow all the grim statistics about the rise in unemployment around here during worship too," sighs a pastor from West Oakland, California. "And I don't want to go on telling, in every sermon, all the oppressive stories about what the people in my congregation are living every day. To me, that would be like doubling our sad daily experiences. I spend the whole week seeing how people deal with the injustice of long-term unemployment, the everyday disasters that happen when a paying job is no longer at the center of life to give it meaning, when the money is so tight that the single mother who lives next door to my rectory knows that the household budget will be used up by the twenty-fifth of every month. It seems to me that worship should be a disruption of daily life; the liturgy should let God's beauty shine out; the *good* news should be palpable. Especially for these people who see so much grayness around them, the worship service should give a foretaste of the heavenly banquet through the shared meal, the music, the light breaking through the church windows and shining in, but also in silence and the echo of the ancient words of Sacred Scripture in sacred space."

∽✥⁀

The theology student leaves the university worship service depressed. Her head is pounding. A gnawing headache is spreading from her right temple. Everything in her is slowly cramping up; she feels crippled. Today the professor preached again about the good news of the justification of the ungodly, that God's grace comes to us as a free gift that we have not earned and yet receive, a gift that shakes our existence from its base and bathes it in a new light. The professor took a while to get to that point in his sermon. He had spoken at length about the desire for self-redemption, the human temptation to shape a good and righteous life through one's own strength, to get involved on behalf of a better world and to encounter God in the process. He talked about godless works-righteousness, human unworthiness, and our inability to contribute anything to our own salvation.

She thinks back to the time when she was anorexic and almost starved herself to death. The words *unworthy* and *incompetent* were always present to her in a big way in those years. And she really did strive then for something like self-redemption. She tried for years to free herself from the voices in her body that told her she was unworthy, shapeless, incompetent. She had always known that she was unworthy to live her life. So what was the liberating message? What did talk about justification and grace mean in her life?

∽✥⁀

The philosopher Christoph Türcke, in his book *Kassensturz* (*Cashing Up*), decries the perverted form of a theology of grace that claims a right to work and suppresses the fact that the destruction of jobs is a component of the processes that promote capitalist "efficiency":

> The capitalist labor society has produced a remarkable reversal. The curse of labor has become a blessing; release from labor has become a curse, and the mechanism that produces this confusion—and yet in it so clearly and implacably blesses and curses like a Calvinist God—is not merely a product of the mind, but a constructed reality that everyone can feel. In its godlikeness and in its power to confuse and obscure

it combines the two central features that theology used to assign to God's opponent. The result is the astonishing fact that the Devil, who existed only as a concept during the era of Christian enlightenment, has been incarnated in an original fashion in the post-Christian era. And just when that is happening, the official representatives of theology say more and more frequently that, enlightened as we are today, we should no longer believe in the Devil. The latest utterances of the churches with regard to work and unemployment are likewise written in the spirit of this new unbelief. The Devil does not appear in them— but the right to work does. Whoever demands that has already been taken in by the diabolical aura that surrounds work in capitalist conditions. It is acknowledged as a blessing, as grace—and is supposed, at the same time, to be a right, whereas it is one of the basic tenets of theology that everyone has a claim to a right, while no one has a claim to grace. Capital, which never stops buying or dropping wage labor according to its own abilities and needs, therefore has to feed the human rights advocates some special education and make it clear to them that grace can never be a right, but is always accompanied by rejection: unemployment is not an industrial accident; it is part of the ongoing cost of doing business. There can be no crisis or added efficiency without firing people, and no capitalist process without crisis and increased efficiency.

All the powerful know that, just as do the church dignitaries. So when the latter urge solidarity between workers and the unemployed and proclaim the equal value of both, what they are promoting is not solidarity, but readiness to accept economic rejection as an alternative grace and so to free oneself from the terrible circumstance of having to grapple with one's fate. The God who we hope accepts us all, with or without work, is supposed to be the God of the Bible, but he looks a damned lot like the power that actually hands out and refuses work. He apparently doesn't rightly remember the curse he once laid on labor; instead, it is his gracious gift. And he has no idea of a *vita contemplativa* as a sign of something beyond work, something that can be realized in the present; that all belongs to the church's ancient past. . . . It is not the abandonment of the idea of the Devil that is enlightened, but the intellectual analysis of the diabolical character that society as a whole has accepted.[1]

The Mexican theologian Elsa Tamez reflects, in her book *The Amnesty of Grace*, on the doctrine of justification by faith from the perspective of those excluded from society and questions its action-oriented dimension:

> Condemnation to physical death by hunger and the experience of "insignificance" were two urgent dimensions of the experience of excluded or marginalized people that moved me to examine the doctrine from its very roots. The first entails condemnation to death due to the nature of exclusion in the economic system currently in force, and the second results from not being accorded one's dignity as a human person.
>
> The study of justification by faith from this perspective led me to take on that doctrine as a concrete affirmation of the life of all human beings. The revelation of the justice of God and its realization in justification proclaim and bring about the good news of the right to life for all people. The life granted in justification is recognized as an inalienable gift, because it proceeds from the solidarity of God, in Jesus Christ, with those who are excluded. Such a life of dignity makes human beings subjects of their own history. God "justifies" (makes and declares just) the human being in order to transform the unjust world that excludes, kills, and dehumanizes that same human being.[2]

With these dissonant voices in our ears: the harsh question of the church-goer in a little town in North Hesse; the longing of the West Oakland pastor for God's beauty and a worship service that interrupts daily routine; the memories of the anorexic theology student who gets a headache from listening to the professor's sermon on justification, and in whom the feeling that her body is unworthy is very much alive; the philosopher's sharp polemic as he traces the cynicism implicit in a theology of grace produced by a capitalist economy; and Elsa Tamez's question about what the justification by faith means for the excluded—with all these voices in our ears—we begin this book.

Justification: An Elementary Reflection in Homiletical Perspective

These voices lead us to search for traces of a homiletic in which our ponderings about divine justice[3] as it is expressed in a theology of justification may be expressed in preaching that is attentive to people who, in the course of economic processes, have been made redundant or expendable. The notion of the "expendable" may well be provocative, but we introduce it here in order to point to the harshness of economic processes, intended to produce efficiency, that "downsize" or "right size" people, as is euphemistically said. There is no place for them in the world of labor anymore; they have been made superfluous, expendable—or else they *appear* to be expendable, for instance, in the case of Mexican immigrants in the United States who apply their labor to necessary work in agriculture and service jobs, but as so-called illegal aliens are dismissed in many political debates as superfluous labor that is "flooding" the land. The concept, however, corresponds also to theological language about superfluity: the abundance of the overflowing grace of God. The connection between these two realities may be sensed in what follows. Central to our project is the question of how the embodiment of grace in preaching justification can take on a living and life-giving form in our sermons and liturgies in times of rising poverty and structural unemployment, and in view of the experiences of the "working poor." We will be asking about the life contexts of preaching justification, which from the perspective of Lutheran theology are pivotal for a theology and practice of preaching.

Our homiletic is body oriented: we want to develop a perspective in which our talk about God's justice is located within the complex personal embodied experiences of people who have been made expendable. *Body orientation* refers to social and economic conditions that affect the well-being of human bodies. It is also about a reflection on the morphology of the divine Word that is not just a disembodied idea but which reaches us in the flesh and which has physical manifestations itself in preaching and worship. A body-oriented homiletic is last but not least interested in the performative dimension of preaching in which justification happens and grace is embodied.[4]

We will begin with some considerations that reduce matters to an elementary level, in the interest of homiletics. For Martin Luther, the great awe-inspiring discovery of God's justice was anything but a merely intellectual insight into a newly-to-be-interpreted *theologoumenon*; it was a deeply shattering experience that resulted in a radical change in his life and even his physical, embodied sense of self. He describes this radical change as a transformational experience—from fear to joy, from slavery to freedom, from despair to assurance, from hatred to praise. Within the broader homiletic context, we will introduce the preaching of justification as performative, reality-creating speech in which the gift of grace is embodied. In this, it is helpful to understand how intensively Luther connected his process of theological discovery with particular emotional states. Looking back at his theological breakthrough, Luther notes that he had learned to hate the central idea of God's justice in Romans 1:17. He had become acquainted with it as a philosophical concept in the Aristotelian sense. In the fifth book of his *Nicomachean Ethics,* Aristotle develops the idea that God's justice was demonstrated by the fact that God punishes sinners and the unrighteous. This notion shaped Luther's mentality as well: he lived with a restless, confused, and tormented conscience.[5] As a sinner, he could never trust that he could be reconciled to God through his own actions. This uneasiness was accompanied by sullenness, a resistance with which he bit into the theodicy question: As a result of original sin, were not all people condemned sinners forever? And if so, how could God bring people to judgment? With "burning hot thirst," he tried to understand what Paul was trying to say in Romans 1:17:

> I meditated night and day on those words until at last, by the mercy of God, I paid attention to their context: "The justice of God is revealed in it, as it is written: 'The just person lives by faith.'" I began to understand that in this verse the justice of God is that by which the just person lives by a gift of God, that is by faith. I began to understand that this verse means that the justice of God is revealed through the Gospel, but it is a passive justice, i.e. that by which the merciful God justifies us by faith, as it is written: "The just person lives by faith." All at once I felt that I had been born again and entered into paradise itself through open gates. Immediately I saw the whole of Scripture in a different light. I ran through the Scriptures from memory and found that other terms had analogous meanings, e.g., the work of God, that is, what God works in us; the power of God, by which he makes us powerful; the wisdom of God, by which he makes us wise; the strength of God, the salvation of God, the glory of God.
>
> I exalted this sweetest word of mine, "the justice of God," with as much love as before I had hated it with hate. This phrase of Paul was for me the very gate of paradise.[6]

Central to Luther's understanding is access to God's *passive* justice, through which, as he says, the merciful God *makes* us righteous through faith. The concept of passive justice is thus applied both to God and to human beings: it describes God's action and also its effects in the human being. Wilfried Härle summarizes his discussion of the passage from Luther just quoted: "Luther understands God's righteousness both as God's action *through* which he makes the human being whole and as that *which* God thereby effects for and in the human being."[7] As applied to God, the concept of divine justice points to God's mercy; as applied to the human being, it refers to faith. Härle argues that Luther can use "righteousness" in the twofold fashion just described because he is interpreting it in terms of the Old Testament concept of *ṣĕdāqâ*, which is best translated as "fidelity in community" or "acting in light of community," or as "a behavior that serves the community context of life": *"Luther's Reformation discovery consists in the recognition that 'God's justice is fidelity to the community through which God makes people righteous, and thus faithful to community, by evoking faith in them.* It follows that God's action that evokes faith (that is, creates human 'righteousness') is done through Jesus Christ. Therefore and to that extent human justification is produced by God *sola gratia, sola fide, solo Christo."[8]* *Ṣĕdāqâ*, or in Greek *dikaiosynē*, therefore refers to a sense of relationality that encompasses a dynamic process—and thus is more than a sporadic moment. It is about a comprehensive understanding of a just order brought about by God that has universal significance. To cite Härle again: "This just order is inclusive in relation to God and in relationships among creatures, in social and cosmic dimensions, throughout the length of history as well as in a contemporary cross-section."[9]

Sadly, our ordinary use of the word *justification* lacks the breadth and depth Härle sketches. Nowadays "to justify oneself" normally means producing evidence of being right in a contested situation[10]—which, of course, is diametrically opposite to the understanding of righteousness or justification just described. When, in what follows, we use the word *justification*, the connotations that envelop the concept of *ṣĕdāqâ* should always be kept in mind. Accordingly, notions like fidelity to the community should likewise be in view.

The ordinary usage also has echoes of the *forensic* interpretation of the doctrine of justification. Justifying, in the sense of recognizing that someone is in the right, points first to the arena of social negotiations and thus also to the fact that the formation of subjectivity happens in interactive processes: how we see ourselves has to do with the degree to which we receive social recognition by others. In addition, ordinary usage points to the legal sphere, where claims to rights over disputed objects as well as punishable offenses by individuals are dealt with.[11]

Forensic usage plays an important part in the history of interpretation of the doctrine of justification, portraying the sinful, and altogether unrighteous, human being as one accused, standing before the divine judge, who declares her or him righteous solely by grace for the sake of Christ.[12]

Although the Reformation discovery of *passive* justice turned all the rules of an orderly judicial process upside down, the Reformers repeatedly used forensic metaphors. This paradox, as regards Luther, may be situated in his own life story, in his profound struggle with the image of the heavenly divine judge, which hounded him and gave him no rest. But for a broader interpretation of God's justice as divine fidelity to community, it seems too restrictive to use forensic metaphors in an exclusive fashion. In his work on the pragmatic linguistic problems of preaching justification, Frank M. Lütze argues along these lines when he stresses that forensic categories are only marginally able to address the relational character of the event of justification.[13] The image of the judge inadequately describes how God utterly spends and surrenders God's self in this event, altogether unlike an impartial judge who must embody disinterestedness. In addition, forensic metaphors scarcely touch the creative quality of the process of justification:

> An acquittal, in the first place, creates a legal fact and need not touch the person acquitted at the heart or change him or her. In contrast, it is of the essence of love to regard the other as a person, and to address him or her in a creative way: "God's love does not discover what is lovable, but creates it. For sinners are beautiful because they are loved; they are not loved because they are beautiful."[14]

Beyond this, Lütze points out that the process of justification is precisely *not* about individual trespasses but about a fundamental falling short, on the human side, of the relationship to God: "The broken relationship to God does not *need—horribile dictu!*—to be punished, because it already carries its punishment with it."[15]

The image of acquittal is not especially helpful as we try to appreciate the healing renewal of the relationship between God and the human in the Christ-event as it happens in the event of justification. After the close of a judicial process, the judge normally evinces no interest in the renewal and deepening of a relationship with the one previously accused. In light of the embodiment of grace through God's righteousness, however, what happens here is just that: the creation of genuine relationship.

These critical considerations on the exclusive usage of forensic metaphors for the event of justification bring us to the further conclusion that it is centrally important both for theological reflection and for preaching to introduce a broad spectrum of metaphors to describe God's saving action. In Luther's account of his Reformation discovery, previously quoted, he himself makes clear, with reference to 1 Corinthians 1:30, that there are many concepts and images that are appropriate for getting closer to the idea of God's saving action. These include, for example, wisdom, justice, healing, power, strength, salvation, and the glory of God.[16]

Thus, an exegetical insight was determinative for Luther's understanding of justification: namely, that God's justice, which according to Paul was revealed in the gospel (Rom. 1:17), does not refer to right action by human beings in the sense of behavior in accordance with the law but a justice that is given by God to the sinner, undeserved and without any human precondition.

But was this not what the teachings of the high scholasticism of the Middle Ages had already said, in their own way, according to which God gives justifying grace to the human being in the sense of a *habitus,* an enduring shaping of the person? Luther's understanding, in fact, is essentially different from what was presented, for example, by Thomas Aquinas. Luther does not understand justification as a process of healing which, although it emanates entirely from divine grace, brings the result that a human being who has been made righteous can also be factually declared righteous at the final judgment. Luther, rather, understands the grace of justification as God's gift that anticipates any change in the life of the sinful human being as in fact a justice which is attributed to him or her in a paradoxical contrast to her or his own reality. God does not call righteous the human being who has been made righteous through divine grace, but instead, and truly, the "ungodly" (Rom. 4:5). The human being, who in and of him- or herself is and remains a sinner, becomes justified because God imputes justice to her or him (*simul iustus et peccator*). The subject of this gift of divine justice is Jesus Christ. That justice is imputed to the sinful human being includes the fact that God unites her or him with Christ, that Christ takes human sin on himself and applies his own justice on the human being's behalf. Justification is the affirmation of the righteousness that belongs to Christ and with which Christ encourages the sinner. Therefore, for Luther the word of the gospel preached, through which the human being experiences this comfort, is the real bearer of the gift of salvation; it is the true sacrament. It occurs in the medium of the word preached, in the embodiment of grace; it is here that God justifies the human being.[17]

Corresponding to this word is the faith in which the human being—*without* weighing up all that he or she can say and judge about his or her own life, without condition—relies on this promise, just as it is unconditionally given to her or him. Faith is not at all about working up a psychic orientation; faith means that the human being as an entire person, as body, mind, and spirit, consents to receive the gift and so is renewed.

This does not mean that Luther would understand the sinner's being proclaimed righteous as a mere relabeling, a simple judgment "as if," leaving the human being unchanged from what he or she is. Rather, he sees the word that declares one righteous as the powerful word of the Creator and Redeemer, who brings about what it promises. Just as God declares someone righteous, so will God make that justice a reality. Therefore, sin, which in God's judgment had already lost its potency to control the human being, is a power that will also be overcome in its reality.

This event is already beginning, so surely is Christ effectively present in faith through his Spirit. Although sin is still present, its rule over the human being has been broken; here the Spirit is countering the power of sin and bringing about the beginning of new life. Therefore, also faith, which in regard to one's own salvation is purely passive—that is, it can be nothing more than receptivity—is in no way passive toward one's neighbor in the world. Faith means entering into the realm of Christ's living power. Therefore, works of love proceed spontaneously from faith. Luther can say that true faith cannot exist at all without such an orientation of love in the praxis of life.

The difference between this fundamental Protestant insight of Martin Luther and the scholastic doctrine of grace is not that scholasticism understood justifying grace as making one "effectively" righteous while Luther understands it as only a "forensic" declaration of justice. Rather, Luther speaks emphatically of the effectiveness of Christ's grace in the life and actions of believers. However, he forcefully opposes addressing this new life as a possession, a *habitus* that becomes a characteristic, a quality of the human person. Instead, Luther insists that justice, even as God's gift, cannot become a human possession; it is, namely, the *aliena iustitia Christi*. Christ remains the subject of this justice through which the human being is proclaimed righteous and becomes a new person.

God's justice streams forth in overflowing grace. God's grace and the justification of the "expendables" belong together in different ways: grace is excess, free and unlimited divine gift. God's grace is incalculable, immeasurable, *per definitionem* beyond human measure and calculation; it explodes all plans, ideas, and reflective abilities. God's grace is a gift belonging to the whole person—and therefore we seek a link to the bodily perspective, because this gift is given not simply to the knowledge or self-reflection of the individual in the sense of cognitive operations, but to the whole person as body, spirit and flesh.

And the second dimension: God's grace belongs to the people who in terms of the market are seen as "expendables" because, according to the Gospels, the good news belongs to all people, and to the poor first of all. In the globalized economy, the poor are that group of people whose numbers are exploding and who, living in insecure working conditions and receiving very little remuneration for their work, do not have enough on which to live; they are the "working poor." These are people who, because they have migrated from one place to another, are shut out from the "normal" opportunities for employment, education, and training; but they also belong to the growing social groups who are repeatedly told, explicitly or implicitly, that they are as insignificant in the "first" labor market as they are among consumers able to pay—insignificant as people who participate in cultural and political lives as subjects, and not only as the objects and trafficked products of their own lives.

Elsa Tamez also argues that the doctrine of and preaching on justification must be made tangible in terms of the experiences of poor people, and not simply spoken of in the abstract:

> Human beings have a face, a social location, color, and sex, and justification intersects that specific social and cultural reality.
>
> Today we are not able to continue engaging in a universal discourse, without taking into account the particularity from which it is pronounced. By not touching on the realities of life of the distinct subjects who live in history, any discourse loses its force. In the present, however, there is no visible human reality that manifests the power of the gospel of which Paul was speaking and was not ashamed (Rom 1:16).[18]

Poverty has many faces. Before we listen to some voices who speak out of their own experience, we seek to sketch out of some structural aspects. However, first we must speak of our own social location: an important aspect of situating the extreme polarization of poverty and wealth in Germany and the United States is that we cannot speak adequately about all these things without taking account of our own situation. As teachers, we belong to the middle class in our countries; we have multiple means at our disposal in contrast to a family on welfare, and considerably more than any normal working-class family. We speak in this book as practical theologians, who reflect on the task and the form of preaching and worship under the conditions described. And we speak as pastors who, in Germany and in the United States, are attempting to sharpen our sensibilities to the phenomena of economic injustice.

"Expendable" People: Contexts of Poverty and Unemployment

Who Are the "Expendables"?

The Organization for Economic Co-operation and Development (OECD) reflects in its annual report for 2009 on social cohesion and unemployment in light of the current economic crisis:

> Many countries registered significant job losses, and many more jobs are expected to be lost globally in 2009 as the impact of the financial crisis continues to affect the real economy. Some groups in the labour market, particularly youth, immigrants, low-skilled and older workers, and those on temporary contracts, are likely to bear the brunt of rapidly rising unemployment.[19]

This global development, which hits especially the just-mentioned groups, is certainly true for the United States as well. What needs to be added is the racial divide within the United States that complicates the picture. It is embedded in an economic development that shows a dramatic deepening of the economic gap between the rich and the poor within the United States over the course of the last ten years. The 2009 OECD document, "Growing Unequal?" reports that of its thirty member states, most of which are members of the European Union, the United States has the largest gap between its wealthiest and poorest households after Mexico and Turkey.[20] That gap has grown particularly large in the United States since 2000—that is, under the administration of President George W. Bush—according to the report, which found that the gap between the U.S. middle class and the wealthiest 10 percent has also increased. The American Dream, which cherishes social mobility, is thus just an illusion that cannot be proven by the economic trends. The OECD report, rather, states that countries like the United States who live on highest standards of economic inequality do very poorly in terms of social mobility. This means that the dishwasher is likely to remain a dishwasher while the son of a millionaire does not have to be too much concerned about his future wealth.

Although the rich-poor divide is not as drastic in Germany, we see similar trends developing. Indeed, the data speak for themselves. What is most obvious is the development in the net monthly income of private households. Between 1993 and 2004, the net worth of the richest quartile of the population in West Germany has increased by nearly 28 percent. In the poorest quartile, during the same period, there was a dramatic 50 percent decrease. In East Germany, the income of the richest quartile increased by nearly 86 percent, although remaining on a lower level than in the West, while the income of the poorest quartile decreased by nearly 21 percent. The current data reported by the federal statistical office confirm that this trend is highly stable.[21]

The extreme polarization of poor and rich in the society of the Federal Republic of Germany has become more radical since 2002. While in the early period of the red-green governing coalition, in view of unemployment and the provision of welfare, the statistics showed a slight decrease, since 2002 the numbers have risen drastically. Since 2000, the number of those receiving welfare has risen from 2.68 million to 2.8 million. At the same time, wealth has radically increased:

> "To them that have, more will be given." And in abundance. In the last ten years increased monetary wealth has accrued above all to those who already had a great deal, and the inequality of division has clearly increased.... A better method (than measuring average individual earnings) for describing developments in distribution remains a comparison of household incomes. It appears that 2002 was a turning point. Until 2001 the share of the poorest fifth of the population in overall income lay slightly below 10 percent; in 2002 that share sank to 9.3 percent. At the same time the share of total income of the wealthiest fifth attained a high of 36.4 percent.[22]

And within this group, a greater and greater share of wealth and income fell to fewer and fewer households. The rigid reform of unemployment and welfare regulations in Germany, known as the Hartz IV concept, radically heightened the situation. For example, they compel a fifty-year-old middle-class worker who has been employed all his or her life and paid into unemployment insurance to leave his or her rented apartment if it is larger than fifty square meters for a single-person household or over sixty square meters for two persons. She or he is required to sell any privately owned family dwelling over 130 square meters, to liquidate any property accumulated through savings, to sign a deed of gift and submit to dependence on so-called case managers (whose fairness and competence are neither guaranteed nor subject to supervision)—in order to receive the prescribed periodic sum of 345 Euros (in West Germany) or 331 Euros (in East Germany)—all this in the face of a labor market in which, in 2004, a few hundred thousand jobs were available for over four million unemployed persons.[23] In 2007—as a result of the effects of a long-awaited upturn in some sectors of the economy—the numbers of unemployed have shrunk slightly. At the same time, the sharp and unresolvable debates about a minimum income and the raising of the allotments under the Hartz IV rules show that the problem of poverty in Germany has lost none of its explosiveness in light of the improvement in the economy; instead, the public is more acutely aware that the fruits of the upturn have been unequally shared.

In 2007, the German economy grew by 2.7 percent, but scarcely any of that landed in the pockets of the workers. Instead, nominal increases in wages lay below the rate of inflation. In the midst of the boom, these people lost in terms of real income. "This has never happened before in Germany and it was not anticipated by neo-liberal theory."[24] The decrease in unemployment, which in the short term, in an expanding economy, has consistently remained below four million, is primarily due to a growth in minimum-wage jobs. Therefore the problem of the "working poor" has become one of the faces of poverty, even in Germany, shaping the lives of larger and larger groups of people—and at the same time, the other side of that face is the visible reality of child poverty. "The sum total is depressing: Even a single mother who waits on tables, earning a gross wage of 7.5€ [Euros] an hour and working full time, cannot manage to escape from Hartz IV if she has two children. She earns too little not to have to apply for supplemental stage-two unemployment payments. Her little ones fall under the statistics of 'child poverty.'"[25] Whole job groups are among the lowest earners, and in them whole families, adults and children alike, are living in poverty: florists, hairdressers, agricultural workers. The president of the Association for the Protection of Children, Heinz Hillgers, reports that, in Germany at the present time, 2.6 million children and youth are poor. He includes in this statistic all recipients of Hartz IV aid under the age of eighteen, including children of asylum seekers and parents unable to work.[26] If we include the reality of the "working poor," the number will be much greater. Poverty is the lot of people in Germany at present who have to live on second-stage unemployment insurance or low wages, and whose support, even for basic necessities, must be partly derived from resources from Hartz IV, which excludes them from various means of participating in society. Vacation trips, newspaper subscriptions, trips to the movies, or restaurants are not included.

The polarization between poor and rich has sharpened in Germany since chancellor Gerhard Schröder's second term (2002–2005) and has by no means decreased under the grand coalition. At the same time, this is a development that has been accelerating in Germany for decades—corresponding, though in a mitigated form, to the worldwide polarization between poor and rich in a globalized economy.[27]

A decade ago, it was already evident that children and youth, above all, were victims of poverty.[28] Klaus Hurrelmann, researcher on youth and society in Bielefeld, names unemployment of parents as the primary cause of this development. "If the trend continues, a majority of the younger generation will be excluded from the welfare society."[29] In the year 2006, this development had sharpened dramatically. This means that

The degree of risk of poverty among children and youth is predominantly conditioned by the social markers of the family of origin. Considered in terms of households, children who live in single-parent households are at the greatest risk of being poor. More than a third of all children in these households live in extreme poverty. In families with more than two children under seventeen it is about a fifth. Children in households with two parents, by contrast, are "only" affected by poverty at a rate of about 6 percent. Although these household-specific differences are already enormous, they yield an incomplete picture. Thus, there are extreme class-specific differences within each of the household types. Families in the higher social classes—in which 46 percent of all children live—have a very small risk of poverty. But if the head of the household is a manual laborer, one in six smaller families with children and one in two larger families with children live in poverty. Among single parents, too, there is a clear class differentiation, with about two-thirds of all poor children in single-parent families having a working-class mother.

In total, 56 percent of all poor children live in working-class households and another 24 percent in families of skilled workers. Thus, it is primarily children of the working classes who bear an increased risk of poverty, and who also represent the great majority of poor children in Germany. This is even truer for immigrant working families. Working-class families with an immigrant background are the largest group of poor in Germany. A quarter of all poor children live in those households.

Poverty is thus embedded in the class- and immigration-specific structures of social inequality. Talk about the "infantilization" of poverty is one-sided to the degree that it looks only at the aspect of polarization between household types with and without children and ignores social and racial disparities. Child poverty is at the nexus of manifold social processes of division: between childless lifestyles and those that include many children, between the working classes and the higher social classes, between natives and immigrants.[30]

Within this long-developing situation, we can discern several constants. For example: in times of mass unemployment, it is primarily women who are affected by job loss, especially over the long term. Poverty has a gender.[31]

It is especially evident in the age segment of those over sixty that poverty is female. Among men, retirement benefits, which are directly tied to earnings, on the whole contribute to a standard of living above that of social assistance. As a rule, women who are now over seventy usually exhibit traditional female biographies, with gaping holes in their employment history created by child rearing, and if their life partners die, they are forced to rely on widows' benefits. Women of advanced age, as a rule, have already cared for their husbands and now, if they have no family members—again, these would be most often daughters or daughters-in-law—who are ready and able to help them, they have to look to strangers for assistance, often in nursing homes or other institutions.[32]

Since the turn of the millennium, the social situation in Germany has been characterized on the one hand by increasing poverty, and on the other hand by an enormous growth in wealth. The social polarization in the United States and Germany, already clearly on the increase since the 1970s, has continued to widen without any relation to business cycles and the character of the regimes in power. At the same time, as far as the poor are concerned, life has effectively become more expensive; the lower the disposable household income, the sharper the concentration on satisfying the indispensable basic needs such as housing, food, and energy. With increasing household income, a higher degree of consumption is made possible; in particular, there is more freedom in the areas of household management, transportation, the dissemination of news, education, entertainment, and personal clothing and care. Rich households have the opportunity to acquire long-lasting, high-value consumer goods; in addition, in this country the savings rate has also increased.

It is not just poverty that is growing; so is wealth. The unequal distribution of poverty and wealth is increasing, and with it, social polarization is expanding.

Poverty as Social and Cultural Phenomenon

It is pivotal to realize that poverty is not merely an economic phenomenon or something that reveals itself in emotions like fear and uncertainty. Poverty means, above all, the loss of social contacts and the means to participate in public life.

Calculable, tangible factors are by no means sufficient for an understanding of poverty.[33] At issue as well is the access to political and cultural opportunities through which women, men, and children are enabled to express themselves as the subjects of their own life stories. Poverty is a multidimensional phenomenon in which economic and noneconomic aspects are inextricably interwoven (e.g., level of income, quality of dwelling, health, sense of well-being). Household income is a central feature of one's life situation because it provides access to the satisfaction of many other needs. The social and cultural dimension places an emphasis on the scope for action and the constraints that are specific to one's life situation.

Consequently, the life-world or situation in socioeconomic terms includes

- the scope of provision and income: this has to do with the quantitative supply of goods and services;
- the scope of contacts and cooperation: this concerns opportunities for communication and interaction;
- the scope of learning and experience: this covers the opportunities for development and realization of interests determined by socialization, school and professional education, experiences in the world of work, and the degree of social and spatial mobility;
- the scope of leisure and regeneration: this includes opportunities to relieve psychic and physical pressures brought on by work, housing, and environmental conditions;
- finally, the scope of determination and participation: this describes the extent of participation and the ability to join in deliberation and decision making in various aspects of life.[34]

If we take these aspects seriously, we can see the answer to the question of what a life in poverty means for the people concerned: a life of subordination, of exclusion from important opportunities for political and cultural participation, of constant experiences of one's own worthlessness and unimportance. Thus, poverty does not begin when people are actually starving or homeless—although we must realize that more and more are experiencing those. Poverty, rather, forces people to exist far beneath the level of their possibilities.

Numbers and data are fairly opaque. Ernst-Ulrich Huster, a sociologist from Bochum, gives some everyday examples in his book *Neuer Reichtum und alte Armut* (*New Wealth and Old Poverty*), now already a decade old:[35]

> An upscale shopping area in a city. Distinguished customers walk determinedly, not hastily, past the goods displayed in the show windows. A

brief glance, a flick of the hand, a curt nod or shake of the head. . . . The picture is shattered. There sits a man begging in this shopping street; to his left are two plastic bags holding all that he owns; "Out of work, no place to live" is shakily written on a little cardboard lid. A little farther along there is a young prostitute looking for customers at the train station. His services for the next joint? A well-dressed, clear-eyed, broad-shouldered man appears. He makes it clear: the bum must clear out. "If I see you here again . . ." The boy prostitute knows that it would be an unequal contest with this man from a private security firm whom the people doing business on the block have hired. He leaves. . . .

. . . Another scene: a residential area in a German community. Snug homes with carefully tended gardens and hedges. Here you can feel at home; here everything is just how you want it to be. After all, you've worked hard for it. Now one house that has changed hands is to be made into a private nursing home. Nothing against old people, of course; after all, you never know what may happen to you, either. But here? In the evening and at night the moaning of old people, then the visitors with their cars, and finally: How often will the hearse arrive? Property is constitutionally protected, including the property of this homeowner. One owner lets his gasoline lawnmower run during the day behind the hedge, at the place where the old people like to sit. "Noise is often found to be disturbing . . ." so it must be possible to run off the old people. There is a threat of a lawsuit. But apparently that's not enough: the cars of the people who work there and those of visitors to the home get scratches on their side panels.

Another scene: in Frankfurt, single homeless people are being struck by hammers during the night, while they are sleeping. Human life is made disposable because of "a-sociality." The perpetrators are not, as a rule, the store owners, the elegant customers, the owners of the little houses, and the like; rather, the doers of the deeds are often those who are themselves threatened with displacement, who are afraid that these people will take from them the last little things they have. Aggression is directed against asylum seekers and foreigners: those who know how their social position within the constantly increasing social wealth is getting worse and worse cling to the "order" of this society and defend it with brute force.[36]

Today groups of people who in the past could expect social advancement with some certainty are affected by an increasing uncertainty about their lives and the threat of unemployment. Academic professions are not spared; nowadays the mass media speak of the "apprenticeship generation." Students, for example, live in a situation that is, at least potentially, conditioned by scarcity; fewer and fewer receive federal student assistance and more and more have to work between semesters and sometimes even during the semester in order to secure their livelihood while they are studying; now university fees are being added. Many interpret this as a temporary phase that has to be gotten through somehow, en route to a permanently secure income. But many students are affected by a mood of anxiety, of fear that, thanks to the uncertain economic prospects and the high rate of unemployment, poverty and dependency could become a long-term perspective for their lives, even in the academic professions.

First the Grub, Then Morality

We are speaking here of poverty and wealth in economic and cultural terms without idealizing the poor. The poor are not per se good or better people. Luis Buñuel demonstrates this strikingly in his film *Viridiana*.[37] One scene shows the poor and the crippled taking possession of a castle while the masters are away. They put on a huge banquet, and in one camera shot, they are grouped at the table in a scene reminiscent of Leonardo da Vinci's "Last Supper." How lovely: the poor are celebrating the Lord's Supper, loudly and joyfully—so one might think. Up to this point, it is almost a religious idyll. If the scene did not continue, the film would probably have become a long-running hit in continuing-education seminars for pastors and church social workers. But it goes on. The figures gobble and souse to their hearts' content, and the banquet becomes a chaotic spectacle. A brutal fight develops; a woman is raped. The poor are not better people. There are circumstances in which people are robbed not only of their opportunities in life, but also of their perspectives, their morals. Bertolt Brecht criticizes a certain morality imposed by the church that does not take into account these harsh realities as he captures it in the phrase: "First the grub, then morality."[38] And very few who are denied food have morals *instead*. The attempt to claim that the poor are better human beings only heaps a lie on top of injustice. Elsa Tamez also rejects the idea of romanticizing the poor as morally superior. She insists that a contextualized form of the doctrine of justification, the appreciation of the relational character of sin, which leaves no one untouched, can sharpen the point: "We are clearly not claiming that the poor are not 'sinners.' Practice teaches us that people who experience themselves justified always recognize themselves not only as sinners but also as responsible for the structure of relationships of sin."[39] We ought not to romanticize but, rather, perceive life conditions as soberly as possible.

With this kind of sobreity, we ask how the promise of grace overflowing can be extended to the "expendables," who are considered to be superfluous, without rendering their life situations innocuous, but also without romanticizing or idealizing them.

Example: A Sermon in the Christ Ambassadors Ministries International–Church of God, Hamburg

In Hamburg, as in other large cities in Germany and throughout Europe, there are more and more congregations made up primarily of men, women, and children who have an immigrant background and often are deeply affected by exclusion from the primary labor market and from opportunities for political and cultural participation.[40] We want to describe one of these congregations in Hamburg and present, by way of example, a sermon made available to us by Pastor Ossai Okeke. Christina Okeke, the pastor's wife, describes the congregation's situation:

The charismatic Pentecostal Church of Christ Ambassadors Ministries International–Church of God was called into being by a Nigerian pastor and his German wife. The congregation fosters intercultural encounters. The great majority of the members come from various African countries: South Africa, Kenya, Tanzania, Cameroon, Ghana, Nigeria, and other nations; ethnic identification within the countries themselves is also very mixed. This is quite different from other so-called African congregations, which are generally monocultural. The number of German members in the congregation has grown steadily since the founding of the church in the year 2000.

The socioeconomic situations of congregants differ widely: from doctors to warehouse workers, from childless couples to large families, from economically established to impoverished women, men, and children. The socially precarious life situations of some of the members have the following aspects:

- Many have left their spouses, children, parents, and siblings behind in the homeland. Because of the often very uncertain status of their residency, the families may be separated for years, without being able even to visit one another. Those who live together in Germany in a nuclear family are often faced with the burden of trying to provide financial support for two families of origin (the husband's and the wife's) in Africa. These immigrants often work in the lowest income sector, since they are perceived as lacking essential job qualifications such as German-language proficiency. Many live in extremely cramped housing conditions.

- Some men, women, and children accept commuting up to fifty kilometers each way and come every week from Lower Saxony and Schleswig-Holstein to woship, in order to praise God and experience a bit of home. The social dimension of congregational life, especially the church's systems of support, are an aspect that should not be undervalued.

The pastor and his wife are frequently called upon in cases where there are marital problems, for the translation of official documents, trips to the immigration offices, job searches, questions about the children's education and upbringing, and a great deal more.

The pastor's duty in our congregation is to offer an appropriate degree of realistic evaluation and aid, and at the same time to give hope through the living word of God. The latter can only be accepted if it is believed and lived by the preacher.

Our congregation does not preach merely material well-being—that is one of many topics. As regards the core message of the sermon that follows, the foreground belongs to a humanly worthy life without fear and misery. Christ Ambassadors Ministries International wants to encourage the members of its communities not to internalize other people's images and in that sense to be enslaved, but, rather, to pursue their own wishes and goals in order to lead a self-determined and worthy life.[41]

In this congregation, Pastor Ossai Okeke preaches on Jesus' parable of the Prodigal Son, confronting the theme of poverty theologically by opposing a false spiritualizing of the subject:

> You have probably often heard that wealth should only play a role in your spiritual life. Yes, you may even have heard that God wants you to be poor so that you will not sin against him. Are you, too, among those Christians who believe that their lives are not meant to blossom, that you are not supposed to develop yourselves in economic terms?
>
> Maybe you find it hard to believe anything else. If that is true, you should try to open yourselves to different ideas. . . . How many people learned that the world is flat before Christopher Columbus taught us better? Turn

your eyes for a moment from your present condition, marked by poverty, deficiency, and desire, and concentrate on the word of God.

HE is the divine source of gifts! God wants you to be able to flourish in all aspects of your lives. Maybe you have already heard many sermons that say differently. But open your heart to the word of God, so that your spirit can be renewed. Then you will see that God intends honor and greatness for you. I learned all that garbage, too: that one can better serve God if one is poor, that we believers must suffer like Christ if we want to go to heaven. I have prayed much and studied the Bible. Now I have come to understand that God did not choose me so that I could live in poverty. No, he created me in his image, so that I may live and exercise power and be rich, like HIM, so that I may represent HIM as his messenger here on earth. I know that I am not perfect, but I know that God's intention for me is not that I should live in poverty.

Be assured, God has not written my name or yours as fated for poverty. You have to deal with poverty every day. God did not choose you to be poor. It is a dissipation of God's wealth that there is not enough for each and every one of us to live, even though he is the almighty God, Creator of heaven and earth. The difference between poverty and well-being is knowledge. Every day you have the opportunity to write the story of your life anew. Dive deep into God's word and know the path out of poverty. Bodily redemption happens in the divine health that Jesus Christ provides for us . . .

That is the good news that the poor, the sick, and those who suffer are to hear. They must hear how they can leave poverty behind them in order to participate in God's wealth. They must hear the good news that God desires their flourishing, their healing and liberation in all aspects of their lives. God has created them in his image. Tell this message to the people you meet, so that they may know the power of the word of God.[42]

The Congregation as Life-World and the Limits of Economization

If we look at the discussions in German practical theology in recent years, we note that, as far as Protestants are concerned, the subject of poverty or the meaning of unemployment receives little attention within a religious horizon of interpretation.[43] There are only a few exceptions to this trend.[44]

On the Catholic side, by contrast, we may mention the work of Norbert Mette and Heinrich Steinkamp, who attempt to bring into dialogue the ideas of practice theory and the current focus on phenomenological questions in light of poverty issues.[45] Mette speaks of the necessary presence of a "Samaritan church" whose life brings together two perspectives: the amelioration of individual needs and distress (as a social perspective) and the broader analysis of the causes of need and distress. "As urgent as it is to ameliorate suffering where we encounter it, we must also examine what can be done, at the very least, to actually prevent avoidable suffering. . . . Most often it is groups within the congregation from which such a solidarity and social-critical engagement in praxis and consciousness-raising takes its start."[46]

The general inclination of the Protestant churches to ignore these questions while seeking to position themselves and establish their view of the world is also strikingly evident in the study of church membership titled *Kirche in der Vielfalt der Lebensbezüge*.[47] Anyone who seeks information in this volume about the social stratification of congregations in Germany will not find much from the perspective of the poor. The sociological models that are applied concentrate on typologies of membership, with their reference points being closeness to or distance from the church, studies of specific lifestyles, and the analysis of worldviews. There is no research on how types of piety and lifestyles or worldviews relate to economic aspects. One gets the impression that economic issues dealing with experiences of unemployment and poverty are accorded no particular significance.[48] We, however, assume from the outset that these phenomena are of central importance for subjective meaning-making processes both in the life of the community members and in the lives of people on the margins of or outside the church's life. Diametrically opposed to this neglected perspective are the attitudes and expectations that church members formulate with regard to the church.

As we seek to become attentive to grace overflowing for people who are made superfluous and to preach the justification of the "expendables," we have to keep the broader church and community contexts in view. After all, we are not preaching in a vacuum. The homiletical perspective needs to be broadened by including the debate about the future of churches and congregations, which goes on against the background of shrinking economic resources.

A change in the image of churches and congregations that is quite powerful today is being brought about especially by the market-oriented economization of the Protestant churches, originating in an increasing pressure of shortages and competition in *the fields of social service*: the church as business or corporation and the *congregation as a branch office*. Major denominations are in the process of *consolidating* congregations in order to obtain "synergy effects" and cost cutting. This entails setting up exemplary procedures in congregations and church institutions and making those processes more efficient through evaluation and control in order, as consultant Peter Barrenstein has said, to advance the modernization and business efficiency of the churches in a harmony of "enterprise, customer, and product."[49]

In this situation, we seek to reclaim the wisdom of the Protestant Reformers in not tying what makes the church to be church to the quantitative success of its daily operations. Church exists where the promise of the gospel is proclaimed and encounters faith, and where Jesus' friends unite with him in celebrating the sacrament of Holy Communion in the intimacy of his body. Church is not necessarily present in successful organizational development, where growth is accomplished against the trend, and where a customer base with ability to pay is satisfied with what is on offer. Rather, church is there where all who have lost their hearts to Jesus Christ live and celebrate belonging to the communion of saints—people from all continents, no matter their social status or level of education, men and women, people of all ages, the living and the dead. According to the Reformers, neither tradition nor political power nor money determines what is church. What is decisive is that people hear the gospel together and are able to accept in faith that God gives God's justice to me, to every individual, solely for Jesus Christ's sake, without my deserving it. Common ideas as well as the realities of power and rule are broken in this community: all who have crept forth from baptism, who let their lives be governed by this gift of God, are already priests. This, in the mind of the Reformers, is the fundamental challenge to the theological legitimacy of church hierarchy.

At the same time, the Reformers' discoveries offer a basic orientation for the question of the nature of the church's life but present no precise answer to that of its social form. We find some important thoughts on this matter in the works of the Reformers, for example the idea of a "priesthood of all believers," but they were unsuccessful in challenging a factual accommodation to their social and political surroundings. In the territory of the Lutheran Reformation, these were the monarchical, rationally governed territorial states; for the Reformed leaders it was bourgeois city structures that were reflected in the churches' internal organizational forms. For centuries, the model of "church as institutional authority" determined its activity, despite repeated upheavals (Pietism, for example) that tried to recall the "fascination of the beginning."

At the present time, the economic question plays an absolutely central role in innumerable debates among congregational leaders, in regional churches, and in the offices of the state church bodies. These debates are often not only about problems that can be analyzed and must be solved but also about a fundamental sense of the church's life: it is not only the business talk about quality assurance, theme management, customer orientation, and so forth that assumes a higher value than biblical and Reformation-theological reminders of the communion of saints. We, rather, want to suggest that the primacy of the economization debate must be disrupted if congregations are to become alive, attractive, and liberating for the people in their neighborhoods. We need to continue to work on a variety of ways of how we are church in the world today. Local congregations, as well as community services offered by the church, are crucial. They all have a center for worship, but depending on the context, each has an independent face and can augment one another in their essential tasks.[50] For example, congregations—more than other social locations—will be seen as spaces in which civil society can take form, for example in the actions of *group initiatives* (e.g., engagement on behalf of immigrants and the victims of globalization, for sanctuary, communities of and for AIDS victims, peace groups, "social-pastoral" work).[51] The ordinary congregation is a community of narration, celebration, and also of friendship that, in fact, can be called upon as a reliable life-world, more than other social locations, by people who are being damaged by the conditions of achievement and competition in late-capitalist society: congregations can be exemplary places for the preservation of lived relationships. The central question is: How can the destructive consequences of a "total" market economy—which no longer has to compete with any other—be met in domestic political perspective as regards mass unemployment, destruction of the environment, the surrender of liberal assumptions, and in global perspective as regards the issues of hunger and poverty? How can these issues be addressed without oversimplifications that will in turn have problematic consequences?

We see such a tendency to oversimplification in various places and in numerous contexts: it can be about the temptation to preserve "what properly belongs" to the church, so that explosive political issues are dismissed from "what is properly our function" or, on the contrary, are redefined as the kinds of problems that, like confessional questions, determine the very identity of the church. A sense of helplessness can appear either as blind activity or as a retreat from burdensome and problematic areas of knowledge and action. But there are also many congregations where, in spite of conditions of financial scarcity, there is a vivid openness to life, the competence, and the engagement of the local people are valued, solidarity is practiced, and at the same time, space is left for the development of individual lifestyles.

Congregations will only be able to fulfill their social and individual duties if they are likewise a spiritual place. It is not a matter of constantly discovering something new but of paying attention to the richness of spiritual practices and of constantly filling them with new life. Fulbert Steffensky speaks of the "ordinary charm of faith."[52] The community of narration and celebration in the local congregation is in urgent need of the vibrant *forms* of divine liturgy and the foreign language of prayer. As Steffensky says, "When I pray, sing, or give words to my faith I can expand myself. One prays with the stammering articulation of one's own faith in the words of sisters and brothers and with the gestures of the dead. . . . That is what church means: being more than a lonely subject; being able to believe more than one believes individually."[53]

The congregation is a community of narration and celebration, a place in which to experience community without excoriation from outside; a space in which the search for clarity in content and forms that can be inhabited. This happens in the manner of ongoing retelling and ongoing celebration of the biblical story, but also in political action. The congregation is a space both for giving form to spirituality and for empowerment for certainty in life—and so for perceiving the "power" that can be separated from economic and political interests and hierarchical structures and taken possession of as "courage for life" and shared.

Vibrant congregations will not see their activities and attention directed only to the church. The contextual faces of their neighborhoods are part of their own identity.[54] Engaging with ambivalent economic developments should be part of their daily bread. The processes that are leading to a snapping of the sinews of society are destructive in many respects, but by no means is their effect unilinear. In the niches of such developments, we can repeatedly perceive alternatives and countertendencies. For example, in sociological studies on urbanity, the development of a neighborhood is not only viewed in terms of its economic infrastructure (e.g., the presence or absence of institutional facilities or the tendency to impoverishment, gentrification, the failure and closing of shops in a particular part of town); attention is also given to interactive spaces that are accounted as part of the "social" or "symbolic capital" of a neighborhood or village context.[55] This could be a snack bar where young people meet, without regard to nationality; a newsstand where people stop to chat; or a retired teacher who donates her time to visit lonely people on her block. From some point on, the existence and expansion of social capital in a neighborhood or rural village will constitute an effective counterweight to destructive local developments, which always represent a risk of becoming sources of violence (e.g., confrontations between youth gangs, the attractiveness of radical-right ideas and violent behavior, for example in East German housing developments). Here congregations can become important places, and often they already are.

Under certain conditions, Christian communities can become spaces for interaction that will strengthen the social capital of such a place. Congregations always exist in the *internal interaction* of organization, milieu, and communion of saints. Their spiritual presence and effectiveness as "energetic networks"[56] will become a social reality to the degree that people live *within* (and not outside) their actual life as organization and milieu, and that spaces for interaction are made available—places that reveal themselves as such by their respect for people and their vigilance against destructive forces.

People's readiness and ability in this regard will depend on many things, but in any case, on a continually successful answer to the question: Is there an open, accessible spiritual center in the congregation that embraces everyday life concerns?[57] Is a lively worship service available, one in which openness and honesty is practiced with regard to the brokenness of peoples' lives, as well as an openness to receive the forgiveness of sins and the promise of new life in the encounter with the presence of the triune God? Are people empowered and encouraged to face their everyday life issues? Do the pastors entrust active members of the congregation with self-directed projects, and are they ready and able to appreciate and support the talents of others and to surrender authority? And: Are there crystallization points in the congregation's milieu—people who can take the time to have a conversation? Are there open households "where one can visit" (with clear boundaries, but nevertheless there), people who like to engage in conversations with others, people with courage and the ability to deal with conflict?

Under economic macroconditions in which more and more people are being "released" from paid work and thus are considered to be expendable, there will also be more and more people in every place who, at any rate, have one thing: time on their hands. Many will welcome the chance, after a history of rejection and the disappearance of social networks following the loss of their jobs, to enter a new field of interaction and take on limited responsibilities—provided there are people who see them, welcome them, and entrust this to them.

In fact, it is unthinkable today to carry on daily congregational work without delegation of tasks, so that volunteers take over whole segments of the work and carry it on independently—often without pay and outside of clearly delimited processes of delegation of responsibility. There are a great many parts of the work that only survive because of the engagement of volunteers from the congregation. Visits to elderly members celebrating birthdays, and work with the older parishioners in general, management of the cemetery, preparation of the parish newsletter, direction of and membership in the choir, youth work, the organization and supervision of building and repair projects—all this and much more is regularly done by people who keep the congregation alive through their own initiative and with a high degree of commitment.

We envision congregations that are exemplary life-worlds in which respect, cooperation, and above all a transparent approach to power can be practiced. Often enough, it is just here that problems and conflicts arise and may undermine the self-confidence of those affected. It is all the more necessary to be clear at this point. We see it as a central task of pastors to act as nodal points in the local system of communication. Dealing with power is also, and above all, a *spiritual* problem: religious leaders need a spiritual practice in order to be able to distinguish their own desire for power from the power of God. That is the only way in which they will be able to transmit the healing power of God to others without dominating them. There is a crucial difference between the encouragement and empowerment of others, enabling them to value their own life contexts and stories, to love themselves in times of weakness as well as in strength and to be open to others, and a dominating mode of communication. Pastors will play a special role in this local network for the simple reason that they have a theological education and bring that knowledge to the congregation in both an instructive and a critical fashion, and do the same in fields of work beyond the congregation itself. In addition, many of the clergy possess additional training in psychology and sociology. None of this will lead to strains in the power structures pertaining to the daily life of the congregation if the circulating power is recognized and used in such a way as to strengthen and encourage, to educate and build up self-confidence in other people who live and work there. It is about the acknowledgment of power and about the ability to surrender power—not only in a respectful style of communication but also in the trusting recognition of the work of volunteers.

Example: The Christian Center in Berlin

In what follows, we want to give an example of how the congregation can be seen as a Spirit-filled space in which the justification of the "expendables" can take concrete form in the connection of social ministry with worship.

This example illustrates the opportunities that may exist here for a renewal of congregations. We will quote extensively from an account by Waldemar Sidorow of a community of homeless people within a free-church congregation in Berlin, the *Christliche Zentrum Berlin e.V.* (CZB):[58]

In the Easter service on March 26, 1989, the congregation ordained an evangelist. This was the first internal ordination of a pastor, and it was done so that the "*service to the poor* and homeless" could be "affirmed as a particular priority of the gospel." . . . This ordination was meant to give concrete form to the "responsibility of the CZB for the poor" in the city. This responsibility for the poor of the city was given to the congregation in 1985 by a prophecy through a woman prophet highly regarded by the charismatic groups.

For a while it was not clear how the congregation should respond to this prophecy, until it was "discovered" that the poor had already been present for quite a while in the congregation. About forty homeless people came to the weekly "prayer breakfast" of the members of the immigrant mission team. The team had been meeting weekly for years, every Thursday, for breakfast and prayer. One day a homeless woman came to the group because she found the door unlocked. The next week there were two homeless people. In a few weeks there were forty of the homeless who were sharing in the team's breakfast and prayers.

It didn't stop there, with the homeless people's sharing in the spiritual life of the team. The members reacted spontaneously to the material needs of their visitors and collected clothes and donations for food from the congregation. But they sensed that it had to go farther, somehow. The team members moved their prayer time to a different day, and the original meeting became a gathering for the homeless. At the beginning they kept the usual time for prayer, though it was shortened, and there was more singing; breakfast became the more weighty matter. This is how a structure arose shaped by the needs of the group being served. Donations of clothing and money for food, simple counseling, and sometimes accompanying people to the local authorities—all this became part of a regular offering.

The pastor who was called in the spring of 1989 was glad to take up this initial work. First he built up a collegial group of his own. In the middle of this opening phase, on 9 November 1989, the Berlin Wall fell, and the young church was faced with new challenges in the wake of those events. The West Berlin neighborhood of Kreuzberg, which lay next to the wall, was suddenly at the center of the city now growing together. Although the congregation, thanks to its history, was scarcely rooted in the social ghetto of Kreuzberg—only a very few of the several hundred members of the congregation lived in the neighborhood—the congregational leaders decided to assume a stronger presence in the community in order to meet the challenges of increasing poverty. Extensive renovations of the side aisles and in the galleries were undertaken in order to set up spaces for socializing, for the kitchen, clothing distribution, counseling offices, a bookstore, and a place for children in the church building. The original meeting that began with forty homeless people was now transformed into a weekly worship service for the homeless, followed by breakfast. Counseling, spiritual advice, the distribution of food and clothing, as well as emergency medical services provided after worship services, all added to what was on offer. Attendance at worship quickly rose to more than 150.

The demands on the ministry team began to exceed their strength. New and appropriate team members had to be found quickly. They came from different congregations, building an ecumenical team of thirty to forty colleagues. The numbers of those being served continued to grow. Homeless people from that whole quarter of the city came to worship every Thursday. Everything that the worship service and the associated programs had to offer thus became in time, for one group of the city's homeless, a part of their lives for one morning a week. The set-up team arrived at seven A.M. to prepare for the Thursday morning worship at nine and the breakfast and distribution of food and clothing that followed. The pastor and his team conducted the worship service for the homeless together. As is usual in charismatic worship, there was a lot of space given to singing and common praise, as well as to prayer. The proclamation, in preaching and witnessing, was strongly concentrated on the biblical promises to the poor and the weak. The perspective of hope was only partly directed to the immediate present; future anticipation dominated.

Heaven was richly portrayed to the homeless in many sermons as their future dwelling. For many of the homeless, Thursday morning became "their" spiritual meeting place. Over the years they celebrated many worship services, Christmases, and Easters, sharing joys and sorrows. Homeless people who died were buried by "their" pastor to the homeless. Couples who wanted to marry were counseled by him, and their marriages were celebrated at the church. Homeless people came to faith and were baptized. Everything that was important to the homeless community and needed fixing was addressed on those Thursday mornings.[59]

Listening to the Voices of the Unemployed: Traces of Cultural and Religious Interpretation

Following our sketch of the congregation as a life-world in which grace unfolds and the justification of the "expendables" is preached, we will consider in this next section the voices of those who are counted among the "expendables." Susanna Kempin, in her important study *Leben ohne Arbeit?* (*Life without Work?*) considers the question of how people affected by unemployment deal with the fact that paid work can no longer be seen as the center of their lives which provides meaning, the locus of their social and personal identity. She is also interested in how experiences of work-related insecurity in life are dealt with. This is about the dilemma that it is increasingly difficult to develop long-term life plans based on employment.[60] Kempin locates her empirical investigation against the background of two major changes in the sociocultural structure: the end of the employment society and the dissolution of the so-called normal biography. The thesis that the employment society comes to an end is based on the fact that immense increases in productivity, brought about by newer technologies in the second half of the twentieth century, have led to the destruction of jobs on a grand scale. Unemployment will be a constant structural factor in people's lives. Transformations in the area of industrial production, the service sector, and information technology will not change the situation. With the end of the employment society, marked by the belief that full employment was possible, the concept of a normal employment history dissolves as well. Even a generation ago, three phases of a professional biography were assumed: preparation, an active phase of full-time occupation, and then retirement. This construction of the "normal" biography was probably always a fiction, especially for a great many women. It is no longer possible, for the majority of the population, to order and interpret one's life in this way around anticipated employment as a constant factor in one's biography. In this situation, individuals must deal with the dilemma that the sociocultural system of values, which emphasizes the importance of paid employment for personal life and for the associated respect bestowed by society, is still in full effect, while at the same time, the end of the employment society is taking concrete form.

In her empirical work, Kempin identifies two major thematic groups: on the one hand, the experience of unemployment as a *stigma*, and on the other hand, the interpretation of unemployment as *transitory*. People in the first group are mainly those who experienced the so-called economic miracle after World War II. Many of them internalized the illusion of an endless economic expansion as well as the ideal of the "normal biography," which promised an enduring continuity of and ability to control the events relevant to one's life. The confrontation with unemployment is correspondingly experienced as a breakup, a shock, or a deep crisis; the value of work in one's life is described as a center, something to hold on to, and the real purpose of life.[61]

One of the persons interviewed by Kempin, Jürgen, describes his own biography as a continual ascent, until the crisis.[62] In cases where there is no continuing work history, the person's own life story is painfully compared to the ideal: Kempin quotes from an interview with Jürgen:

> So, and now of course I am in the process of applying, but I still don't have a job. And the longer it lasts, the greater the danger that I will drift off again and then I'll be more or less at an end again, as I have been all my life. Then there will be a kind of hole again, a gaping thing like a wound, y'know. And trying to find a reason for it again: yes, why were you out of work for such a long time, again, and what were you doing during that time? That's another problem, always having to justify yourself, to explain what you've been doing.[63]

Jürgen presents an impressive picture: the discontinuity in his life, which brings on unemployment, is described as a gaping wound; it represents a deeply wounded self.

Unemployment is experienced by many as wasted time: "You just putter around," says Mr. Wagner.[64] The day is often tinged with depression and massive sleep disruptions:

> So it goes. I often wake in the night . . . it's a torture [he begins to weep]. To put it quite clearly, it gets to the point that you have an upset stomach, with vomiting and all. Okay. That goes on for an hour or so and then. But sometimes it's so bad that you just can't stand it. And now, to get away from it, sometimes I get dressed at four or three o'clock and go out, walk around in the fields.[65]

Mr. Wagner, too, describes the collapse of personal identity in impressive fashion. Without work there is no possibility of living unscarred: "Because you have to make something, otherwise, I think, you just go kaput, totally kaput. So I'm scared."[66] Gianna's fundamental feeling that her life is illegitimate is only intensified by the link with unemployment: "Who are you without work? . . . You're nothing."[67]

Kempin summarizes with regard to the group who experiences unemployment as stigma:

> What they all have in common is that the difference between the real and the ideal moves them deeply and is the source of personal suffering; only the reference points by which they experience the difference vary. The situation of unemployment places them all . . . under an enormous internal pressure to justify themselves. For them, the fundamental legitimacy of their existence lies only within the horizon of employment, or the labor market. Their internal experience swings between a corrosive depression and intense efforts to find work.[68]

In the horizon of religious models of interpretation, Kempin posits that, for the group who interprets unemployment as stigma, the extreme importance assigned to work in shaping personal identity has an almost religious dimension. When religion is defined as that on which one hangs one's heart, or that on which one experiences oneself as totally dependent, we can say that work has religious features. Work becomes a symbolic representation of that from which recognition, legitimacy, or comfort must be drawn.

Gianna, a young Italian woman who thinks that God is only a product of human needs, attempts in one of her deep crises to return to the Roman Catholic Church: "So then I tried, after I had lost the children and my mother, too, I said well, I'll try to believe. But it really didn't work for me. I tried to talk to a priest, but I couldn't speak freely with him. I had a constant feeling that I had to pretend to be what he expected me to be. And I couldn't [painful sigh]."[69]

In another case, the interviewee answers a question about his understanding of God in a somewhat formal and abstract sense, with the notion of the providence by which God shapes human fate. But then he immediately expresses doubt about that idea, since the work world has taught him to be realistic about things like that.

The second group, who sees unemployment as *transitory* in their lives, has long since accepted that the major changes in society and culture mean there will be no security in their own working lives. These people have in some way accepted the limiting conditions of dynamic poverty, leaving only partial access to the labor market. The sociologist Ulrich Beck speaks of "high-wire biographies":

They are all attempting, in the face of a constant danger of falling, and with a larger or smaller share of artistic self-awareness, to master their own lives—few of them with much success, many with very little. A society in which high-wire biographies are compulsory is characterized by a situation in which a significant degree of accommodation, alluring artistry, and *fear* draw all into their course and hold them there—and a great many fall.[70]

In one interview, Kempin lets Mark tell about the various stages of his work life. Mark has made numerous attempts to find the right profession or job. He tried learning to be a gas and water installer but gave it up, took jobs in several businesses, and finally completed a course for metalworkers. But he could not find a job in that line of work. During the time when he was unemployed, he completed his high school diploma at night school and then studied English as well. Mark found no work as an English teacher, and for the last three years he had again been working intermittently.[71]

Mark has found the concept of "patchwork identity," which had migrated from the social sciences to popular idiom, a key for interpreting his own work history: "Well, I didn't see it as all that bad. . . . So I can live with this whole patchwork business. Not, of course, when I think what all these patchwork people will do when they are sixty-five or seventy—where they're going to get their pensions. That's something else. But otherwise I'm okay with it."[72]

Mark makes it clear here that it is by no means his work history that is a problem for him but, rather, material anxieties with regard to aging; those are what trouble him. For him, various reorientations in his value system are a fact. After an intermediate orientation to the measures of the capitalist economy, there comes a setting of priorities with regard to private life. The ability to deal creatively with crisis situations becomes an implicit religious theme; it opens for him a horizon of meaning against which he can see his bumpy life's road in a positive light.

Anne, who has always had a fairly sober and pragmatic attitude toward the meaning of unemployment, is in a position to make creative use of the free time she gains during her period of unemployment. She is one of the few who articulates an explicit reference to the subject of faith. She formulates her belief in a very personal way and at the same time gives it a social shape through her work in a church congregation. For her, going to church has a critical function as an interruption in the daily round. Anne expresses her trust in God, in view of her unemployment, as follows: "If the good

God thinks: 'That's the job!' then I'll get it. If not, not. It's that simple for me. And I haven't thought any more about it. Not at all. . . . It's been okay, this time when there's been no work. Or I won't get my job, not as a teacher . . . but the one that's meant for me."[73]

Kempin makes it clear in her study that there is certainly not one single model according to which people deal with crises in their work lives. A great many answers, strategies, and practices are proposed for dealing with the challenging situation. For the preacher, it is therefore vitally important to understand what horizons of meaning the hearers create when they find themselves in life situations in which they are suddenly counted among the "expendables." For it to be possible to approach the manifold forms of these horizons of meaning, spaces must be opened in congregational life in which people can talk about their experiences with poverty and unemployment.

Preaching Grace in Life-Worlds Scarred by Poverty

Embodying grace by preaching justification in life-worlds scarred by economic marginalization must take people's experience into account. It must meet them, address them, but above all take them seriously as the subjects of their own lives, their own narratives, and their own agency. These are especially people who live on the margins of economic society and for whom the promise of liberal democratic culture is in fact constantly being broken: the promise of sharing equal opportunities with everybody else. The proclamation of the superfluous grace of God today means above all announcing this gift to those who have been made superfluous in relation to the market, those who by economic measure count for nothing, achieve nothing, and add nothing.

Preaching the gospel means announcing the grace of God in such a way that people are addressed, touched, and enveloped in their inner selves as well as in their outer selves, in their opportunities to understand themselves and the world just as in their sensibilities and physicality, in their being-for-themselves as well as in their being-for-and-with-others. Our central question is: How can this kind of preaching be put into practice? How can that offer be cashed in in such a way that it does not become merely an empty promise? How can the act of proclamation in the worship service become such a powerful and embracing event in which divine grace is poured out onto God's people? What are the liturgical forms in which the gospel of the justification of the "expendables" finds expression? This is the horizon of questions within which the following thoughts are developed. We have achieved a great deal if the questions are posed in such a way that one can take hold of them—and they do not contribute to an unhappy awareness that constantly arises in view of the actual situation of our churches and our worship services: of an unmistakable mismatch between the fullness, the wealth, the superfluity and overflow of God's grace that we as preachers have to proclaim, and the timidity, skimpiness, and the lifelessness of sermons that are sometimes preached. It is probably not hard to experience this mismatch pretty often.

Martin Luther was already aware of the challenge of how to make the preaching of grace and justification relevant to people's life experiences. So he complains: "And you have sure evidence of it: when one preaches on the article of justification the people sleep and cough; but if you make an effort to speak of stories and examples, they prick up both ears, are quiet, and listen avidly."[74]

This kind of storytelling needs to be sensitive to ordinary life experiences, especially as they pertain to the experience of being made expendable. It is pivotal for the homiletical task to gain insights into the meaning-making processes in which hearers engage, in order to understand where the stumbling blocks and barriers to a preaching of justification that is relevant to their lives may lie.[75]

In light of the voices interpreted by Susanna Kempin's study, it appears that one great stumbling block is that the values shaped by the paradigm of the employment society that are relevant to the stabilization of one's personal identity are diametrically opposed to the idea of *iustitia passiva*, to a justice that is given by God as a gift and not achieved through accomplishments or assertion of self. In the world of labor, personal identity is associated with one's own ability to work; this creates both personal satisfaction and social recognition. In the case of *iustitia passiva*, however, we are talking about an understanding of the constitution of the person that happens not through personal achievement but in the act of receiving a gift.[76]

Being recognized as a person in the act of divine gift giving is a dimension of faith that is hard to grasp since recognition is, for many people, almost exclusively achieved through work. The idolization of work hinders access to an understanding of life and the world in which the ex-centric nature of life that results from being-in-Christ can be emphatically articulated.[77] The idolization of work prevents access to the givenness of the gifts that are bestowed on us in order that we might live.

For those who do not surrender themselves to this "trip" of idolizing the work world, there is increased pressure to design an autonomous personal identity within life's various high-wire acts. Here too, the voices that could respond to the givenness of gifts and the gift of grace in freedom are marginalized.

Within the phenomena we have described, the question of the gracious God seems in many cases to be pushed into the realm of interpersonal human interactions. It is not the search for God's grace but the issue of the gaping wounds in one's own work history, the feeling of being illegitimate, or fear of poverty in old age, that become the inner voices that tyrannize individuals.

It is of critical importance in preparing sermons that we ask the question: Where are the concrete barriers in the immediate life situation that render preaching grace and justification of the "expendables" irrelevant, stale, or cynical? At the same time, we have to ask, how can we make this kind of preaching plausible so that a space of deep listening is opened up?

Accordingly, it is necessary to engage in liturgical forms that have the potential to express *iustitia passiva*, the givenness of gifts, and overflowing grace, all within the horizon of the experience of poverty and unemployment; to articulate this in our preaching; and to celebrate it in the sacred meal.

The Homiletical Perspective: Interweaving Content and Form

When we situate our homiletical reflections in the context of economic process and discourse, we are pointing to the fact that the homiletical question—What shall we preach?—is directly connected to the question: How should we preach? The questions of content and form cannot be answered sequentially—first the content, then the formal structure. It is equally unhelpful to locate the relationship between content and form in an *explicatio-applicatio* model.

The German homiletical tradition did distinguish between fundamental, material, and formal homiletics.[78] According to this classic division, fundamental homiletics engages questions like these: How should we consider the relationship between Christian faith and language, given that preaching is a speech-act? It should be kept in mind that the concept of "word" in the theological sense—understood, that is, as "the word of God"—is always only partially coextensive with the meaning given to human language and human communication, even though the two are mutually related.[79]

The traditional formulations of foundational homiletics present us with a central problem. The principles of preaching are themselves not valid for all times because theological reflection, like the preaching of the gospel, always acquires its form, power, and significance in specific historical-social contexts. But if the situation and context are themselves subsumed in the idea of "principles," we cannot at the outset formulate abstract, metahistorical principles that can only be examined at a second stage in terms of their *consequences* for contexts and situations. Rather, attention to the situation—and that means the situation of the listeners as well as the historical and social context in which they live—must be incorporated in reflection on the preaching of the gospel, and that must happen at the very beginning.

Material homiletics traditionally seeks to relate the foundational reflections about the theological significance and purpose of preaching to the articulation of aesthetic criteria and rules to enhance the concrete form and content of a sermon. This is precisely the task addressed by traditional material homiletics. It is traditionally at this point that consideration is given to the relationship among text, hearers, and situation: Can listeners find themselves reflected in the biblical text? Or is there a deep abyss separating the text as transmitted from the present situation? Theologians are generally well trained in how to exegete a biblical text with historical-critical tools. But that by no means gives us an answer to the question of homiletical presentation. While historical-critical exegesis examines the parts and elements of a text, and in what situation and from what perspectives (of the tradents and the redactors) a text originated and was transmitted, homiletical inquiry asks what it says *here and now*. The field of material homiletics also includes questions such as: Is the text from which the sermon is to be preached given by the lectionary order, or is it chosen for a particular purpose? What should be the relationship between textual exegesis and thematic concentration in a sermon ("thematic preaching")? Should one preach on large blocks of text, sometimes in a continuous reading of whole biblical books, or can there on particular occasions be a "sayings sermon" in which a single verse gives the impulse for taking the situation, feelings, and perspectives of those affected (e.g., by a golden wedding anniversary or a confirmation) as one's subject?

In addition, material homiletics asks: When are preachers in their own individuality, their self-reflexivity, and theological conviction an impediment to the preaching of the gospel? Or is the "I in the pulpit" the only real basis and foundation for a good sermon? Should sermons teach, appeal, or narrate, explain or build up and console? And when and in light of what situation is this or that choice to be made? What occasions an idea in the mind of a preacher that, through development and structuring, can lead to a well-formed sermon?

The label "formal homiletics" is traditionally applied, for example, to the discussion of the relationship of preaching at worship to rhetoric in general, that is, the relationship of preaching to the genres of classical rhetoric:

- *genus iudicale* or *docendi* for legal discourse, in which clarity is to be established concerning some subject;
- *genus deliberativum* or *movendi* for the common assembly, with the purpose of bringing about a political decision;
- *genus demonstrativum* or *delectandi* for a solemn speech expressing sorrow, hope, joy, elevation, or another sentiment; in any case, this is related to feelings.

A sermon is a speech;[80] this conviction was part of the reflection on preaching from earliest times. Preaching (unlike speaking in tongues) must be comprehensible and accessible to human understanding; it must be possible to test it for content and purpose. Like any public speech, a sermon is located within a web of relationships among the speaker, the hearers, and the subject. At the same time, the special situation of preaching distinguishes it from other genres of speech: formal homiletics must take into account the fact that the locus of preaching is Christian worship; that preaching takes place within the framework of a worship service; and that it must be examined, as it must also be shaped, within that space and its communicative possibilities and limitations.

The distinction we have sketched between foundational, material, and formal homiletics has become problematic. Because of a variety of theoretical concerns but also and above all because of practical experiences, the irreducible connection between the questions of "what" and "how," between the content and the method of preaching, has been emphasized. In what follows, we will sketch some contributions to the academic discussion on preaching in which, most recently, the indissoluble connection between "what" and "how," "object/content" and "method," in the work of preaching has been discussed from different vantage points.

Manfred Josuttis locates the questions about the connection between content and form within, inter alia, the creative process of sermon preparation. How can a preacher understand the stages of such a process—preparation, incubation ("being pregnant with it"), illumination (breakthrough to an idea for the sermon), and development—so as to arrive at a well-prepared sermon?[81] How can the mysteries of our faith be handed on in such a way that they will not be betrayed?[82] How can preachers bring the Bible's stories in contact with individual life stories (as well as social myths about daily life) so that a healing flow of life will be set in motion: so that destructive powers that attack the personal center of the human being can drain away and God's healing power of grace may be called upon to fill human hearts and minds?[83] In this process there, is little sense in trying to make a clear distinction between the questions of "what" and "how." They are interwoven, a mutual back and forth, a flowing process in which both sides influence one another with equal intensity. The questions of "what" and "how" are still distinguishable, but they are connected in the most intensive way possible.

What Josuttis has described as regards the *production* of the sermon, Gerhard Marcel Martin has described for the sermon's *reception*, in his inaugural lecture at Marburg, a text that has also been highly influential and indeed has become famous: "Preaching as an open work of art."[84] Martin sees that, as far as the production side is concerned, there is an analogy between the work of preaching and *aesthetic* activity. Individual activity does not bring about an artistic work merely through the correct use of general rules—and the same goes for a sermon. The efficacy of the gospel unfolds in the act of reception through the hearers. They participate in deciding what the sermon says by the way in which it becomes important and effective in the context of their own lives.

Wilfried Engemann understands preaching as the setting up of signs.[85] Martin had already related his reflections to the work of the semiotician Umberto Eco, and that perspective has been rendered more profound by Engemann. "Semiotics," he writes, is the name for the theory of signs. Its central thesis could be: people understand something, or make themselves understood, only through signs. "So we *have* a sign when something is apprehended 'as significant,' i.e., when a meaning is given to an expression"[86] and the reverse: when a linguistic figure or a gesture or the like is associated with a particular content. "Sign" should thus be understood as the link established in a particular act of recognition or communication between a particular expression and a particular meaning. What does this mean for preaching? Offering signs in a sermon opens up the possibility through which the hearer can apprehend more than what she already knows—and also more than what is in the manuscript. The attempt of a preacher to say everything in her sermon would miss the most important aspect of the preaching event: namely, speaking in such a way that the audience can expand on it. Preachers should not regard the need for their sermons to be expanded upon as a dilemma; rather, they should embrace it. Thus, in terms of the theory of signs, a sermon to which nothing can be added is profoundly suspect. A sermon is not a work that can be finished at a desk but something that requires the engagement of the hearer in order to be effective. In other words, a sermon should challenge and enable the hearers to take *their* part. The congregation should be able to *find something* in the sermon that furnishes them with a starting point.[87]

Martin Nicol develops the concept of a "dramaturgical homiletics" that is heavily influenced by David Buttrick's work:[88] the sermon should become an "event" and be rhetorically staged as "movement." Preaching itself is movement, a speech that is both moving and moved, drawing the audience into its movement. Martin Nicol advocates the incorporation of aesthetic techniques, for example, from cinema and theater, or the reflections of the culture section of a major newspaper into the process of a "dramaturgical homiletics." He develops his concept of preaching in conversation with modern homiletics in the United States:

> If I were to summarize the intention of a major part of North American homiletics . . . I would say that film has replaced the lecture as the paradigm for preaching. One could, of course, think more of theatre, because it involves live performance on a stage. But film is much more representative of the modern (mass) media. The sermon should be inspired by film rather than following (usually unwittingly) the classic paradigm of a lecture.[89]

The intent of preaching, to be an effective event and movement and to draw the audience into that movement, is conveyed through specific formal principles. Thus, Nicol suggests that the sermon should be constructed of separate sequences—images, scenes, symbols—which he calls "moves" (by analogy to film technique), and the sermon as a whole—the "structure"—should be conceived as an overall movement of several separate moving segments. In this concept, too, the "what" and "how" questions are inextricably connected.

One recollection may be helpful in the contemporary context of homiletical discussion. In 1921, Eduard Thurneysen posed a challenge to his contemporary "modern" homileticians that we may want to recall in the present situation: this was to concentrate more on the question of "what" and less on that of "how" in preaching. His challenge to those tasked with preaching at that time was: the content and center of preaching mean *a new respect for God*, and *the human being qua human being must die*.[90] Thurneysen thought at the time that every sermon had to say these same things. Always the same thing: that in itself is a rhetorical problem for preaching. We could not adopt that formula word for word today. We stress again that a separation between content and form—between "what" and "how"—is not possible for the preacher. But there is a question of weighting the relative importance of the two. In view of the situation of church and society, in view of the current boom in theories of preaching and their concentration on the "how," we believe that a more thorough concentration on the "what" question is unavoidable.

The elemental question is what preachers of the gospel have to say, in divergence and clarity, what others do not and cannot say, at least not with this kind of clarity. To return to our central consideration: the grace of God, which we as preachers of the gospel are to convey, is a free gift, pure superfluity. The task of preaching is so to convey this superfluity that it is not soaked up by the strategies of devaluation and consumption in which people today are fettered but so that it remains a truly free and overflowing gift that can make life new.

Manfred Josuttis has said that it is the task of the sermon so to convey the mysteries of faith that the gospel will not be betrayed. That is the issue. The question of the relationship between preaching the grace of God and superfluity arises in an equally urgent manner. In a situation in which more and more people are being made expendable, superfluous—as employees, as consumers, as culturally and politically active contemporaries—the elementary task of preaching today is to announce the promise of justification to the "expendables," or more precisely, to people who have been made superfluous.

The demand that we concentrate more on the "what" of preaching is not an affront to aesthetes among homileticians. What and how, content and form, in preaching belong together. *Within* this inextricable connection we stand for placing more weight on the "what" question.

From the outset, to preach the gospel as preaching the justification of the "expendables" involves, for us, a commitment to the biblical narrative tradition, which is to be made audible in the preaching of the gospel, here and at this moment, in this situation and in this worship service, for these particular people here and now. In its whole narrative sweep, the biblical tradition conveys God's justice, revealed in God's overflowing grace that explodes all expectations and boundaries. God's grace is pure superfluity, and it belongs first of all to the "expendables," the "superfluous" in society. That God's affection and promise are first for the poor is told, promised, and demanded throughout the whole Bible—from the social laws and prophetic writings of the First Testament to the Gospels and letters of the New Testament. People who open themselves to God's promise, rely on it, and let themselves be embraced and enveloped by it are surrounded by the flow of divine grace. It is first of all the "superfluous," the "expendables" who are gifted by this superfluity. The Protestant tradition has repeatedly attempted to say that the announcement of divine justice must be received and understood as God's free gift to human beings: it cannot in any way be "earned" by them. Those who are excluded from the social processes of "earning," those who fall out of the system of production, consumption, and opportunities for political and cultural participation, are today the first recipients of God's gift.

What sort of *preaching* of the gospel can really convey this divine gift? How can we preach so that we speak not only *about* God's overflowing free gift but *from within* and in a way that it can happen: here and now for the people gathered for worship? That is the question that we seek to pose as clearly and invitingly as possible and for which we are seeking the traces of a plausible answer.

In the next chapter, we will expand on the doctrine of justification as a form of embodied relationality and inquire about its homiletical relevance. The third chapter will engage more closely with the preaching of justification as overflowing grace for people who are considered superfluous within the resonance of Sacred Scripture. In a fourth chapter, we will, in conclusion, concentrate on the embodiment of grace as performative event.

2
GRACE AND JUSTIFICATION
IN RELATIONAL TERMS

IN WHAT FOLLOWS, WE seek to deepen our understanding of grace and justification in relational terms.[1] We will begin with a theological and homiletical reflection on God's self-communication; this will be followed by a consideration of the preaching event as a movement within the realm of grace that needs to be made explicit in several directions. This movement pays attention to the life experiences of the *homo incurvatus*. The image of the *homo incurvatus* captures the human person twisted back upon herself in a state of desperate disconnect and isolation; it pictures the human person being affected by sin as alienation from God, self, and other. Preaching as a movement within the realm of grace attends also to moments of profound bliss in light of the event of justification, by means of homiletical imagination as anticipatory and disruptive speech. This kind of preaching is sensitive to the traces of divine grace in the face of the other. Foundational for these reflections is the question of how we can speak about God as subject and about human subjectivity in the dialectic between distinction and reciprocity. Finally, we will engage our ideas on the corporeality of grace in the act of preaching and the economy of faith as an economy of intimacy.

God's Self-Communication: Grace as Flow Experience

What does God communicate about God's self when God recognizes human beings as righteous? This question can be illustrated in a theological debate between August Hermann Cremer and Karl Barth.[2] Before being called to Greifswald in 1870, August Hermann Cremer was the pastor of a congregation near Soest; during his professorship, he continued to pastor a congregation in Sankt Marien in Greifswald. Cremer wrote a little booklet titled *Die christliche Lehre von den Eigenschaften Gottes* (*The Christian Doctrine of the Attributes of God*, 1897) in which he developed the doctrine of the divine attributes as the result of the self-communication of a loving God in the Christ revelation. Cremer suggests that the concept of the divine attributes should be defined as "the particularity of God's appearance in his actions through his essence as love . . . or the particularity of his appearance in his actions—in that in him, the original and eternal reality of the Good and direction toward the realization of the Good are one, that he is the highest Goodness and the highest Good."[3] He emphasizes that the doctrine of the divine attributes communicates most appropriately God's own proper being. Knowledge of the essential attributes of God results from God's self-actualization; it is thus not the product of human theological thinking. God makes God's self understood as love in the divine essence, and that is in itself an expression of God's freedom—for love happens out of freedom and in freedom, or it is not love.

It is only when God communicates God's self in the act of divine revelation that we understand something of the uniqueness of God's *existence*. When God communicates divine essence, God acts as God. The *subject* of the divine revelation determines, at the same time, the divine *predicate*. Through this self-communication, God's essence is shown to be love: "In [this self-communication] he appears and acts as the one who is wholly love, not one who simply has love and gives love, but is love. That is, God wills to be and is everything that he is for us and with us, and wishes to have us for himself, or is entirely realized in being and willing to be for us and in community with us."[4] Cremer describes the divine essence as without restraint or reservation, unconditional and free, proexistence for others; it is free love that has found its authentic expression in God's self-surrender in Jesus Christ. In Christ's life, death, and resurrection, this love has broken through the world's self-enclosure, by which it is destroying itself, and it has made human beings themselves capable of faith and love.

Karl Barth took some of these considerations as the basis for his own theology but rejected others at a crucial point. Theological reflections like these, that see God's attributes as entirely realized in God's relationship to the world and understandable only through the appearance in the world of divine essence, evoked Barth's most vehement opposition. "God is not realized in his relationship and attitude toward the world and to us, as in the event of his revelation. The dignity and power of his works, his relating and conduct to them depends rather on the fact that in relation to them he is himself, without being any other than the one who acts in them—that in revealing himself to them he always remains superior to them."[5]

Barth is most deeply concerned that both aspects of God's self-communication, God's freedom and God's love, should receive the same emphasis. He speaks of God as the one who loves in freedom and is free in loving. This is not a tautology. Instead, God's revelation as love is pure superfluity, pure grace, the free, self-determined expression of God's essence, sufficient in itself because in itself already rich in relationship in the loving relation between Father, Son, and Spirit. Barth writes:

> God is sufficient as his own object and thus also as the object of love. He would not be less the Lover if he loved no object different from himself. Since he chooses of himself to love such an Other, his love overflows, but he does not exhaust himself, his love is not limited and conditioned, but its overflowing is conditioned precisely in this, that it *could* be sufficient in itself and yet *has* no contentment in this self-sufficiency, but as love to an Other can and will be still more than that in which it could be sufficient for itself.[6]

The words *overflow* and *overflowing* are key to this paragraph 28 of Barth's *Church Dogmatics*. Magdalene Frettlöh interprets them thus: in clear distinction from Cremer's interpretation of God's self-communication as love, Karl Barth's concern is that the overflowing, superfluous communication of the divine essence *outwardly* corresponds, as its precondition, to the immanent self-expression, the internal wealth of relationship and the overflowing communicativeness of the trinitarian God in God's self. God is thus altogether loving and overflowing in God's self, in that the three divine Persons communicate themselves to one another. "God does not alienate himself from himself by entering into relationship with another, nondivine living being, but in so doing remains himself, altogether true to his own communicative, expressive, and overflowing essence."[7]

What are the consequences of Barth's reflections for preaching? Above all, Barth's homiletics has been received from the perspective of "testimony," that is, the constitutive difference between the speech of those who give testimony and the object of the testimony in the act of testifying speech. When Barth engages homiletical questions, this receptive mode is certainly present. For example, in his homiletical lectures in Bonn in 1932–33, titled "The Churchly Nature of Preaching,"[8] he derived preaching, as well as the whole of the church's life, from God's *revelation*; preaching is preaching and church is church to the extent that they originate in revelation and point back to it. "Where the Word of revelation creates it and where people live as hearers of this Word, there is church."[9] God's "revelation" is not a metaphor for theological reflection on the relationship between God and the world; it contains a specific, content-filled opening of communication to the human being, revealed and formed by its subject, God. Thus, in Barth's thinking, the entire Sacred Scripture is to be understood as a mediated witness to the communicator of this revelation, the testimony of the prophets as well as of the apostles. Preaching rightly fulfills its obligation when it gives new form to the direction and continuity of the testimony to revelation thus opened to human beings in their current community context. The church as a whole is founded on the utterly unique event of God's action in Israel and in Jesus Christ, and it is from there and nowhere else that the designation of preaching's task as that of witness derives. "Its duty is solely to repeat the testimony by which the church is constituted. It must be testimony to that testimony, to the Sacred Scripture as attested revelation."[10]

It is altogether indisputable that the concept of testimony incorporates the essential intentions of Barth's idea of preaching. The testimony to the God who exists in pure relationality that overflows in self-giving grace is a constructive foundation for a theology of preaching that focuses on the justification of the "expendables." What, then, is the form of preaching in which God reveals God's self in overflowing, self-outpouring fullness?

We can adopt this idea of flowing and streaming as a way to receive, adopt, and reformulate Karl Barth's concept of preaching. Manfred Josuttis, in his essay "Die Predigt des Evangeliums nach Luther" ("Preaching the Gospel according to Luther"),[11] opens a possible path in that direction. It is precisely the event of presence, of happening here and now, that characterizes the gospel in the act of forgiving sins. The word of the gospel reaches hearers in the present. It does not communicate some past history of salvation, it gives no metaphysical information, and it does not find its focus in psychologically rich interpretations; rather, it addresses those who hear it in their own present situation and so changes their lives up to that point. Here and now, sinners are acquitted and made righteous before God.

People are always already tangled up in their narratives, the scripts of their own biographical plots, and the powerful narratives of the world in which they live and the society that surrounds them. A sermon that really intends to be effective here and now must establish contact with those stories. It must do so in such a way that the narrative thread of the biblical tradition goes on being told, enters into contact with the life stories of these human beings, and so brings them into the flow in order that limiting, dominating, and destructive narratives can be washed away and the account of overflowing grace can reach and fill their hearts. Josuttis writes:

> Luther suggests distinguishing the narrative material in light of the christological distinction between *sacramentum* and *exemplum*. In the

prolegomena to the *Kirchenpostille* (*News for the Church*) he writes: "Christ, as gift, nourishes your faith and makes you a Christian. But Christ as a model does your works; and they do not make you a Christian; instead, they come from you after you have already previously become a Christian" [*WA* 10, I/1, 12]. Thus the gospel narrative's aim is not setting legal norms or ethical indoctrination, but animation. It nourishes the human being, by filling the heart and moving the person in many ways.[12]

The art of preaching is just this: in the midst of people's accounts of their lives, a different narrative is told in such a way that one's present story is liberated and can move forward in confidence. People who are tangled up in crippling, oppressive, anxiety-producing, and dominating stories get immersed in a different story that breaks open the possibility of liberation and consolation. Preaching the gospel means freeing people from destructive stories through a narrative that is effective here and now, and leading them into healing stories.

Josuttis thinks that it is above all the understanding of language in energetic terms that gives adequate expression to Luther's discovery; we can adopt in a similar sense the homiletic intention expressed in Karl Barth's understanding of the overflowing, self-outpouring God. The structural elements that constitute the speech-act of forgiving sins are to be interpreted in terms of presentness, their character as address, and their claim to authority, but they cannot acquire their effectiveness solely or primarily from such theoretical attributions because the word of the gospel, which is "in" and speaks to hearts, is not solely or primarily addressing a theoretical problem that can be received first of all through a sequence of cognitive events.

Josuttis suggests that primarily spatial metaphors, but also metaphors of flow, are best suited to grasping the power released in the healing word of the gospel.

> If God's word is "in," is on the move, souls will be raised up and refreshed because they are exposed to life-renewing vibrations that cause proud fools to reconsider and that console despairing minds. In every congregation and every place the word of God must be heard in this healing fashion. It is precisely in the marginal places in the course of the day, at sunrise and sunset, that this life-force must be made audible. When the fountain of life is sensed, the air of common life is filled with the healing grace that is received in faith.[13]

Martin Luther, in his *Freiheitsschrift* ("On the Freedom of a Christian," 1520), explicitly adopted the idea of flowing and streaming to describe the lived reality of faith:

> We give this rule: the good things which we have from God ought to flow from one to another and become common to all, so that every one of us may, as it were, put on his neighbor, and so behave towards him as if he were himself in his place. They flowed and do flow from Christ to us; He put us on, and acted for us as if He Himself were what we are. From us they flow to those who have need of them.[14]

Preaching as Movement within the Realm of Grace

God, who loves in freedom, turns toward human beings in the healing process of the event of justification. It is in this divine attentiveness that the healing of a broken relationship happens. This is exactly the promise that carries the act of preaching. Luther repeatedly points out that it is in the act of preaching the word that God pours out God's grace.[15]

Preaching in this sense is a creative event in which justification *happens*. It is not the analytical-reflective *habitus* that is on scene here; a sermon is not a lecture on the *doctrine* of justification. Rather, we are drawn into the center of the realm of grace as our relationship to God is healed. God is the subject of this event. And at the same time, we as preachers are given the task of cooperating in bringing this about.[16] Within this paradox, there unfolds a dynamic promise that makes room for all.

The preaching of justification as a creative event in which God's fidelity to community takes shape does not represent simply a one-sided subject-object relation (for example, in the sense of "God creates XY"). It is creative communication in that it happens in the mode of address in which God turns toward us: "I have called you by your name, you are mine" (Isa. 43:1).[17] And we are invited to respond as we enter into the sphere of freedom within the realm of grace.[18]

We understand preaching in this sense as a movement within the realm of grace. The intention of this movement is to give an expression of God's fidelity to community in an act of comprehension that is also discovery.[19] Preaching within the realm of grace sets in motion a dynamic in which we are drawn into a variety of movements that must be shaped homiletically. These movements refer to the articulation of *incurvatio* experiences as alienation from God, self, and other and to justification as a fragmentary experience of profound bliss, to a sense of grace in the face of the other and to disrupting and anticipatory discoveries that might unleash critique of economic injustices as well as imaginative potential to envision alternatives.

Recounting *Incurvatio* Experiences

One sphere of freedom relevant to preaching that reveals itself in the movement of grace is the ability to articulate *incurvatio* experiences and to dare to speak about the (self-) destructive effects of diminishment and damaged lives. For preachers, the most important question in this context is the extent to which such bringing-to-speech actually occurs in our worship services and the broader life of congregations, or whether instead it is thwarted.

We rely here on Luther's famous description of the sinner as *homo incurvatus in se ipsum*.[20] "The human person twisted back upon herself" lives in a state of deep alienation and is not able to relate to God and to other fellow human beings. This destruction of relationality can be captured in the notion of sin. The *homo incurvatus* is tangled as well in a state of self-alienation, in a hellish self-centeredness that prevents her or him from turning the heart to God. When justification and thus the healing of the relationship to God happens in the realm of preaching, self-diminishment is disrupted and healed then and there, in that the hearers experience anew the relational character of their personhood. In the Protestant tradition, this is described as a kind of rapturing in the act of hearing the word: "The word that is heard is *in* the event of hearing the creative power that breaks the self-bending of the human—*cor et voluntas*—out of its *incurvitas*, directs it to the praise of God and at the same time 'draws it' in this direction."[21]

The *incurvatio* experience, with its effects of self-diminishment or self-distortion, is multifaceted as regards the relationship of the individual to God. At the very center of Pauline theology, the effects of diminishment and deformation are related to the supraindividual, transmoral power of sin. In the letter to the Romans, the Apostle Paul reflects the totality of sin, which deforms all of human life and brings death, a death that can already be died during our lifetimes.[22] Our thoughts, feelings, indeed our whole bodies, are subjected to the rule of sin. The marks of *hamartia*'s ("sin") tyranny are written on the body of every individual. Redemption from the body of death (Rom. 7:24), according to the apostle's testimony, is accomplished through Christ, for the human being, possessed by sin as by a sphere of power captured, for instance, in the figure of Satan, is not in a position to achieve self-control over his or her own deeds. "He or she is like one possessed, who no longer acts on his or her own initiative, but does what she or he does because sin dwells in her or him" (cf. Rom 7:17, 20).[23] Sin becomes a lawgiver that subjects human beings to its *nomos* ("law"). "The *nomos* of *hamartia* is not Torah but, rather, the compulsion that makes it impossible to fulfill God's will, the Torah."[24] The compulsion is described as world encompassing. This reflection on the link between sin and law speaks not only of the fundamental existential human situation but also implicitly of the power politics of the *Pax Romana*.[25] Paul describes the social situation of *Pax Romana* as a form of structural sin, in which it is not solely the practices of individual subjects but, rather, structures and external forces that mold actions. In this social and existential situation of alienation, the will and the results produced by constrained action are out of synch with one another: "For I do not do what I want, but I do the very thing I hate.... If I do what I do not want, it is no longer I that do it, but sin that dwells within me" (Rom. 7:15, 20). The *homo incurvatus in se* suffers precisely from this contradiction, in which individual intention, action, and the results of action fall out of harmony with each other.

Paul's meditation on sin, agency, and subjectivity can be related to Michel Foucault's critique of the Enlightenment concept of the subject, according to which conscious intentions, actions, and effects of actions are related in a causal and logical way.

> At the moment when one realizes that all human knowledge, all human life, and perhaps the whole human biological heritage are embedded in structures, i.e., in a complex made up of elements subject to relations that can be described, the human being ceases, so to speak, to be the subject of his or her own self. One discovers that what makes the human being possible is an ensemble of structures that he in fact comprehends and can describe but whose subject, whose sovereign consciousness, he is not. This reduction of the human being to the structures that surround him seems to me to be characteristic of current thinking, and thus the ambiguity of the human being as subject and object is no longer a fruitful hypothesis or subject for research.[26]

Sermons that consider *incurvatio*, the distortion of the human being in its personal and structural dimensions in light of the promise of grace overflowing, will speak about the contradiction between intention and the outcome of actions, and the tragic circumstance that derives from this dissonance. Giving explicit attention to this dissonance in light of the event of justification can lift the burden and free people from the compulsion constantly to present themselves as subjects who can control their own lives and the world in which they live.

The theme of *incurvatio* can fruitfully be brought into conversation[27] with various theories of narcissism.[28] Engagement with modern theories of narcissism involves a critique of theological traditions that contrast self-love (*amor sui*) with love of God (*amor Dei*) and so regard the former as an expression of sinful human attitudes.[29] We suggest instead that the access to grace overflowing enables not only liberation from *incurvatio* but also a new freedom for the self, that is, a renewed relationship to the self that is founded in self-love and feeds on one's relationship to God and attitudes toward others.[30]

As regards the myth of Narcissus, Michael Roth points out that Narcissus's problem is ultimately that he cannot love himself: "The myth expresses this by depicting the object of Narcissus's attachment as unavailable to him. The object of Narcissus's love is a mirror image, not himself. But the essential characteristic of a mirror image is that it is unreachable by its owner."[31] The self-absorbed human being who in and of himself or herself cannot turn the heart to God but only to his or her own self-image, which wavers between self-hatred and grandiose fantasies, cannot ultimately attain self-love. The Christian tradition has used the concepts of *hybris* and *desperatio* for this back and forth. Theologically, this inability to love oneself can be expressed this way: "The destruction of the relationship to God consists in the destruction of the relationship between the original lover and the one who loves because she or he is loved. It is thus the attempt of human beings to negate the love-relationship that constitutes them."[32]

Some social psychologists even talk, in regard to the industrialized Western world, of a narcissistic age.[33] These social-psychological analyses suggest that the end of the labor society did transform the paradigm of the normative professional biography, the meaning of family and partnership, as well as the meaning of public life. These transformations tend to produce a change in the fundamental psychic dispositions of the people concerned. We have already mentioned the writings of the sociologist Ulrich Beck, who has worked with the phenomenon of "high-wire biographies" in the context of the so-called risk-oriented society.[34] The drifts toward individualization and pluralization taking place in (post-) industrial societies set in motion processes of erosion of the classic features of human life, such as family and partnership, neighborhoods, workplaces, and communities, that bring individuals into a newly immediate relationship with the market and society. The compulsion to assert, realize, and reproduce oneself socially and economically is sharpened by the experience of insecure jobs. This process might imply some more flexibility and liberty to shape one's own life. At the same time, many people are driven in view of economic insecurities by a strong sense of fragility.

It is a fundamental characteristic of this process of social transformation that structurally conditioned crises appear as personal. One's own guilt at "choosing the wrong profession" and one's inability to manage family conflicts arising out of the attempt to balance paid work, childcare, and required mobility are often experienced as personal failure. "There has come to be—paradoxically enough—a new kind of immediate contact between the individual and society, the immediate contact of crisis and sickness in the sense that social crises appear as individual crises and are no longer, or only very remotely, perceived in their social character."[35] Regarding our topic, it is important to note that in this same process the compulsion to self-justification of one's own decisions is also intensified. The less the clan, family, or tradition prescribes how one is to shape one's life, the greater the spotlight on the actions and choices of the individual. This apparent elevation in the value of subjective agency is, however, a highly ambivalent matter. On closer inspection, we see that the pressure to become more flexible can evoke new compulsions and conflicts as it can easily be studied in the conflicts brought on by the combination of parenthood and paid work that the majority of women must still endure.[36] Likewise, for those who are considered superfluous by a market-driven society and whose life situation is constricted by the fear or the reality of poverty, the processes of individualization and pluralization do not necessarily contribute to an expansion of their subjective agency. This, however, does not mean that the ideology of free choice ceases to be an effective factor in their own meaning-making processes.

From a psychoanalytic point of view, the dissolution of traditional ties thus described and the disappearance of parental authority attached to it represents a weakening of the ties of the superego. Correspondingly, the anal conflicts that were, at least as a tendency, decisive for the psychic disposition of the bourgeois white Western European middle class in the first half of the twentieth century recede into the background. The orientation to command and obedience, power and subjection, has given way to a conscious orientation to one's own interest. The development of the superego as the instance reflecting the tyrannical strictness and irrationality of the paternal superego and the demand for identification with the father has undergone a decisive transformation since Freud's days.[37]

The alteration in the conflicts within the self that force many people today into therapy confirms these observations. In his research on the alteration in symptoms of neurotic disturbances informed by social psychology and social history, Joachim Hohl asserts that the classic neuroses resulting from conflicts in the construction of the superego and the associated repression of sexual needs are no longer central to therapeutic processes. Those seeking help are troubled not so much by phobias, hysteria, or compulsion neuroses as clearly identifiable symptoms but, rather, by diffuse fears, anomie, inner emptiness, and feelings of insufficiency. The theme of guilt associated with the repression of "drives" and inspired by the existential questions—What do I want, what may I do?—is being replaced by feelings of shame associated with the theme of the insecure self and evoking questions such as: Who am I, and what am I worth?[38]

This new personality type bears strongly narcissistic features: its presentation is marked not by feelings of guilt but by vague fears and the suffering caused by an existence emptied of all meaning.[39] Such a person does not seek redemption but present satisfaction of his or her personal need for well-being. As Christopher Lasch writes:

> Plagued by anxiety, depression, vague discontents, a sense of inner emptiness, the "psychological man" of the twentieth century seeks neither individual self-aggrandizement nor spiritual transcendence, but peace of mind, under conditions that increasingly militate against it. Therapists, not priests . . . become his principal allies in the struggle for composure; he turns to them in the hope of achieving the modern equivalent of salvation, "mental health."[40]

Because of their self-preoccupation, however, strongly narcissistic personalities are often not in a position to love themselves or to make real contact with other human beings. They use the world as a mirror for their search for recognition, desiring to know that their supposedly grandiose self is affirmed by the admiration of others, or taking a primary interest in people who have charisma and power. Such a fixation drives a self that must always be hungry because it constantly needs new people who can assume the function of mirrors.[41]

It is not merely the formation of private relationships that is influenced by this. The meaning of one's public life also shifts in that it centers not in the creation of tradition as the construction of a collective identity but in the stylization of the passing moment. The sphere of public, political life thus becomes a terrain for self-disclosure and self-presentation. The cultural sociologist Richard Sennett writes in this connection that the intimate community is driving out public life:

The reigning belief today is that closeness between persons is a moral good. The reigning aspiration today is to develop individual personality through experiences of closeness and warmth with others. The reigning myth today is that the evils of society can all be understood as evils of impersonality, alienation, and coldness. The sum of these three is an ideology of intimacy: social relationships of all kinds are real, trustworthy, and authentic the closer they approach the inner psychological concerns of each person. This ideology transmutes political categories into psychological categories. This ideology of intimacy defines the humanitarian spirit of a society without gods: warmth is our god. The history of the rise and fall of public culture at the very least calls this humanitarian spirit into question.[42]

In what follows, we will assume that the fundamental existential questions of a sociocultural milieu steeped in narcissistic tendencies shape the questions of many of the people who attend church. This is especially true of the shift in the question of the authoritarian personality of what is permitted to the question of personal self-worth. This is, of course, not to say that all those who listen to preaching are troubled by profound narcissistic personality disorders. The problem of narcissism is, however, virulent in all communities. It affects those who have been made expendable and those who still have work.

Tilman Walther-Sollich, in his analysis of sermons for Good Friday and Easter in the twentieth century, makes some interesting discoveries touching on the problem of narcissism.[43] He shows how the shift from the oedipal theme of the classic bourgeois subject to the narcissism of the post-traditional subject brought in its wake a change in the theological orientation of the sermons. From his historical analysis of sermons, working with categories borrowed from psychoanalytic theory, he concludes that, in Good Friday sermons until about 1930, the central focus was on the oedipal themes of guilt and obedience. The idea of sin to be found in those sermons assumes an enduring rejection of the divine will by individual human beings, manifested in moral failings in daily life. The confession that Christ has died for our sins supports a relief from individual guilt. The oedipal interpretation of Good Friday in this phase indicates the "emotional ambivalence of love and wrath, judgment and mercy, punishment and reconciliation in the relationship to God, and working through this ambivalence makes present . . . the assurance of God's love."[44]

By contrast, the sermons since the 1960s are increasingly marked by the narcissistic problem, leave the personal level, and speak of sin primarily in the structural sense: the individual is entangled in structures of violence. Correspondingly, the narcissistic theme of powerlessness is articulated: the cross reveals the love of God, who takes the part of the powerless sufferers. The question of personal guilt and the associated threat of losing one's own life are strongly repressed or vehemently rejected.[45] The preaching of the resurrection, which at the beginning of the twentieth century was still strongly connected to the theme of guilt and interpreted as the completion of Christ's redeeming death, also changes in the narcissistic age. From now on, the narcissistic need for self-expansion and the erasure of boundaries is taken up and applied to an empowerment of the individual for action. This tendency indicates that the theme of individual guilt has been replaced by an experience of powerlessness, which reflects the transpersonal entanglement of the individual in the mechanisms of global destruction of the resources necessary for survival.

In contrast to these experiences, the Easter sermons stress the present-eschatological risen life of believers, oriented to the deeds and words of Christ:

> Easter no longer signifies a process of completion to be understood primarily in future-eschatological terms, but the present-eschatological overcoming of personal and transpersonal limits to the development of one's life. Correspondingly, the sermons do not interpret God's power as a normative authority for the preservation of the Christian life, but as a behavior-oriented ideal whose translation and fulfillment is the goal of Christian existence and in whose liberating, life-creating potential Christians participate, through the grace of God.[46]

A historical-psychoanalytical appreciation of the preaching models just described can be a help to preachers in locating themselves within a broader homiletical narrative picture and illuminate their own theological assumption regarding the problem of narcissism in relation to preaching justification.[47]

We now return to our initial thesis, according to which the preaching of justification is to be understood as a creative event in which the disruption of distorting experiences finds its gestalt.[48] In terms of fundamental homiletics, this event is grounded in the power of the Holy Spirit, which enables faith, lifting us into the realm of grace.

How can we talk, within this realm of grace, about *incurvatio* experiences in such a way that people are really seized by the message of justification? How can we talk in a healing way about what is often suppressed by silence and shame? If we are to undertake this task, talk about the *homo incurvatus in se ipsum* must first be freed from its moral connotations. This image is powerful precisely because it describes people who live in a state of bending of body-self, willingly or not. If we listen to people who have been made expendable, we sometimes hear echoes of dreadful voices in their struggle to tell their own life stories in the tension between the ideal of the normal life and their own lived experience: the gaping wounds, the feeling of being an illegitimate or broken woman—we hear about wakeful nights and stomach cramps and the constant longing to go back to the old job.

These experiences, which are often very stressful to articulate, describe the social experience of diminishment of self and growing isolation, even when there is no direct reference to God in the context. In addition, there are experiences in which self-isolation is not caused only by processes of marginalization but is an active expression of participation in the power of sin.

As regards a focus on *incurvatio* experiences of distortion and diminishment, the biblical texts can potentially provide a vivid space of resonance for what initially, at the individual level, had to be shamefully hidden. In Romans 3:10-18, the apostle Paul begins a lament over the *homo incurvatus in se ipsum* who cannot escape the power of sin. His vivid language is impressive:

> "There is no one who is righteous, not even one;
>> there is no one who has understanding,
>> there is no one who seeks God.
> All have turned aside, together they have become worthless;
>> there is no one who shows kindness,
>>> there is not even one."
> "Their throats are opened graves;
>> they use their tongues to deceive."
> "The venom of vipers is under their lips."
>> "Their mouths are full of cursing and bitterness."
> "Their feet are swift to shed blood;
>> ruin and misery are in their paths,
> and the way of peace they have not known."
>> "There is no fear of God before their eyes."

These dramatic images reveal the torment that can be suffered in sin's clutches. The physicality of these images can help the preacher to shape a mediating space in which experiences of distortion and diminishment can be articulated.

We assume that many biblical texts can function as intermediary spaces in which things that have been concealed or are difficult to speak about can take shape and what is absent can be transformed into presence.[49]

The courage to address *incurvatio* experiences, things that are meant to be kept secret, ignored, or concealed, in sermons can be owned in the light of grace overflowing poured out onto our lives so that we are unbent and raised up before God.

This ambivalence of the *simul iustus et peccator*—that we stand before God as justified and at the same time continue to sin in the world—is something that must also be powerfully presented in worship. Luther describes this courage for ambivalence in his third disputation against the Antinomians in terms of the Our Father:

> If you are holy, why do you cry out? Because I feel that sin is clinging to me; and therefore I pray: Hallowed be Thy Name, Thy kingdom come! O Lord, be gracious to me. And yet you are holy. And yet you are holy? In this sense: insofar, that is, as I am a Christian, to that extent I am righteous, devout, and belong to Christ; but insofar as I look back at my sin, I am miserable and a great sinner. Therefore it is true that in Christ there is no sin, and in our flesh there is no peace and no rest, but enduring struggle.[50]

If you are holy, why do you cry out? The perception of sin is for Luther an all-encompassing event that is profoundly sensual, because I *feel* that sin is clinging to me. This deep-seated perception of sin can only occur if the distinction between person and work is repeatedly addressed in our preaching. This seems to be the key to a preaching of justification that can help us not simply to permit the narration of *incurvatio* experiences, in view of the ambivalence of *simul iustus et peccator*, to descend into a depressive and perhaps also a voyeuristic depiction of life's realities. *Fides facet personam*: faith makes the person, not the work—and not the seamless and polished résumé we think we must present to describe our employment history. Human personhood *coram Deo* is constituted, in the first instance, not by our achievements but by the fact that God has regard for us. This, however, does not mean that human works are to be demonized. The faith that is at home in the event of justification instead frees us for an attitude that must no longer be directed by a narcissistic impulse but, rather, can be developed in a genuine encounter with the other. Michael Moxter points out that we are urgently required to make a further distinction regarding works:

> Work and play, sports and entertainment, production and work, effective and expressive action, political activity and church participation—none of these can be summarized without distinction in the simple contrast of person and work. The cultural significance of the doctrine of justification can, therefore, not consist in summarily calling all activities "work": rather, the difference between works must be perceived and maintained.[51]

This discourse on works is not simply subsumed under the concept of paid activity, as often happens when theologians attempt to establish a right to work. Human creativity and imaginative ability extend far beyond contexts of paid employment.

The articulation of *incurvatio* in preaching should go hand in hand with the depiction of profound bliss as it flows out of the reception of grace as a gift. We will turn to this in the next section.

Grasping Bliss

The theologian Jörg Lauster, in his book *Gott und das Glück* (*God and Bliss*),[52] reflects on the connection between justification and the experience of bliss. First, setting aside the types of reflection that are peculiar to the Christian religion, he speaks of what an experience of joy is, beginning with the bliss of a moment—in contrast to the joy that may arrive as the result of a success-oriented action. Bliss in this context is something uncontrollable that happens of itself, and the timing—suddenness—reveals this uncontrollability as a moment of surprise. Bliss comes, unhoped for and unsought; it cannot be striven for; it can only happen of itself.

> Very few of life's goals can be reached by the determined following of a life-plan; situations continually arise in which one needs precisely this kind of joy in order to arrive at one's goal. Bliss is thus more than simply the arrival at a preconceived goal. . . . There is, then, an unavoidable dimension of bliss that extends beyond human accomplishments and cannot be attained by any combination of wishes, plans, and their completion. In this perspective we may say of bliss that it is not created, but given. Bliss exceeds the bounds of human self-determination because its preconditions and conditions are never precisely determinable,

because they are, at least in part, unattainable and uncontrollable. But this uncontrollability is itself the special attraction and charm of the joy of the moment.[53]

This instant experience of joy reveals an affinity to aesthetic experience, in which we discover the liberating release from a strictly functional connection, an instantly occurring certainty that makes the question of "what for" meaningless because here, in this moment, the words, sounds, colors, or forms are sufficient in themselves. Aesthetic experience contains the moment of interruption, and therein lies what is freeing, the sigh of relief, because the complex functional relationships of the modern world seem suddenly to be partially disempowered. A person experiences something that is good and beautiful in itself, and therefore in itself sufficient. This is the experience of an unexpected entry into reality. A sudden, uncontrollable, unsought moment of fulfillment unfolds that stands outside the causal relationship to what was previously wished for, striven for, sought for.

In analogy to aesthetic experience, the experience of bliss can be described as a twofold experience of freedom:

> It frees from what lies outside this moment; that is, it frees and relieves from one's own intentions, goals, and the functional contexts in which the individual is embedded. At the same time, this experience frees one for what is happening in this moment and invites to linger. In the moment of bliss I am freed from the fixations of my situation, precisely in that I am fascinated by the gift of this moment.[54]

Besides aesthetic experience, there is also an analogy between the joy of a moment and sensual experience. Lauster refers to Plato's idea of the Good: what a person experiences in the joy of the moment as the overcoming of one's own efforts and one's own life orientation can be interpreted as a "self-revelation of the Good itself." The sensual experience of momentary bliss, or better, the bliss of a moment as sensual experience, is congruent with the fundamental Platonic experience in that the soul, through beholding the ideas, is lifted beyond the conditions of its own life and thus sees the light of true beauty, exalted above all mortal things: being, endurance, and eternity that fill the human being with longing to get beyond the limitations of his or her existing state.

To this point, the focus has been on philosophical considerations. Next Lauster stresses the link between the joy of the moment and religion: the moment's joy rests on self-transcendence. At the moment when one is aware of one's own life as a good one, at the moment of joy, there occurs an experience of meaning that exceeds everything the human being can "make" of herself or himself. In this way, the joy of the moment is revealed as an experience of transcendence. The moment's bliss is thus also an experience of the holy, an experience of the incommensurable that can be neither derived nor demonstrated. Wilhelm Schmid argues similarly in his book on the art of living: "Bliss breaks through the limitations of mortality and allows the mortal being to share in the experience of eternity. . . . The individual is imbued with a strength that is more comprehensive than that of the individual self."[55]

Lauster continues by saying that the joyous realization that one can take control of one's own life does not stand alone; it is based on another fundamental assumption that is always prior to human planning and acting. Human beings must be aware of themselves as accepted by some other before they can accept themselves. In Protestant theology, the doctrine of justification provides the classic theological formulation of this central connection in the theology of grace. In instantaneous fulfillment, a person experiences the immediate presence of an ultimate, unconditional, and infinite dimension of reality that, by far exceeding one's own will and efforts, simultaneously reveals her or his own limitedness. The fulfilled moment liberates the human being from every kind of megalomania, every destructive overreaching of aspirations toward self-sufficient ability and fulfillment. The bliss of the moment in conjunction with the embrace of one's finitude and limitation constitutes a liberation from megalomania, the compulsion to self-realization through one's own efforts and will—into the freedom to develop one's own self. This self develops in a manner that is constantly aware of being already surpassed, set on a foundation that it never posits for itself but on which it can always trustingly assume that it is benevolently sustained and supported. Reformation theology formulated this connection as the amalgamation of freedom and justification grounded in communion with God.

Justification, communion with God, and freedom are the fundamental and mutually determinative moments of this experience. Human beings experience the fulfillment of their lives as a moment in which they behold their lives as something good and fulfilling, before they seek or even could seek, on their own, to make good and successful lives for themselves. By the mediation of the life and message of Jesus, the Christian religion interprets this experience as an experience of God. It opens up a sense of life, a sense of being held in the love of God that corresponds structurally to what philosophers regard as the illumination of a higher reality, a self-revelation of the Good. The religious interpretation of it as an experience of justification differs from the philosophical interpretation by being a higher level of determination: it is God's self who becomes present in the sustaining sense of life experienced by the human being and so enters into communion with her or him. The experience of certainty that one's life is lifted up in God frees the human person from the desire to try to establish independently the foundation of her or his being and life fulfillment. Human persons experience their own lives as sustained by a power and a meaning that is not at their disposal and that they themselves cannot ascribe to their own lives—nor do they need to do so. The human being experiences that his or her being is fulfilled not through having certain goals and aspirations but as founded and lifted up in the love of God and therefore sufficient in itself. That is an experience of reassurance by which the human being "comes clean," gets things straight with herself or himself, although she or he cannot establish the conditions for this harmony but only receive them. This relieves individuals from having to chase after self-chosen or imposed powers and ideals. This experience frees one, in the course of one's own life, to develop that life as something that it already is: on my crooked path and in my half-baked dreams, I can know myself as loved by God and so learn to walk with dignity.

Lauster underscores that it would be absurd to assert that *every* dimension of the experience of justification is joyful, just as it would be absurd to describe every momentary bliss as an experience of justification. Rather,

> there are certain forms of the experience of bliss that can plausibly be understood in terms of the theology of justification. This is true both of the content and of the foundational context of these experiences. . . . In the uncontrollable arrival of bliss, in the purposeless coming-to-oneself, and in the breakthrough to an acceptance of meaning that sustains one's being there are striking structural analogies that permit us to translate the idea of justification from its previously rigid dogmatic encrustations into the language of present experiences of life.[56]

What does this mean for preaching? We suggest that above all we should consider the *attitude* of the preacher and not primarily individual abilities, skills, or techniques. The attitude of the preacher is apparent in these dimensions, surrounds her and at the same time goes beyond her, because it affects her whole existence. One does not simply "have" an attitude; it must be practiced, and without practice one will lose it again. Two perspectives seem especially important to us for preaching that is able to get its hearers in touch with the joy described: opening oneself to the uncontrollable, and being able to perceive and shape experiences of flow.

Rolf Zerfass titles one chapter of his book on preaching: "How Do I Arrive at Insights? Or: Drinking from One's Own Wells." Creativity is something I cannot approach primarily through certain techniques like those currently being taught in management seminars with the motto "Through creativity to greater productivity." One can observe in many fields of creative work, including music and art but also in preaching, that adhering to strict training regimes can improve organization and technique but tends at the same time to close off contact with the creative moment.

A sermon inspiration is a creative event and opening oneself to this event requires an inner relaxation such as that needed for play and sleep.[57] In theological perspective, Zerfass writes, we may regard these inspirations as the Holy Spirit's playing field. The Spirit blows in us as she will, and her greatest opportunities happen when we do not cling stubbornly to our own concepts and learned rules of logic but are open to what arises out of the depths. This is why an internal release plays a central part in all forms of meditation: it is about opening oneself to the Spirit's speaking. Here, too, exercises are needed, and they are provided by many religious traditions: for fruitful inspiration, there is a need for a concentration of the heart and the body, for a process of internal tuning. Often, there are small steps to be taken; these are about a careful apprehension of one's own sense of time and body and may correspond with a careful organization of one's daily life:

> Develop a feeling for the specific conditions surrounding your own creativity: When and where do good ideas come to you? More likely in the morning or in the evening? While you are walking or when you are lying down? Learn to protect your creative times (at least two hours per day!) and to keep them free from superficial work and other disturbances! Many good ideas occur when you awake early in the morning ("for he provides for his beloved during sleep," Ps. 127:2!). If you make space for them right away and note them down (even before eating breakfast, reading the paper, listening to the radio, etc.) and meditate on them, you will work very economically.[58]

Zerfass then suggests, for the further process of shaping the sermon, the practice of "phrase-thinking": one idea at a time is written on a slip of paper; the preacher experiments with various ways of arranging these slips in sequence until a good solution is found. The preaching is then done extempore, with the chain of ideas noted on the slips providing the framework.

In this way, one can learn and practice opening oneself to the uncontrollable. As regards the preaching of the gospel as the opening up of the possibility of blissful experience, we want to suggest a second perspective: learning to preach also means opening oneself to experiences of flow and giving shape to them.[59] Flow, in the sense intended here, is both an experience and an attitude that can be practiced by perception and attention to techniques available in play, in art, and indeed in all creative processes and in religion. With "flowing" or "flow," we describe

> the total sense perception we have when we act with total commitment . . . [it is] a condition in which action follows action according to an internal logic that requires no deliberate intervention on our part. . . . We experience this condition as a unified flow from one moment to the next. In this condition we feel that we have our actions absolutely under control and there is no separation between self and environment, stimulus and reaction, past, present, and future.[60]

Action and awareness melt together, and attention is focused on a particular field of stimuli; the actors are "plunged" into the flow; there is a loss of ego and simultaneously the greatest intensification of physical and spiritual presence. Being in the flow is satisfying in itself. Those who have experienced this in creative situations (e.g., when painting or playing the piano or in sports) know that experiences of flow can be associated with great feelings of joy. In a certain sense, I can practice opening myself to experiences of flow, even in polishing and delivering a sermon. I can make it present to myself by accepting the image of a "flow channel": when I am insufficiently challenged, lack ideas, am poorly prepared, have no desire to work, and so on, I will fall "down" out of the flow channel; in situations of high demand, stress, but also when I try to achieve too much in a theological or dogmatic sense in my sermon, I slip out of the flow channel "upward." Swimming in the middle of the flow channel is joy, from a homiletical point of view.

The interpretation of the event of justification as an experience of bliss leads us now to the next aspect: the interpretation of homiletical imagination as disruptive and anticipatory speech.

Homiletical Imagination: Anticipatory and Disruptive Speech[61]
The assembly's worship in which justification of the "expendables" takes concrete form is in many ways a staging of disruptions, which opens new spaces for imagination.[62] The ideology of the *homo laborans*, for example, is hereby disrupted. The preaching of justification, which focuses particularly

on those who have been made superfluous, will again and again give clear expression to the fact that human personhood is not exhausted by employment and social status, and that being accepted by God has nothing to do with the ability or readiness to produce or with one's position in the job market.

Such proclamation will seek homiletical and liturgical forms in which the receptive responsory existence of believers is given expression. It will not favor productive and calculating activities in life stories but, instead, those ritual actions that inculcate and make space for the *habitus* of receptivity and listening.[63] It will be sustained by the energy of the Sabbath rest, of Sunday as the day of the *kyrios* who created heaven and earth, and spaces for creativity and for rest. In worship, which physically disrupts the busyness of unemployment and employment, we have the opportunity to experience ourselves, in awe, as those who receive, and God as the one who gives. In this sense, we can join in Eberhard Jüngel's question:

> Can we cease to be *doers* and *owners* and once again become *beings* who, *astonished*, become visible to themselves? Can we once again discover ourselves as God's children: as *newborn children* who can do nothing, absolutely nothing, for their own being? Can we finally discover that all our doing must come from a *not-doing* if it is to be a helpful doing and not one that, by its very success, is destructive? The work week lives in an unfathomably deep sense from the *Sabbath rest*, which Christian faith not accidentally identifies with *Sunday*, which celebrates the resurrection and has moved to the beginning of the week in order to make it clear that being and letting-be is the origin of all activity.[64]

In this sense, the Sunday worship service can be seen as a healthy disruption in which the attitude of balanced responsory receptivity can be practiced as a central element of a *vita contemplativa*.

In addition, proclaiming grace overflowing for those who are considered superfluous will constantly bring to the fore the prophetic resistance that is not reconciled to economic conditions in which the maximization of profit is set above opportunities for human development and life. It disrupts by rejecting the ruling economic logic whereby the accumulation of capital and the maximization of profit are described as God-given natural mechanisms. Prophetic speech within the horizon of preaching grace cultivates this kind of irreconcilability, which does not forget the victims of profit or reduce them to passive recipients of the church's charity.

The preaching in which justification happens also disrupts rigid and static self-images that are constantly reproduced. In this sense, it can be understood as anticipatory speech. It addresses the hearers not simply in some sense such as "I'm okay, you're okay," nor like the advertising slogan of some diet margarine: "I want to be the way I've always been." Since it is creating speech, it sees and addresses the hearers in their *potentiality*, in what is *not yet* realized in their lives and strives to take a gestalt in them and is not content with the narrowing of horizons that the *incurvatio* brings forth.

This applies also to the development of the individual self, which in the eyes of God is filled with potentiality. In 1 John 3:2, we read of the glory of the children of God, which introduces a concept of the subject that has a process-oriented character and is open to God's future. In eschatological perspective, identity is totally given in the promised seeing of God: "Beloved, we are God's children now; what we will be has not yet been revealed. What we do know is this: when it is revealed, we will be like God, for we will see God as God is."

This becoming-a-subject is effected through ex-centric identity that does not strive for self-sameness. Becoming a subject is, rather, related to the Other, the revealed Christ. Knowledge of one's own person happens in an eschatological perspective, when believers shall see God. Becoming a subject in relation to the Other, to Christ, happens in and is at the heart of the preaching of justification. Michael Moxter remarks:

> In contrast to concepts of individuality that are linked to identity, self-possession, and an independent self-control, another picture emerges in the horizon of belief in justification. In a somewhat problematic summary one could say that just as the difference between the *idem-* and the *ipse*-identity belongs to the human, so in relation to the God who justifies, the human self encounters her- or himself as Other.[65]

Moxter is speaking of the encounter with the Other, with Christ, as an act of healthy loss of self.

This open-process-oriented concept of subject constitution is contrary to the violent construction of identity in which people are identified in terms of a particular gender, a race, or a social status. Especially in the modern era, identity is constructed with a specifically forceful logic that subsumes multiplicity and contradictions into a constricted monotony and subjects all special traits to a single logic. The principle of identification is, then, more than merely a form of knowledge. It takes shape in ritualizations and cultural forms that demand accommodation and smooth out all dissonant experiences.[66]

These considerations about the construction of the subject as an open process can be brought into conversation with various social-psychological concepts of fragmented identity development in such a way that value is given to the ability to allow different and sometimes partly contradictory constructions of identity and their associated social roles to exist alongside one another.[67]

The philosopher Judith Butler has applied her deconstructivist thoughts on constitution of subjectivity as an open and incomplete process to the construction of gender: "The subject is never fully constituted, but is continually subjected and produced anew. This subject is thus neither an origin nor a mere product, but the constantly present possibility of a particular resignifying process."[68] Butler's critique of normative, mainly binary concepts of identity aims to lay bare the abjections associated with those concepts and the politics of identity connected with them. In light of Christian theology, however, the processes thus described have a direction founded on the eschatological expectation of seeing God.

The preaching that justifies, like the distribution of the sacraments, is an embodied performance of undoing *incurvatio*, the undoing of bending of self. Baptism, as a ritual presentation of undoing *incurvatio*, frees human beings from the destructive compulsion to constitute their own subjectivity in solely self-referential terms. The baptized are joined to Christ, the crucified risen one, by being acquitted of the compulsion to justify their own life stories. But this does not happen through an individualistic action; instead, baptism conferred in the name of the triune God, is aimed at incorporation into the body of Christ.[69] The ecclesiological dimension of baptism is linked to the church's ethical obligation not to allow the unity of Christian community to be called into question, whether through gender differences, race, or social status, or even by confessional differences.[70]

I do not receive my life from myself. In the light of ex-centric baptismal identity, it is not even my biological parents, through whom life is given to me. In baptism, an act of dislocation takes place, not my "blood ties" but the immersion into the body of Christ, the dying and rising with Christ—this is where life is given to me. Paul in particular articulates the ex-centric constitution of human subjectivity when he addresses the subject of the body. Baptism is incorporation into the body of Christ.[71] To put on Christ like a new garment, in the act of new creation as it occurs in baptism, is a ritual action of eschatological imagination par excellence in which binary-ordered hierarchies are transcended. The baptismal act was intended in the primitive Christian communities as a ritualized transcending of static identity by means of dramatic gestures (disrobing, immersion, robing). Unfolded in baptism was "the power to assist in shaping the symbolic universe by which that group distinguished itself from the ordinary 'world' of the larger society. . . . A factual claim is being made, about an 'objective' change in reality that fundamentally modifies social roles."[72]

The anticipative mode of preaching justification embraces eschatological imagination, which refers to the cosmos, the well-being of the planet, and the life-worlds in which we are at home. It paints the picture of the new Jerusalem, in which God will wipe away all tears, and points to the time in which people will be able to harvest what they themselves have sown. It describes the moment in which God will be all in all.

Eschatological imagination seeks to respond to experiences of human distortion, in collective and global perspective as well, with the treasures of imagery and symbols in which the risen Christ shares his life with us. Eschatological imagination is nurtured by *ṣĕdāqâ*, God's fidelity to community, directed to the healing of relationships.[73]

Zerfass, in the second volume of his textbook on preaching, chooses the word *intervention* to emphasize this disruption, and particularly the ability of preaching to disrupt violent and destructive life situations. "Preaching interrupts not only the course of the worship service, but the course of life, by inviting us to look carefully at what is going on. It draws our life's context into the light of the Word of God: 'Your word, Lord, is a light to my path' (Psalm 119:105). After that, life itself is again in view."[74] Zerfass takes Jesus' act of speaking in parables as a paradigm for this disruptive form of speech, and also the way in which Jesus resolves destructive situations in arguments and other interventions and in this sense brings a liberating clarity to those who suffer from these situations. Zerfass gives an example in order to make clear how explosive this speech is, and begins with a disturbing story:

> One of the Pharisees asked Jesus to eat with him, and he went into the Pharisee's house and took his place at the table. And a woman in the city, who was a sinner, having learned that he was eating in the Pharisee's house, brought an alabaster jar of ointment. She stood behind him at his feet, weeping, and began to bathe his feet with her tears and to dry them with her hair. Then she continued kissing his feet and anointing them with ointment. Now when the Pharisee who had invited him saw it, he said to himself, "If this man were a prophet, he would have known who and what kind of woman this is who is touching him—that she is a sinner."

Jesus knew what the Pharisee was thinking. He let the woman go on with what she was doing, but by catching Simon's eye and through his own manner he let him know that he knew what kind of woman she was, but he did not want to make a fuss and disturb the dinner, the conversation, and the atmosphere. Simon was reassured. He thought: While the man is a little too generous, he is polite and clever. He will get rid of the woman as soon as he can. This man is one of us.

Meanwhile, the woman had used up her oil. As neither Jesus nor anyone else in the room took notice of her, she stood up and silently left the room.

From that day on, many Pharisees found the young itinerant preacher quite agreeable.[75]

Jesus resolves the embarrassing situation by being in solidarity with the Pharisee and letting the woman drop. Zerfass offers two further possibilities for an intervention by Jesus that would have been problematic and humiliating, especially for the woman: Jesus gives a wild, revolutionary speech in which he enters into solidarity with the woman and attacks the Pharisee, Simon—and in so doing mistakes the particular anointing and, after this scene, delivers her up to public aggression; or, Jesus does not enter into solidarity with anyone, but instead seeks to save his own skin by beginning to preach platitudes about the goodness of God, who lets even such a sinner live. "Thus the woman is turned into even more infamous object than in the first variant: she is made a means for demonstrating how bad people are and how good God is."[76]

In fact, Luke's Gospel tells of a quite different outcome:

Jesus spoke up and said to him, "Simon, I have something to say to you." "Teacher," he replied, "speak." "A certain creditor had two debtors; one owed five hundred denarii, and the other fifty. When they could not pay, he canceled the debts for both of them. Now which of them will love him more?" Simon answered, "I suppose the one for whom he canceled the greater debt." And Jesus said to him, "You have judged rightly." Then turning toward the woman, he said to Simon, "Do you see this woman? I entered your house; you gave me no water for my feet, but she has bathed my feet with her tears and dried them with her hair. You gave me no kiss, but from the time I came in she has not stopped kissing my feet. You did not anoint my head with oil, but she has anointed my feet with ointment. Therefore, I tell you, her sins, which were many, have been forgiven; hence she has shown great love. But the one to whom little is forgiven, loves little." Then he said to her, "Your sins are forgiven." But those who were at the table with him began to say among themselves, "Who is this who even forgives sins?" And he said to the woman, "Your faith has saved you; go in peace." (Luke 7:36-50)

Jesus resolves the situation neither by harmonizing nor by polemicizing or generalizing but by confronting the people gathered here and now, through the parable, with the premises of their own acts and their relationship to the world, bringing them to see the scene now present before them, but also themselves in the whole sweep of their lives, with new eyes:

> In this way he confronts Simon with the question: Who is your God? Is God the highest principle, metaphysically legitimating all the differences in this world, between men and women, Jews and Gentiles, good and evil? Is God the ultimate ground of justification for the social barriers we set up against one another? Or is God the one who crosses all those boundaries, or undermines them, because he is God, the friend of life?[77]

Preaching as intervention finds its model in this disruptive form of speech practiced by Jesus: a wise intervention, in words, that clarifies and opens apparently closed, inescapable situations in the eyes of those who are humiliated, that confronts people with the ultimate, often unconscious premises of their relationship to themselves and the world and their actions, and invites them to look at themselves, other people, their ways of interacting and living together, with new eyes.

Attending to the Traces of Grace in the Face of the Other

Becoming a subject in light of the event of justification describes the ex-centric orientation of Christian existence. It encompasses a form of relationship in which the encounter with Christ draws us into encounter with the other: in the other, we encounter Christ. The idea is expressed in Matthew 25:36 as follows: "I was sick and you took care of me, I was in prison and you visited me."

Luther also, at the end of his work *On the Freedom of a Christian*, writes: "A Christian man does not live in himself, but in Christ and in his neighbor, or else is no Christian: in Christ by faith; in his neighbor by love."[78] Ingrid Schoberth interprets this love of which Luther speaks as attentiveness to the other.[79] Referring to Emmanuel Lévinas, she writes:

Lévinas here takes an explicitly biblical view: the other is *not* a threat to my subjectivity; rather, he is the occasion for my subjectivity in that through his presence he opens to me an elementary human relationship. For Lévinas it is the countenance, the face, the whole being, a hand or the rounding of shoulders, in the perception of which the other approaches me.[80]

John S. McClure sees the rupture of sameness that occurs through the encounter with the face of the other and the infinite responsibility that flows from this encounter as foundational for preaching:

Our deconstruction of preaching will seek to re-envision preaching at its deepest level, as what Lévinas calls a "saying, that is a sign given to the other, peace announced to the other, responsibility for the other, to the extent of substitution." We will search for a form of preaching that is constantly interrupted by the proximity of the other, by an obligation to the other, and by what Lévinas calls "the glory Infinite" given in the face of the other.[81]

Attentiveness to grace in the face of the other also means to realize that the other is not dissolved in the encounter with me, that he or she can never be fully grasped in my perception, but remains other. It means, as far as preaching grace is concerned, that we try to look as sensitively as possible into the faces of the justified, so that the ontological reflections on justification as relational event do not descend into abstract discussion. This looking-into-the-face means perceiving the complexity of experiences of distortion, respecting the complexity of physical and social experiences, and giving them their value—and being attentive to the resonant space they open in worship. This attentiveness practices the humility of not knowing as we seek to ask what justification through faith alone means for an unemployed single mother and for the manager who tries, for more than fourteen hours a day, to manage the business of his department within a huge corporation. What does it mean for the immigrant from the Congo with a German passport, who can hold three academic degrees and still cannot find a job because he is rejected on account of his origin and the color of his skin?

Cultivating attentiveness to the traces of grace in the face of the other in preaching also means giving careful expression to the disparities and experiences of marginalization associated with particular social positions. For example, Helga Kuhlmann speaks of what it means to develop a gender-sensitive theology of justification in which a multitude of women's life experiences are neither simply subsumed under the androcentric category "[hu]man" nor essentialized and homogenized.[82] Her purpose is "[to interpret] women's current experiences in terms of a theology of justification that is helpful and life-sustaining."[83] Among other things, she considers the particular forms of social pressure to justify themselves experienced by many women in their lives and how the conflicts that thus arise can be discussed within the theology of justification. She is also concerned to modify the theological model of *iustitia passiva* against the background of the still-current stereotypes of femininity: the notion that the nature of the female gender is primarily passive. Kuhlmann proposes, instead, that we should speak of a *iustitia receptiva*:

> If, as we have explained, being justified means being delivered from misery and what is damaging, justification is especially needed by people in trouble, caught up in guilt and weakness. It is given to those who think they must prove, and yet cannot, that they are worthy enough to be loved, even though they are blemished and feel themselves weak, imperfect, and guilty. It also belongs to those who have sinned against others. It surprises, it consoles in despair. Does it presuppose passivity? Is it appropriate to call justification a *iustitia passiva*?[84]

In the concept of a *iustitia receptiva*, even listening, receiving, and accepting the proclamation of grace can be understood as activity.

> Actually to allow a gift to do one good contradicts the modern expectation that one should constantly be remaking oneself, and also the expectation that we must always be helping others. Adopting others' appreciation as part of one's own self-concept so that one values oneself, imitating the way God beholds oneself: this is justification as *iustitia receptiva*.[85]

Example: Good Friday in the Tenderloin: "Stick Us with a Needle of Reality"

Every Good Friday in San Francisco, men, women, and children gather to walk the way of Christ's cross through the poorest part of the city and the centers of political and economic power. San Francisco shelters about 150,000 people who experience poverty and food uncertainty in their own bodies every day. The soup kitchens at Glide Memorial Church and the San Francisco Metropolitan Community Church are always full, and starting around the twentieth of every month, one sees more and more families with children in the queues, waiting to enjoy a hot meal at least once in the day. San Francisco Network Ministries and other organizations like the Temenos Catholic Worker[86] invite priests and pastors, homeless people, families, those holding public office, people with HIV, and drug addicts to join in procession on the way of Christ's cross through the streets of San Francisco. Here the justification of the "expendables" is set on its feet and put in motion. This way of the cross practices attentiveness to the traces of grace in the face of the other when Jesus' lament in the Garden of Gethsemane is recited while, at the same time, people are standing on the sidewalks and begging: "Can you spare some change?" or when the pastor who has placed herself at the end of the procession joins her deep alto voice to that of the others: "Were you there when they crucified the Lord?" and then accidentally steps on a discarded needle, looks down, and shudders, terrified.

Here it is proclaimed: Jesus is crucified in the poor, in the children living on the street; his face shines out of the faces of the drug addicts, the prostitutes, the "working poor," the people sick with AIDS-related causes. The message of the justification of the "expendables" here is: God, you give life in the midst of death. You forgive us in the midst of our unholy entanglements. And here life means the material essentials: bread, a roof over one's head, a hospital with open doors, a safe, clean place to exchange needles. "Stick us with a needle of reality" is the prayer for the ability to look each other in the face.

The Good Friday procession in the Tenderloin is impressive because walking through the neighborhood is already half the sermon: it gains its depth because the life-world found here is not perceived simply in terms of good and evil, but instead, complex situations are named without denying political responsibility. This Good Friday procession is also a physical exercise of *iustitia receptiva*. It confronts us with our own feelings of powerlessness and guilt, and at the same time opens a space in which the message of reconciliation and the resurrection of the body can be grasped in the streets of San Francisco's Tenderloin.[87]

∽◉∾

Station 1: Jesus Prays in Agony in the Garden of Olives (City Hall on Polk) (Mary Lou Geppinger)
  We adore you, O Christ! Because by your holy cross you have redeemed the world.

How many sleepless nights do we spend in prayer, O Jesus? How many sleepless nights do we spend in prayer, O Jesus? How many nights of agony and fear over our health and economic well-being? How many sleepless nights do we spend over worrying about feeding our children and retirement? How to end senseless bombings? How many sleepless nights do we spend over worry about people sleeping on the streets, not having health care, or anyone to speak for them?

Help us, Holy Redeemer, to join our agonies with yours. Sanctify our suffering with your own. Amen.

Station 2: Judas betrays Jesus and Jesus is arrested. (Municipal Court, 350 McAllister) (Pastor Maria Carone)

We adore you, O Christ! Because by your holy cross you have redeemed the world.

It is a bitter truth that those closest to us betray us. The ones who should love us, the ones who should protect us, the ones whom we love deeply. . . . It is a bitter truth that those we have shown trust to by electing them to high office betray us and betray themselves. Children are abused by their parents. Teach us to recognize and to intervene in this horror. We weep for you, Jesus, as you walk the path of a human being, vulnerable in all ways as we are. May the tears of betrayal lead us to everlasting waters of life.

Station 3: Jesus is accused by the Sanhedrin (Warren Burger State Office Building) (Father Stephen Bartlett-Re)

We adore you, O Christ! Because by your holy cross you have redeemed the world.

There are times when we feel cut off or separated from our family of faith. Where accusations like conservative, liberal, activist, and reactionary are used to hurt and cut our very souls. May we remember your words in the Sermon on the Mount: "You're blessed when your commitment to God provokes persecution. The persecution drives you even deeper into God's Kingdom. What it means is that the truth is too close for comfort and they are uncomfortable. And know that you are in good company. My prophets and witnesses have always gotten into this kind of trouble." (Matt. 5:11-12).[88]

Station 4: Jesus is denied by Peter (Federal Building) (Mr. Jeff Mezzochi)

We adore you, O Christ! Because by your holy cross you have redeemed the world.

Jesus, help us never to deny you alive and present in each person we encounter. Help us not to deny you through our representatives. We know that our president proposes $528 billion for military spending and for the wars on Iraq and Afghanistan but cuts in help to the poor for housing, health care, and violence prevention. Teach us to speak up and speak out against those abominations.

May we find you in those who repulse us. May we find you in the person sleeping in the doorway, the person on death row. May we find you in the rich and the powerful. May we find you in the broken part of ourselves. May we speak out of this brokenness in truth.

Liturgical Resonance: Petition, Thanksgiving, and Lament

As the example of the Good Friday procession in the Tenderloin shows, not only the sermon but the whole worship service is the place where *iustitia receptiva*, responsory receptivity, finds an embodied form.[89] Accordingly, we think it is helpful to situate the proclamation of grace in the broader context of worship.[90] So the Lord's Supper, but various forms of prayer as well, can be understood as a liturgical amplification for the message of justification. We will sketch this very briefly in terms of three types of prayer: petition, thanksgiving, and lament. In these prayer genres, homiletical movements within the realm of grace find their liturgical resonance. The articulation of experiences of distortion happens in lament and petition; the moments of bliss take liturgical form in prayers of thanksgiving and praise; petitionary prayers have the potential to cultivate attentiveness to the traces of the other. In all three forms of prayer, the ex-centric persona is expressed. In prayer, believers express the truth that they are *not* the sovereign makers of their self-designed lives. Instead, relational existence is embodied in the address to God: the relation to God, to the other, and to the world is only possible in the mode of calling on God. Intercessory prayers can sharpen our attentiveness to the traces of the other. In the other, we encounter Christ: I was poor and you fed me. When we pray on behalf of the "expendables," for people who are unemployed, who experience social and economic marginalization, we do not simply imagine them as objects in need of help; we ourselves are drawn into the encounter with Christ. In this encounter, we can learn to discover traces of grace in the face of the other, and two things can happen: our apathetic view of the world can waver for a moment and our perception of the suffering of others may be sensitized; second, intercessory prayers open us to the interdependence of all living things in that we enter into them in the name of God in a relational, namely a trinitarian, space. Marjorie Suchocki describes the perception of interdependence as follows:

> All things relate to all other things. In this interdependent world, everything that exists experiences to some degree the effects of everything else. We are so constituted that very, very little of all this relationality makes it to our awareness. But we are connected, nonetheless; it is sure. Praying lifts these loose connections to our conscious awareness in the context of God's presence. We begin to feel an echo of that divine meeting and weaving, no matter how distant the one for whom we pray.[91]

Suchocki articulates her reflection on radical interdependence in light of the practice of intercessory prayer in the following insight: "Prayer creates a channel in the world through which God can unleash God's will toward well-being. Prayer puts you in the way of the channel, and you will become a part of God's rolling waters."[92] Images like this, nourished by process theology, attempt to develop a different perspective to counter the danger of objectivizing the "expendables" in our petitionary prayer, of which we have already spoken. When we petition, we enter into a creative process in which God's will for the well-being of humanity is unshackled. Petitioning can open us to the still-hidden possibilities that God has prepared for our life together; our intercession is ultimately sustained by the hope that God's will may be done.

If we always pray only for *the* poor, *the* persecuted, *the* oppressed, we remain in a realm of abstraction in which human suffering and the oppressive structures that surround it are unrecognizable. It is thus very difficult for us to seize the opportunity to bring concrete names, faces, and places into view. Susanna Kempin's study, for example, makes it clear how different people's coping strategies are, their needs, and their self-images, when they are unemployed.

We would like to give an example from the Episcopal Church of St. Gregory of Nyssa in San Francisco. In the classic order of the Prayers of the People, which include petitions for the world, the church, local communities, those who are suffering, and the dead, the priest always asks the people present to mention concrete names and places: "Tell us, for which countries where war is raging shall we pray? For which women, men, and children who are persecuted? For which bishops, which congregations, and which people excluded by the church shall we pray today?" After each petition, individuals in the community evoke places, times, countries, names, and faces. An anamnetic process is set in motion, so that the network of those praying is drawn closer and closer together with those for whom they are praying, sometimes softly and hesitantly, sometimes with rage, disappointment, and tears.[93] Sometimes the prayers are full of grief that we know neither the names of the American soldiers nor those of the Iraqi women, men, and children who have perished in the week just past; that we do not know the story of the woman who took her own life because living on the streets of the Tenderloin in San Francisco had become unbearable. This praxis of prayer is an impressive example of intercessory prayers that are healing because effortful, because they demand that we overcome the abstractions through which we perceive the "others." At the same time, this form of prayer is a movement within the realm of grace because, in view of our limited and damaged abilities to perceive, remember, and live empathetically, we pray in the hope that ultimately our prayers will find their place in God's memory and gracious presence.

Prayers of thanksgiving and praise that are raised up in worship can also be seen as the embodiment of responsory receptivity. In giving thanks and praise, we are made aware that we have our life not from ourselves; rather, it is a gift. We thank God for the gift of life we have received, that keeps us alive and makes our lives worth living. We give thanks for the gifts of creation, for all that is essential to life, for our relationships to other people who are crucial in our lives. Thanks and praise to God arise out of amazement and reverence for the life God has given us, amazement at the reconciliation that has been given to us. Praise of God is inspired by the hope for redemption in which God will be all in all. Thus, prayers of thanksgiving are a concentrated expression of the experiences of joy that can illuminate the horizon of justification by faith.

Lament is the place where experiences of distortion can be articulated. As we have already described, the experience of the world that is indicated by the idea of self-distortion is usually characterized by isolation and the collapse of relationships to God and to the people around us. This radical experience of the loss of relationship, which can also be associated with negation of one's own personal worth, finds its multifaceted, concrete expression in the psalms of lament in the Hebrew Bible and in the prayers of lament that people formulate in worship today. Prayers of lament make possible a balance in worship, countering a naive theology of happiness and telling of damaged lives; lament gives a liturgical form to our struggle with the God we feel is absent. In this way, they become an embodied form of the theodicy question. Laments and litanies, in the second or first person plural, embody the paradox that God, experienced as absent or punishing, is nevertheless the one on whom we call.

The liturgical theologian Matthew Boulton writes:

> Lament, as the primary liturgical witness to divine absence in times of human need, functions in worship as a discipline of negation and disruption through which what might be termed the God of glory— the God installed by liturgical gestures of "praise"—is opposed and denied, in effect forsaking God by clinging to God's promise over and against God. This denial, impassioned as it is, is nevertheless no mere cancellation of praise; rather, in the choreography of Christian worship, the negative gesture of lament—the movement against God—makes possible the positive gesture of genuine praise—the movement toward God—by reworking the doxology of triumph into its properly eschatological form.[94]

The God who is experienced as absent is called upon, in the laments of those who pray, to show divine mercy and maintain divine fidelity to community. This appeal can also be understood as a movement within the realm of grace; it can only be seen as a limping, halting awareness that it lives from the faith that God will show God's self, that God's goodness will be revealed. Prayers of lament open a space of liturgical resonance in which dissonant life experiences in the face of economic marginalization can be expressed.

The Tension between Distinction and Reciprocity: God as Subject and Human Subjectivity

Reflecting on grace and justification in relational terms, in the interest of homiletics, requires that we cast a searching light on the relation between God as subject and human subjectivity. The connection between God's self-communication in the event of justification and the expression of human subjectivity in the act of faith response, as an entry into the realm of grace, has also been discussed in homiletics. The tension between distinction and reciprocity in the description of God as subject and the depiction of human subjectivity has also had its effects in the history of homiletics and has provided some definitive impulses in the development of homiletical reflections in the German-speaking discourse in the twentieth century.

Let us again recall Karl Barth's fundamental dictum on the work of preaching: "1. The sermon is God's word, spoken by himself. . . . 2. The sermon is the attempt, commanded by the church, to serve . . . the word of God . . . in announcing what they [people of the present time] have to hear from God himself."[95] Note, however, a sharp difference between the first and second statements: in preaching, human speech follows that of God, or more precisely, if the sermon is successful, human speech becomes transparent to God's speaking.

If we follow through some of the stations in the academic discussion on preaching since Friedrich Schleiermacher, we observe that there has been a constant swinging of the pendulum, a back and forth in preaching between an emphasis on God as subject and a stress on human subjectivity—or, we might say, between the first and second parts of Karl Barth's famous formulation of the task of preaching. Let us look at a few examples.

Since Schleiermacher's *Praktische Theologie* was posthumously published in 1850[96] and Alexander Schweizer presented the homiletics appropriate to this "practical theology" in his *Homiletik*,[97] some constellations of discourse have emerged that, although they each have individual characteristics, are very similar. Schleiermacher presented a conception of preaching in the context of cultic worship that can be summarized thus: a sermon should strengthen, express, and uplift the religious feelings that are circulating in a congregation; it can be understood as the religious discourse in which a preacher articulates his devout "inner life." Preaching and worship are understood as evocative, not effective, actions, and the focus of attention lies on human subjectivity—the preacher's devout inner life and that of the congregation, which in the worship service is brought into circulation. This idea contrasts with another conception that, despite all the other peculiarities and differences of those who have advocated for it— Claus Harms, Johann Hinrich Wichern, and Theodosius Harnack[98]—has a common thrust: it is by no means the pious feelings of the congregation or the preacher that can be the basis and criterion for adequate preaching; it is the word of God. This is associated with a reevaluation of what kind of action preaching is: preaching, rightly understood, is not an action that *depicts*, but one that *effects*; in that sense, it has a missionary purpose.

A generation later, there was another shift in emphasis. Around the turn of the twentieth century, there was an intense discussion within practical theology about the contemporary conditions of life in church and theology; the most important conversation partners, Friedrich Niebergall,[99] Otto Baumgarten,[100] and Paul Drews,[101] called for a "modern preaching." Preaching should be interesting and not boring, thematically concentrated, and not merely follow an official ecclesiastical sequence of preaching texts; moreover, the sermon should be socially engaged and should take people's religious sensitivities seriously. This revolutionary homiletical movement was directed with equal intensity against cultic preaching in Schleiermacher's sense and against the dogmatic self-satisfaction of the opposite stance, in which the character of the sermon as the word of God was eliminated. Preaching would only succeed and "be received" if it took the religious piety, and also the empirical life-world of the hearers, as seriously as it did the forms in which their subjectivity was expressed.

Only a few years later, at the beginning of World War I, there was a new theological revolution, the point of which was *not* to take human subjectivity and religious feeling as the starting point for reflecting on preaching. In early texts of Karl Barth[102] and Eduard Thurneysen[103] on homiletics, we already find in concentrated form the proposal that would take shape in the debates on "dialectical theology" in subsequent decades. "Modern preaching" attempts, according to their articulation, by the use of every possible rhetorical device, to build a bridge between the human being and God, but because God is God and the human is human, such a thing is, as far as humans are concerned, entirely impossible. Against modern preaching, which concentrated on the "how" question, Thurneysen and Barth demanded a strict concentration on the "what" of the sermon, its object and subject. Preaching the word of God only begins where its obligation to the needs of cultural and moral-religious elevation has been satisfied. We can only speak of preaching in the true sense where and when the pastor has laid aside his role as village or town leader and begins again to take the duty of preaching seriously. New respect for God! and: the human, especially the religiously and culturally engaged human, must die!

Since the 1960s, in various fields of practical theology—religious education, pastoral studies, and liturgics—there has been an empirical turn, and the same is true for homiletics. In practical theological reflection, but also in individual and social religion outside institutionalized forms, there has been a movement away from dialectical theology. So once again, the "how" of preaching is at the center of attention. In this period, the situation of the listeners,[104] the subjectivity of the preacher,[105] as well as communication processes between preachers and listeners were major topics.

Among the homiletical positions thus sketched are a great many peculiarities and differences in detail. Nevertheless, we can observe a back-and-forth movement, a pendulum swing from one homiletical orientation to the other, each of which is dominant for a time and then is again replaced by its contrasting counterpart. This has a number of theological, ecclesial, as well as sociopolitical reasons that we can leave aside. We want to emphasize that this controversy is necessary. It cannot be resolved in such a way that one side surrenders its claim to the truth of its position. On the one side, God is seen as the subject of preaching, and human subjectivity, whether that of the preacher or of the hearers, is at least potentially viewed as risky. On the other side, human subjectivity is regarded as the indispensable starting point for all speaking about God.

A doxological distinction between God and the human being seems to us to be necessary, for the honor of God and the good of humanity.[106] If God were nothing other than a basis for human subjectivity, then God could be dispensed with. Some current discussions on subjectivity in practical theological discourse are all too often drawn into a thesis about individualization—without attention to the social background, especially the question of the limits of validity of this thesis of individualization, particularly with regard to the impoverished in society. On the other hand, an emphasis on God as subject cannot be claimed on behalf of a specific theological position. In this way, too, and particularly so, what is being defended would be damaged: for the communication of God's creative word through human creativity is the work of the Holy Spirit; especially in preaching, it remains *God's* action on behalf of human beings in that preaching intones *the name of God* over all life.[107]

Our fundamental consideration in this regard is: human subjectivity, above all in its depth dimension, cannot be articulated as self-reflexivity but only in relation to its other. What Fulbert Steffensky says of spirituality is especially true of human subjectivity in its existential dimensions:

> There are things that one cannot acquire by seeking, self-exaltation, and self-intensification. One cannot focus on oneself without missing oneself. . . . We do not need to testify to ourselves, and this is one of the great reliefs in life. We do not need to seek ourselves, because we have been found before we sought. This insight might infuse playfulness into our lives and might free us from all the compulsions of self-seeking.[108]

People today may find the other of their subjectivity in different places. This is the great offer of Protestantism, with its rituals and symbols and spaces for interaction: being able to find in the language of prayer and song, confessions and biblical stories a space into which I can allow myself to enter, where I do not need to make up anything in order to be able to "express" myself, because I have already been found and because I encounter a language that our ancestors have spoken for centuries of centuries and into which I can enter with my feelings and thoughts, my self-seeking and self-failing.

Nevertheless, reflection on subjectivity, especially as regards the work of preaching, is not utterly free from contradictions: for precisely when I, as preacher, want to honor God as subject, I can only learn to preach if I trust somewhat in my subjectivity—the subjectivity of the preacher as well as that of the hearers. And that means for those who are learning to preach that they must be seen and appreciated by those who instruct them in their liveliness, their creativity, but also in the distortions of their lives.

Preaching the gospel means joining respect for God with valuing the subjectivity and lived experience of people, especially when life's security is threatened, when life feels fragile, creativity and joy are undermined, and people cannot embrace their creative potential. This preaching is not exhausted in an analysis, however accurate, of the conditions of life and political or social programs. As anticipatory preaching, it seeks to open up a space and time in which all people—contrary to the facts of their life situation—are seen and addressed as God's beloved children, as friends of Jesus, as saints in the community of saints, as members of the body of Christ. They are surrounded by and lifted up into a reality in which, even where daily pressures and promises speak against it, people are regarded with the eyes of God's tenderness. This includes, as regards human interaction, an unconditional esteem for the human being, also and especially where that esteem—as communicative but also as economic and social valuing—is denied them. Then the preaching of the gospel is to be affirmed as protest, as lament, and as challenge, sometimes also as a scream against the conditions by which people are being deprived of their lives' opportunities and hope for the future.

The Corporeality of Grace in the Act of Preaching

The promise of justification is enunciated through the preaching of the gospel, that is, by oral speech—here and now, face to face. Martin Luther describes it as an embodied event that is not just about interpreting a text or reflecting on one's own life story in religious terms. At its center, it is neither about cognitive operations nor about self-reflection. Rather, grace overflowing is poured out onto those who allow themselves to receive it through oral speech. In the Reformer's sense, this is more than and different from an external act of communication. Speaking and hearing are regarded as physical forms of expression, indeed, as indispensable bodily forms of action. The gospel thrusts itself through the ear into the heart and so into the physical center of the human being—the center of a differentiated unity of soul, heart, spirit, and body.[109]

This perspective makes it possible to describe the embodiment of grace in the act of preaching justification more comprehensively than by use of the conceptual context of "forensic event," which has played a major role in theological debates about how to understand justification. As a forensic event, the sinner's righteousness would be declared. Through the lens of performative speech-act theory, we could say this declaration creates the reality it expresses, and does so in the action and in the moment of speaking.

The speech-act theory is helpful at this juncture, but there is something different at work here. We want to suggest that the metaphors used in the Bible and at the core of Reformation theology that speak of *corporeality*—of the incorporation of the Christian person into the saving realm of Christ's power—are not to be understood as merely figurative speech; here we find a search for a form of language to express a truth that cannot be otherwise named, except at the price of losing its full reality. The body of Christ, the communion of saints, dying and rising with Christ, new creation, putting on Christ—all these and many other body metaphors aim, always and each time, at absorbing human corporeality into the event of overflowing grace that changes the whole person. A phenomenological approach can be helpful in our efforts to express the indispensable body orientation of the event of justification through preaching, beyond the limits of dogmatic-theological discourse.[110]

Considerations on the felt sense of space can take us farther: the human's first experience of space is that of the body. Christoph Bizer suggests that we should regard the correspondence between external space and the internal space of the human body as the proper locus of religious experience.[111] This means, among other things, that the external space that is as much determined by the expulsion of breath, by the preaching of the gospel becoming audible, as by the surrounding, symbolically charged space of a church, is taken up into the body-space of those who listen to the sermon, the intellectual, cognitive dimensions but also emotionality, sense, vitality. The inner body-space is the field of resonance for preaching that is building up in the room.

Observations regarding the experience of time tend in the same direction. Phenomenologically, time is interpreted as a contrast between the experience of duration as the undivided singularity of the individual and what was and is present in our relationships with others and different realities with such intensity that one can speak of an "incorporation." That is one side of the experience of time. In contrast to that is the suddenness and momentary orientation of each particular experience and encounter, which, coming from the future, strikes against this experience of duration and, through a process of retention and of the reappearance of similar experiences, makes possible an identification of this particular time as opposed to all the other times that have been subsumed in duration. The question that arises from this notion of time is: What does it mean, and what happens if, in eschatological time, there are no more events coming from the future that encounter this experience of duration? The preaching of the gospel places the justified sinner within Christ's time as the real eschatological time, that is, the time when God's time is already present under the conditions of earthly-worldly reality. If this eschatological time in which there is no more future to come is already present,[112] the human subject is drawn back into sociality and at the same time into an intimacy with all creatures, the living and the dead, that can never be lost—and in this experience of incorporation will be able to see the face of God.

Experiences of space and time point toward an incorporation: the preaching of the gospel of justification is always more than just a communicative act. The verbal, external word that is spoken here and now through the voice of the preacher opens a reality and spreads out a saving realm of power in which Jesus Christ is present here and now.[113] The unconditional love of God fills space and time, and the assembly is enveloped, just as it is, bent over and with their half-developed dreams, into this reality: into the body of Christ, the new creation.

According to Martin Luther, this event, captured in the metaphor of incorporation, intensifies the human-divine relationship in a peculiar way. He refers to the intimacy of bodily union in order to capture the quality of this encounter. This intimate encounter does not lead to dissolution; instead, the difference between God and humans is emphasized. This is so because *in* that union there can be *no mixture*. God remains God; God's love to the human being in the context of the created world is free, overpowering love precisely because God is by no means exhausted in the self-revealing of God's love. And the human being remains a human being also in the utterly transformative experience of joyful incorporation into the realm of grace. Another aspect that this kind of incorporation without dissolution brings forth is: the human being *remains* a sinner as long as it is not true that "all is in all"—even as one who, in this union, has been declared righteous.

The special designation for communication between God and the human that results from the *binding together* of the two—that of union ("one body") and the enduring difference (God remains God; the human being remains human)—was summarized by Martin Luther in the metaphor of the "happy exchange." This form of relationship in the event of justification will receive fuller attention in the next section.

The Economy of Faith as an Economy of Intimacy

How do the self-giving God, whose grace is overflowing, and the human being who receives this gift come together in faith? With this question, we want to recall that at a crucial point Martin Luther chose a metaphor from the sphere of economic communication to comprehend this kind of transformative relationship. He speaks of exchange, or more precisely, of the happy exchange in the relationship between the Christ who gives himself to the human being in his righteousness and the soul, the personal center of the human being, opening itself to that gift. How can we understand what Luther has in mind here and is trying to communicate?

In one of his best-known writings, the *Freiheitsschrift* (*The Freedom of the Christian*, 1520), Luther develops an idea he repeatedly attempted to grasp in his writings from that period, for example, in his lectures on Hebrews two years earlier.[114] In the *Freiheitsschrift,* he discusses an event that happens to the "inner person" who hears God's word and is made new by that contact in two ways: through God's word as command and as promise. When an individual hears God's word as command, a sense of despair is released as the hearer is confronted with his or her inability to respond to it appropriately. Centrally, for Luther, this profound despair is related to the first commandment: the human being cannot admit that *God* is God, because the human being wants to be God. The point of this idea, then, is that human despair is not caused by inability to act right ethically (that is, to keep the commandments of the "second table"). Rather, the awareness emerges that the self is taken captive by original sin, which expresses itself in the megalomaniac fantasy to be God.[115] Because this hubris is destructive, the felt despair can be understood as necessary.

But the individual is not left alone in this despair,[116] for the word of promise gives the human being what the commandments require. The promises fulfill what the law commands in such a way that they lead to an intimate contact, an inner union and mingling, between Jesus Christ, who is communicated in the word of promise, and the personal center, the heart of the believer:

> Then it follows that all they [that is, Christ and the soul] have become theirs in common, as well good things as evil things; so that whatsoever Christ possesses, that the believing soul may take to itself and boast of as its own, and whatever belongs to the soul, that Christ claims as his.
>
> If we compare these possessions, we shall see how inestimable is the gain. Christ is full of grace, life, and salvation; the soul is full of sin,

death, and condemnation. Let faith step in, and then sin, death, and hell will belong to Christ, and grace, life, and salvation to the soul. For, if He is a Husband, He must needs take to Himself that which is His wife's, and at the same time, impart to His wife that which is His. For, in giving her His own body and Himself, how can He but give her all that is His? And, in taking to Himself the body of His wife, how can He but take to Himself all that is hers?

In this is displayed the delightful sight, not only of communion, but of a prosperous warfare, of victory, salvation, and redemption.[117]

In this part of the text we find an obvious closeness between the metaphors and ideas of "exchange" and "union in his body," of the exchange of gifts and of intimacy. Luther describes a process of mutual communication and mutual exchange of gifts between God and the human being, a process that intensifies to such a degree that it results in the most intimate relationship between the two. Luther made that intimacy so strong that we can almost speak of a melting together of the two. Faith has the power to join the human soul to Christ as the bride to the bridegroom. Christ and the soul become one flesh. Luther has now arrived at the metaphor of marital union: between Christ and the soul, there is a marriage of such an intimacy and intensity that human marriages are only pale reflections of it. Everything, the entire life, but also everything both partners have, is common to both.[118] This "happy exchange" has its model and basis in the mutual exchange between the two natures in the one person of Jesus Christ, the *communicatio idiomatum*. This is also the reason why Christ can take on human sin without himself being affected by it. In the process of exchange between God and the human being *in Christ himself*, sin is in a sense devoured.[119]

Luther describes faith in his *Freiheitsschrift* as a union but also as a dynamic relational event between things that are enduringly different. Let us look more closely at the particular dimensions of this relational dynamic:

- Faith joins the human soul with Christ as the bride is joined to the bridegroom. The result is an inner, intimate communion: Christ and the soul become one flesh.
- This inner communion is expressed through the metaphor of an earthly marriage between a man and a woman, but as its intensification: where human marriage is imperfect, this marriage is perfect, and in turn human-earthly marriage is its reflection.[120]

- In this inner relationship, everything that belongs to one partner becomes common to both, and reciprocally so: the human soul acquires everything Christ has and vice versa. Here, too, Luther has in mind a process that develops its dynamic in a series of stages:

1. First, we observe the absolute difference of the two partners: perfection on the one side, nothingness on the other.
2. Faith appears as the element that binds the two partners. This begins an exchange interaction: in this exchange, Christ acquires the nothingness (sin, death, and damnation) of the human partner, while the human soul assumes the perfection of Jesus Christ (grace, life, and salvation).
3. There is no exchange of specific, limited things but, rather, of everything belonging to the partners to the exchange. "For, in giving her His own body and Himself, how can He but give her all that is His? And, in taking to Himself the body of His wife, how can He but take to Himself all that is hers?"[121]
4. In spite of the infinite qualitative difference between the partners to the exchange, which is maintained throughout the process of exchange, there occurs a mutual transfer that is even described as an exchange of positions: "sin, death, and hell will belong to Christ, and grace, life, and salvation to the soul."[122] The *intimate communion* between the partners to the exchange (they become one body) makes possible the exchange of positions, the complete transformation of the human being: as the inner person, the believer is completely free, has power, as priest even shares divine power. Outside this intimate communion in faith, we remain within the description of haunting relations of dependency: as an outer person, the Christian is subject to everyone as an altogether subordinate servant: taking both aspects together, the believer is *simul iustus et peccator*.

The metaphor of "happy exchange" represents the intimate relationship of faith, and in Luther's perspective, it also and primarily contains economic dimensions. Luther's metaphor of the "happy exchange" in the act of justification is thus embedded in a vision of a just form of economic life that includes not only the inner self of the believing individual but also the life-world and its social dimension in a common life transformed by the justifying gospel.

Luther—for example, in *The Large Catechism* in the explanation of the First Commandment—set this form of relationship clearly against the economics of money, the economy of goods. The God-question is decided, so Luther says here, by whom one *trusts* at the core of one's being, what one hangs one's heart on. "Many a one thinks that he has God and everything in abundance when he has money and possessions. . . . Lo, such a man also has a god, Mammon by name, i.e., money and possessions, on which he sets all his heart, and which is also the most common idol on earth."[123]

The alternative between God and money, which appears in Luther's interpretation of the First Commandment, has broad consequences. Wherever life arises and grows, it must be cared for and protected; wherever there are loving relationships, friendships, and neighborhoods, relationships between parents and children, teachers and students, and wherever religion is lived, a compulsive orientation toward money will disturb or even destroy those relationships. There continues to exist an economic form that in some societies once, as *total institution*, shaped the exchange between person and person, person and nature, person and deity, and that was forced by the expansion of the money economy into the niches of intimate, and also religious, communication: the economy of *gift exchange*. The economy of gift exchange is constantly threatened by colonization and exploitation through the money economy that dominates society as a whole.[124]

Under these conditions, *Christian freedom* can be understood as *absolution from the obligation to give back to other people*: God gives to all life, to every individual visage, immeasurable wealth as well as each individual thing. The demand to give back would destroy the human being as human being. Christian freedom means this absolution: we need not "make things up" with God. But it does *not* mean, and this is crucial, *the dissolution of the connection to God and other people in the interest of achieving individual purposes*. At the core, the Reformation's "Christian freedom" is an alternative model, a life-advancing and—as becomes ever clearer—possibly a lifesaving alternative model to capitalistic notions of freedom, because the freedom of the individual is unavoidably viewed in connection with the enduring power and fascination of *relationship*.

Money is the real danger to the human relationship with God and thus to the center of one's self-assurance as well as one's common life with other people. Hence, Luther's alternative stands within a broad stream of biblical narratives and social laws. Accumulation, saving, self-control, avoidance of luxury and profligacy: these are the maxims of the capitalist economy, but they are *not* the maxims of biblical religion.[125] Religion, rather, lifts up the awareness that without constant profligacy, without expenditure, without freedom from care, human life, and all life, is impossible.

"Do not store up for yourselves treasures on earth, where moth and rust consume and where thieves break in and steal; but store up for yourselves treasures in heaven, where neither moth nor rust consumes and where thieves do not break in and steal" (Matt. 6:19-20). In this passage from his Sermon on the Mount, Jesus of Nazareth formulates a relationship between human beings and their social environment—and especially the place and value of economic activity—without which Martin Luther's alternative, "God or money," would be unthinkable. In this statement and elsewhere, Jesus also opposes an attitude of constant worrying, and against an attitude that measures relationships between human beings as well as their relationship to the creatures of the world in which they live according to criteria of usefulness, efficiency, growth, and economic success—and indeed, tends to use those criteria before and above any others. Why?

We suggest engaging a conversation with the French philosopher George Bataille as we meditate on justification as an economy of intimacy and outpouring that is not solely individual, solely internal, but also includes economic dimensions. Bataille, in his fundamental work on economic exchange, describes outpouring and profligacy as repressed, but still effective, principles of every economy.

> I proceed from the elementary fact that the living organism, thanks to the circulation of the power of energy on the surface of the earth, receives more energy than is necessary to maintain life. The excess energy (wealth) can be used for the growth of a system (e.g., an organism). But when the system cannot grow any more and the excess energy cannot be altogether absorbed by growth, it must necessarily be lost, without advantage, and be thrown away, willingly or not, in glory or in catastrophic form.[126]

Life is constant outpouring and spending, a rich, overflowing stream of energy that can always be only partly channeled by the orders of work and reason. Every attempt to translate the whole of the excess wealth of life's energy into growth must fail. Life energy will, from a certain point onward, overflow the orders of accumulation, control, and saving. We remember the cry of a proponent of chaos theory being pursued by a Tyrannosaurus Rex in Stephen Spielberg's *Jurassic Park*: "I hate to be proved right. . . . Life does what it's going to do." Therefore, expenditure, profligacy, and open-handed generosity belong necessarily to the stream of life. Societies that attempt utterly to repress and extinguish this necessary side of life are condemned to failure.

Do not store up for yourselves treasures on earth, where moth and rust consume and where thieves break in and steal; but store up for yourselves treasures in heaven, where neither moth nor rust consumes and where thieves do not break in and steal. For where your treasure is, there your heart will be also. . . . No one can serve two masters; for a slave will either hate the one and love the other, or be devoted to the one and despise the other. You cannot serve God and wealth. Therefore I tell you, do not worry about your life, what you will eat or what you will drink, or about your body, what you will wear. Is not life more than food, and the body more than clothing? Look at the birds of the air; they neither sow nor reap nor gather into barns, and yet your heavenly Father feeds them. Are you not of more value than they? (Matt. 6:19-21, 24-26)

In this passage from the Sermon on the Mount, Jesus of Nazareth expresses the wisdom of a basic economy that is repressed and forgotten in the constrictive and special economy of capitalism but naturally also in the growth-oriented economic acts of a planned economy. Religion is the place where the necessity for life to give freely, to expend and empty itself, is protected against being limited by efficiency-directed economic orders.

You cannot serve two masters. You cannot serve God and mammon. In the Sermon on the Mount, Jesus sets the life orientation of the gospel, of the reign of God, against the life orientation of putting aside, of care, saving, accumulation. Have no care. Live your life today. Give yourself freely and receive freely. What you need for your life the Father in heaven will give you. The lilies of the field, the birds of the heavens: they show the overwhelming wealth of God's creation and the preservation of life. Contrasted to this is the mammon-god, money, the order of care and concern, of precalculation, of piling up and keeping-for-oneself. Mammon is the god who makes people into self-seeking beings, twisted into themselves, people who are *not* free givers.

"Don't worry"—Jesus' urging, raised up in the face of the reign of God that is so rapidly approaching, contains a way of living economically that is completely different from that of the money economy. This demand characterizes an economics of outpouring excess, of giving and receiving, whose subject—and Jesus says this, too, with perfect clarity in the Sermon on the Mount—is the God of Israel. Biblical religion (and also the other world religions, each in its specific way) is even today the place where the economy of excess has its place in society, against the dominant ways of the market economy.

Grace and Justification in Relational Terms   91

The alternative "God or money" can be concretized, above all, in the way two attitudes can be distinguished in face of a situation of scarcity: the attitude of expenditure and the attitude of worry. The economy that dominates in biblical religion can be understood as an economy of excess. Everywhere the gospel is preached, one should also speak of the woman of Bethany: she poured a flask of precious oil on Jesus' head, and Jesus praised her action against the claims of the men among his disciples who objected to this waste (Mark 14:3-9). In his parables, Jesus compares the kingdom of heaven to a treasure accidentally found in a field and to a valuable pearl that one can only obtain by giving up everything one has—but for the treasure, one must also give up everything (Matt. 13:44-46). From these and similar constantly recurring passages, we can see that Jesus' urging, "Don't worry!" is anything but a passing encouragement; it aims at the center of Christian existence. "Don't worry!"—this demand summarizes biblical economic logic in concentrated form. God has given life in fullness. Whoever believes in God also believes that there is enough for all, that God cares for all living things. In contrast, a lack of trust in God, a rupture in relationship with God, sin, is characterized by a situation in which people live with a sense of scarcity: an attitude in which all look after their own lives and attempt to grab as much as possible for themselves. Martin Luther speaks of the attitude of the *homo in se incurvatus*; this "existence twisted back upon itself" is the precise counterimage to Christian existence, and it also describes the content of the biblical word *mammon*. Mammon is something that is laid aside, and dependence on mammon characterizes a lifestyle centered on securing oneself and individual planning. This is precisely the attitude toward life that corresponds to the capitalistic money economy and is appropriate to it: worry about scarcity. Against this attitude to life, faith in the God of abundance is evoked. In biblical perspective, the law opens a way to share this abundance justly.

The new form of relationship founded on faith, which includes everything and therefore also economic relations, is characterized by recognition of the human being as a person, as a unique countenance. For the capitalistic economy of goods, in contrast, the particularity of things is as much a matter of indifference as is each individual face of a living being. The fundamental law of this economic logic is that everything can be exchanged for everything else. Each individual good can be translated into money; in this, and not in its concrete use for particular human needs, its value lies. And human ability to work is also seen as a good whose value lies not in the individual's particular charisms, creativity, and strength but likewise in how much money it is worth. According to this economic logic, money becomes the proper subject of social reality and exclusive measure for all relationships.

The economy of biblical religion, in contrast, opens up an alternative. It tells of the God who made heaven and earth and is not indifferent to the work of God's hands. God approaches each individual human being in her or his uniqueness, accepts us in our half-realized dreams and incomplete life stories. This relationship is not about an exchange of goods. Indeed, this relationship *transforms* abstraction toward people's unique life stories, particular life situations, and concrete needs. Those who let themselves be touched by the biblical narrative tradition are taken into a relational space in which God is concerned precisely for these people: God chose this one people, Israel, living on the margins of the political and cultural empires of the day, as the partner in God's covenant of friendship, and Jesus' friends are incorporated in that covenant as well. In this relational space, the value of every unique countenance is acknowledged and treasured, and people are accepted in their desire to live: corresponding to the Noachic covenant after the great flood (Gen. 9:9-16). God's covenant of friendship is for *every living thing*. In the world of goods, all things, and by tendency all people as well, are made the same, namely interchangeable like money, an abstract value. In contrast, the biblical narrative of the relationship between God and God's people always values the *uniqueness and difference* of all life. This is true from the first beginnings to the end of time: God has created all life according to its own uniqueness, and see, it was very good. Likewise, judgment and redemption are not indifferently applied to creatures but according to their unique form, in their life stories and net of relationships, which cannot simply be exchanged one for another.[127]

Martin Luther, in his *Freiheitsschrift* of 1520 and in many other texts, describes the special form of the relational space between God and the human being that is conveyed by the incomprehensible breadth and manifold character of the biblical narrative, using a theological figure: the distinction between law and gospel. One can explain the *religious logic* of this difference by saying that it is about a twofold movement of flowing out and calling in, a flow movement in which the relationship between God and the human being shows itself to be alive.[128]

The law is an aid to touching the center of our destructive concepts of life, the human megalomaniac fantasy of wanting to be God. This is made concrete in a variety of fields: economic, political, social, and cultural, in which people who cannot accept their own limitations and confuse themselves with God make themselves and other people unfree, caught up in and entangling themselves in control mechanisms. There is a tendency for such concepts of life to threaten the freedom and uniqueness of all life. Identifying this way of life as sin can create a disruption of this destructive self-definition and pattern of relationships.

The word of the gospel, then, when this destructive model of relationships has lost its power, opens a healthy relationship to God and other people, and even to oneself: God gives me, as one who believes in Jesus Christ, God's justice, and takes on my sin: an exchange in which *everything* is exchanged for *nothing*. The economic logic of capitalism is broken here, just as is the logic of the economy of gift exchange, according to which everything that is received has to be given back.[129] The promise of the gospel opens a space for relationship into which all may enter who believe in it and lose their hearts to Jesus: a space of freedom in which, at the same time, the relationship is maintained and, differently from the capitalist model of freedom, relationship does not dissolve into individual self-assertion. Instead, enduring, living relationship to God and other people and fellow creatures is bound up with the acquittal, the release from having to "make up for" everything through one's own action, one's own achievement, one's own ethical behavior. The *joining of relationship and freedom* is the Christian alternative to the model of freedom as individual self-assertion.

In the year 1935, Karl Barth—in an explosive historical situation, after German fascism had penetrated every phase of life and the destruction of the Jews as well as many other groups within the population had become an obvious aim of the German regime—suggested that the sequence and logic of talking about "law" and "gospel" should be reversed, and we should speak of "gospel and law." The purpose of this reversal was to achieve greater precision, a clearer view of Protestant faith and theological existence in a destructive social milieu. For in broad segments of German Protestantism, things had reached such a state that the elementary communication of the biblical message had been torn asunder in the relating of "law" and "gospel."

Theological discourse about the "law" had been disengaged from the irreplaceable tie to Torah and the biblical proclamation of God's will in the Old as well as in the New Testament; some theologians at that time could even go so far as to pretend to see in the figure of the *Führer* and in the German *Volksnomos* (the "law of the people") the true face of what theology means by the "law." And in this connection, gospel was understood as a promise of consolation and, beyond that, only a perception of the world that, in relation to "the people" and the state, had no right of its own as such and above all no right to make any claims. For example, the theologian Emanuel Hirsch, who was very influential at the time, wrote in 1933:

This means, as far as theological teaching is concerned, that Lutheran theology and the present hour of the people and the state belong together. It is misperceived, with all its exhortative and approbative seriousness, when one sees *National Socialism* as "only" responding to a political movement, only a part of human existence, for example the establishment of a sound natural-historical ordering of common life. As a will to renewal breaking forth from a historical and public crisis encompassing all of humanity, it must necessarily will to be more. The very consciousness of the holy limits of humanity makes it the Last and Highest, the fate of all humanity. Through this alone it has become the hour of decision for Lutheran christianity, forcing us to a change of attitude, to a seeking of the divine will.[130]

And a year later, in 1934,[131] he wrote: "The Law in which God reveals himself touches us through the reality of human social life itself"[132]—that is, not primarily as "law" in the biblical sense. The gospel, Hirsch continues, shows God's goodness, but in doing so it explicates the human historical awareness of God only in a special sense. "The gospel revelation is . . . a gracious 'yes,' affirming our sanctification from God, to the people and their history [authors' note: both of which are part of the reality of the Law] as the opportunities given to us to know God and serve him."[133]

The explanation of the sequence and logic of "gospel and law"[134] that Karl Barth presents in opposition is meant to help us to preserve the joining of both dimensions in Luther's condensed form of the entire biblical narrative and to emphasize clarity and specificity as well as freedom in the shape of Christian life, also and especially against totalitarian political, ideological, and economic claims to power. In Barth's theological argumentation, the "law" is the "form" of the gospel; it is the form of divine grace that is communicated to and can be experienced by human beings. In Barth's thinking, grace means that Jesus Christ alone has said yes to God's judgment on humanity: that is, he said yes to God's being God and to the truth that human beings are not God and do not conform to God.[135] The grace of God conveyed in the gospel is that God has revealed God's freedom as divine love for human beings. The "law" is the form of this promise visible to humanity.[136]

How can we reiterate this ordering of gospel and law to one another in such a way that it does not remain an abstraction? How can we preach in such a way that this theological idea can come into contact with the experience of our listeners? Perhaps in this way: we can trust God, for the sake of Jesus Christ. That is the central point, the central content of the gospel and at the same time the strength it conveys. And: we *should* trust God. That is the law: the communication of God's will that we trust God—and bind our hearts, ultimately, to no other competing power figure. When God demands that we trust God alone, the possibility opens up that we can assume a critical distance toward all other promises to which the hearers of the sermon are exposed in their own particular life situations and in their relationships at work and in the consumer world.

When Karl Barth formulated his thoughts, those were above all else the claims to power of the "total state." Today they are primarily the promises and demands of economic society, which extend from advertising offers through the achievement demands of the professional career to the altogether real fear that threatens so many, the fear of unemployment. These promises always seek from people, first of all, something quite different from what they promise.

The preaching of the gospel, the *invitation* to trust God and the *demand* to trust God, in contrast, open up an alternative sphere of relationship: All who rely on this God and hang their hearts on God will be lifted up into the space of divine, life-grounding, and life-sustaining power that demands nothing but what it promises. Both the promise and the demand are that we trust in the love of God. That is the good news, the gospel. The promise and the demand of the God of the Bible are effective when those who hear them let themselves be woven into the narrative thread of the whole Bible and be "taken in hand" in the best sense.

The freedom of a Christian is realized in daily life in learning to distinguish between the promises and demands of the God of the Bible and the daily promises and demands that claim our hearts and minds. The preaching that conveys the flow of God's gifts, that makes the story of the Bible so present here and now that it comes into contact with the people's life stories, the preaching that in *law* and *gospel*, in *gospel* and *law,* opens the freedom of Christians as a sphere of encounter and shows it to be distinguishable from bourgeois-capitalist freedom, opens up opportunities for life, opportunities for desensitizing ourselves against all other possible promises and demands. Nothing can be so powerful for my individual life context and for my relationships to friends and family, work and consumption, unemployment and overwork, that I must allow myself, in my inmost being, to be lured away from this and to be made afraid.

3
SCRIPTURE AS SPACE OF RESONANCE FOR PREACHING GRACE

WE CONSIDER PREACHING JUSTIFICATION of the "expendables" as a relational and embodied movement within the realm of grace in which *incurvatio* experiences and experiences of joy can be articulated *coram Deo*. In this movement, hearers are addressed as justified people in an anticipative and disruptive discourse, which sharpens the attentiveness to the traces of grace in the face of the other. In light of our theme, we have focused on the corporeal and economic form of preaching justification. We have attempted to speak about God as subject and about human subjectivity, both in distinction from and in relation to each other.

In this chapter, we will situate the preaching of the justification of the "expendables" within the space of resonance of Sacred Scripture. We want to ask what it means to take the Bible as the basis for preaching, to engage historical as well as social and economic difference—and so to exercise responsory receptivity.

We emphasize that the justification of humans who have been made "expendable" is a central message of many of the biblical writings and the orientation to the life of the poor associated with that message. In the preaching that justifies, the embodiment of the word becomes a performative event.

The Bible as the Basis for Preaching

In this section, we will address the question of what it means to start from the Bible as the basis for preaching the justification of the "expendables." We begin with some reflections by Manfred Josuttis on "the Bible as the basis for preaching."[1] The relationship we see as indispensable between the preaching of the gospel and a biblical text could seem so obvious that no further thought need be given to it. On the other hand, this agreement could be too much a matter of convention and common sense whose validity has to be fundamentally tested for that very reason, because the agreement is rarely disputed.

Our reflections will be presented in the following steps: we begin with a biographical note in which a practical theologian in the Reformed tradition gives an account of the significance of the Bible for his faith. Then we consider the horizon within which biblical narrative and life story are interrelated. Next, we take up an aspect of the biblical metanarrative—namely, that life is a gift—in order to face the fundamental problem of how we are to perceive, respect, and then engage difference so that the biblical text can be a living word for us, both in the microcosm of our own individual perceptions, in the world around us, and in the global context. The Bible is the basis for preaching, of course, primarily because of its content: the biblical writings themselves attest that the pouring out of divine grace in the life of the "expendables" is fundamental.

A Biographical Note

We begin our reflections with a biographical note. The Dutch-Swiss practical theologian Hans van der Geest has written an unpublished booklet in which he tries to take account of his own faith.[2] Van der Geest meditates on the meaning of Sacred Scripture for his faith:

> My experience of meeting God in stories that are told to me has (from my earliest childhood) continued till today. I cannot seem to find him in any other way. He remains for me fundamentally a hearing experience, and my reaction is literally ad-*hear*-ence [lit.: ob-edience, from *obedire*, to obey, derived from *audire*, to hear].
>
> I don't get to God by logic and thought. Perceiving and experiencing the world outside and inside myself does not bring me to the idea of a divine being outside myself. Some say: "There has to be something." But what does there have to be? It could be nothing but blind fate.
>
> Nor does my immediate life experience let me see God. I have never seen a trace of God's finger, and his voice has never reached my ears. Some people think that accidental happenings are God at work. I sense no inclination of that sort; it always seems arbitrary to me.
>
> My feelings are no more help to me in finding God. I never feel or sense God, even though I am a person with strong and diverse emotions. My wife's pregnancies and the births of our children were overwhelming experiences; Mozart's music touches me at the depths of my soul; a sexual encounter gives me an indescribable feeling of joy; and an Alpine landscape makes me catch my breath in awe. In these

experiences I feel myself overcome with the beauty of human life, the majesty of the earth and of humanity. But I never feel the need to call them divine, as if the human and the earthly were too little in and of themselves. Some people say that they encounter God in music or in sexual ecstasy. I believe, instead, that they lack the right words for the emotions they are feeling, and that they reach for the word *divine* to express their sense of awe.

God, as I have learned to know him, comes to me through the biblical proclamation. That is why I go to church nearly every Sunday. I need to renew the experience of faith. I myself am surprised that it does not bore me, after so many decades, and in spite of the usually deficient work of the preachers. The mystery is totally in the power of the message. It remains new and fresh for me; it continues to grab me. If I did not experience its renewal I would evaporate among my own thoughts, until it would cease to grip me. The biblical story takes me outside my daily perceptions of life and leads me into a different world. But it is not really a different world; it is the same world of my daily life, but seen in the light of God. I believe that my daily routine, my life, my fellow human beings, my fears and hopes belong to this divine world. I had no conscious need of God when I found him. I stumbled on him unexpectedly. I did not seek him; he found me. . . .

I experience the biblical stories as testimony to God's encounters with human beings. Through that testimony he sought me, too. I experience no direct encounters with God. I only receive the testimony to the encounters that Israel's prophets and Jesus' apostles experienced. The accounts, through their inner power, have become for me trustworthy paths to the knowledge of God. . . .

The power of the biblical word has deep roots. I am not guided by some principle that says the Bible is always right. I find that it would have been better if some biblical sayings had not been written. My reverence for the biblical word has not led me to a fundamentalist attitude. . . .

God is evident to me in the way Jesus lives and speaks. That has become, for me, the most important knowledge of faith. God, this great, unknown mystery inaccessible to human beings, becomes visible, enlightening, and trustworthy for me in the encounter with the man Jesus.

I am continually discovering anew what this "like Jesus" includes, as far as my knowledge of God is concerned. Remarkably enough, I then continually forget it again. Obviously, I could write it down, but that would not help me. I believe it has to be this way. I cannot "preserve" Jesus and the divine. It evades my grasp. But it shows itself again. It is in this tension that faith happens for me.[3]

The Shared Horizon: Biblical Narrative and Life Stories

How can the Bible's narrative tradition and the lived reality of human beings speak to each other today?[4] This is nothing less than the central problem of preaching. The formula "the Bible as the basis for preaching"[5] indicates first of all, according to Josuttis, a fundamental perspective that implies multiple stances. Classically, one would first point to the *normative* claims of the text with regard to preaching. The biblical text should protect preaching from the private convictions of the preacher and to that degree help to secure the communal character of the act of preaching. This model assumes that the preacher should be seen as a potentially disturbing factor in the preaching event. The risk of such a view is that the constructive links themselves disappear in the apparent oppositions of Bible and congregation, institution and individual, God and human beings.

Something similar can be said for a second model that tries to apply the claims of the biblical text not primarily to the preacher but to the congregation: namely by saying that the Bible exercises an *authoritative* function as a text for preaching.[6] According to this position, the connection of the sermon to the text determines its relevance for bringing preacher and hearers together into a state of mutual commitment. However, the validity of this argument is already limited by the fact that the majority of those who get into the pulpit on Sunday can no longer count on a guaranteed fund of trust on the part of the hearers as regards what the Bible says. Their sermons must, first of all, demonstrate the significance of the biblical tradition for life's current problems.[7] Still more important is another consideration: the perspectives of the preacher's mental and social life will always enter into the act of interpreting the biblical text before and within the sermon. Therefore, the authoritative claim of the sermon that arises out of its link to the text must in any case remain connected to the previously mentioned normative view. The reading of Scripture in worship should be considered for the preacher and for the congregation as an authoritative source that helps to critique the sermon.[8] We assume, however, that this critical function of public reading of Scripture is often not recognized.

It seems necessary to identify alternative points of contact between the Bible and the overall life of the congregation. Josuttis mentions first the *creative* function of the text for preaching. The biblical text provides the sermon with an abundance of stories, ideas, and images that can shield the congregation from the monotony of the preacher's dogmatic or even ethical thinking. Through the sometimes unsettling movement of the Spirit, Scripture can become for the preacher a source of inspiration and also of critique. The creative function of the text for preaching is about the confrontation with the foreignness of the text, which offers the preacher a challenge and impulse to her or his own speech. The text becomes a partner in a dialogical encounter. The creative expansion of the preacher's life and his or her communicative skills become effective in overcoming previous barriers to perception and expression. In spite of and in view of all individual and collective deficiencies in ideas and language, the biblical text offers challenge, inspiration, and ideas for the sermon. In this realm of creative expansion, the biblical text imparts critical impulses without stifling thoughts.

Another constructive proposal is that of the *communicative* function of the biblical text in preaching. Here Josuttis alludes especially to Ernst Lange's homiletical reflections, to which we will refer below. The biblical text creates community, not primarily by establishing a controlling authority by means of which the preacher can judge the life of the congregation and, in turn, the congregation can judge the correctness of what the preacher says. Rather, the power of the biblical text to create community consists primarily in the fact that it becomes a platform on which a theological understanding for the sake of the present relevance of Christian faith can be developed.

Finally, a further link between the biblical text and our present life situation lies in the Bible's function of *creating identity* for the Christian church. Using a biblical text in a sermon for the sake of the gospel inspires the articulation of faith out of which the community can become church. That such effects really come about cannot be taken for granted, of course. Rather, the ritual act of reading the text is carried by the hope that what may happen will be not merely a speech-act inspired by Christian ideas but that it may inspire a way of living in the light of the gospel—which takes in the direction, line of thought, and action given in the biblical stories, prayers, promises, and commandments.

Life as a Gift

The Bible is the basis for preaching: for Christians, it is a binding narrative tradition. The Bible offers a multitude of narratives of origin and departure—where life comes from and how life is anticipated. It evokes stories of creation and stories of survival—how life is a gift that can be celebrated. The Bible is filled with diverse genres that expose this gift—narratives and poetic texts, commandments, prayers and songs, reflections and meditations, and much more—that can take on new form in a sermon.

Life is a gift.[9] The Bible is filled with stories that give witness to the embrace of this gift. Life is a gift: this deep passion for the givenness of life is shared by Christians with many other religions and worldviews. What is really important in life is something I can never create for myself. I cannot achieve it, and I cannot buy it. Being born, being loved, and being buried in God's soil and held in divine grace in the end—all this is a gift; in Jewish-Christian tradition, it is a gift from God, who makes a covenant of friendship (*bĕrît*) with God's people and all creatures. This gift creates a relationship both binding and liberating: it is an overflowing stream of life energy. It can be handed on to all who are alive, and especially to those among us who need it desperately—in Scripture, these are represented by the poor, primarily widows and orphans. This gift is also offered to the rich man who finally does not understand how to follow Jesus. The relationship God opens up with the gift of life frees from the powers that occupy and cloud the hearts, senses, and minds of people: political totalitarianism, economic concentration of power, ideological reduction of the reality of life as lived. In the Bible, and also in many treatises of the Reformation, it is especially and repeatedly *money exchange* that, as a perilous and threatening way of life, destroys the binding and liberating relationship between all living things and with their origin. For the Reformer Martin Luther, money—in biblical language, *mammon*—is explicitly the anti-God. "There are some who think they have God and enough of everything when they have money and goods. . . . See, such a person also has a god; it is called mammon, which is money or goods, on which he sets his whole heart, which is also the meanest idol on earth."[10] When people lose their hearts to money they are open neither to one another and the fullness of life nor to God.[11] The great critiques of capitalism in the nineteenth and early twentieth centuries showed that money, as capital, had become the real subject that mediates social interactions and made all things and all people equal in a bland and empty fashion.[12] What could not yet be foreseen in this way in the nineteenth century was not only the dark and destructive side of capitalism (the proletariat have nothing to lose but their chains) but also its fascinating side. Consumption carries temptation, at least everyone who can afford it—and there are some who can afford more and more, while at the same time the number of people increases who have too little to be able to participate in the consumerist culture. Against this god, the God of the Bible steps in.

The Bible is full of stories about origins of life, how life can be sustained and nourished. The Bible says: *God* freed God's people, Israel, from oppression in Egypt and provided life for them in the promised land. *God created all life, and see: it was very good. God* is present in the final suffering, present with Jesus, dying a martyr: God makes God's self one with those who are failing and opens for them a new life that devours death.

It is characteristic of biblical storytelling that life's ambivalence is not denied; the problematic side is always revealed as well. It is precisely at central turning points that it tells of a *saving escape*: life can only be preserved and rescued because it is wrung from its destruction by powers that are life's mortal enemies.[13] Contact cannot be made with these narratives primarily through recognition, knowledge, or insight but, rather, through an attitude of trust. The biblical narratives yield answers to questions about the ground, the path, and the goal of life if people let themselves get involved in them, be touched by and wound up in the narratives, if they let themselves be "taken by the hand" and so borne along by them. Then it can happen that people let themselves be enticed to reflect on life from the perspective of the biblical narratives and to retell them for themselves so that their lives can be reshaped in thanksgiving, celebration, and attentiveness to those who bear the tragic side of life's ambivalence to an excessive degree.

Even as tales of liberation, the biblical stories do not deny the tragic side of life. The jubilation at the freeing of Israel from their oppression and slavery in the Egyptian empire cannot destroy the memory of the tragic side of the event: the killing of the firstborn sons of Egypt and the dreadful end of the soldiers swallowed up by the waves of the Red Sea. Indeed, the liberation of the one group is purchased at the expense of the miserable end of the other. This connection between liberation and destruction has constantly inspired new interpretations, especially in rabbinic debates. In one of these stories, from the Talmud, we read that God answered his serving angels, when they broke out in heavenly jubilation at God's liberation of the people Israel: "But remember my Egyptians!"[14]

Or we may consider another characteristic of biblical narrative in which life's ambivalence is more than clear. The creation narrative in the first chapter of Genesis has a particular *Sitz im Leben*. God has created life in seven days and see, it was very good: this is proclaimed among the Israelites at a time when, as far as their daily lives were concerned, there was nothing "very good" about it. The political and religious structures of the kingdom of Judah had been destroyed by the military might of imperial Babylon. The land was laid waste, countless people had been slaughtered, and a large portion of the upper classes of Judah had been deported to the heart of the distant empire of Babylon. Realistically speaking, everything indicated that, with the political end of the kingdom of Judah, its people ought to accept their religious subjugation as well. But instead of acknowledging that the Babylonian god-king Marduk had created life by conquering chaos in his battle with the sea dragon and so establishing order in the cosmos, or accepting that the sun and stars are heavenly powers that bring forth life on earth, the people from the subjugated nation of Judah told themselves a unique, obstinate story: Listen, it was God. God separated the inhabitable world from the waters. And God also made the sun and the stars in heaven; they are not gods. God created life in all its beauty and variety, and saw it all as good.

The Jesus narratives are full of tragic and surprising turning points as well. After a brief phase of public activity, the young man Jesus of Nazareth was executed by the Roman occupation forces as a political agitator and religious heretic. Everything would point to the destruction of the hopes of the men and women who had left everything to be with him and who had seen in his shared meals—often regarded as offensive, for religious and political reasons—and in his stories and promises the healing, liberating, and transforming power of God's reign. And then this disastrous end on the cross: by all odds, they should have abandoned hope and despaired of believing. In this situation, after a brief phase of flight and despair, Jesus' friends began obstinately to tell a story that by every reasonable measure was nonsense, in which life retained its power over death: this death was not the end. God raised Jesus, and death was swallowed up in life.

This story retold redefined the obvious, as did the other narratives we have mentioned. A person brought to his death by judicial murder and pogrom had given up his life for love of his friends. A failed heretic and political agitator—he had lived the overflowing vitality of life and so made the face of God visible. And God had identified with him, even in face of his failure, and transformed death into life.

How can this narrative strand of the Bible be brought into contact with the life of people today? We suggest that the preaching of the gospel must above all be about God's *promise* that is given for all people and so for those gathered here and now for worship: your sins are forgiven. God wants to come to you—in your daily reoccurring inability to accept the gift of God's love, in your wandering ways and with your half-realized dreams. Christoph Bizer describes disempowerment of commodification and freedom from deception and lies as characteristic of the gospel promise—in contrast to the many promises people encounter today in the context of consumerist culture.[15]

The promise conveyed in the biblical narratives, which demands nothing but what it promises—that I trust in God—helps us to develop a critical view of the shallow promises that are all too clearly present in our daily reality. The promises of consumerist culture also trap those who trust in them through their compelling power. Many of these promises are deceitful; they work with lies and demand advance payments (often in the form of lifelong debts) from those who rely on their promise. *Gospel* promises help us to keep our distance as we develop a perspective on the deceptive promises of *consumerism*.

But it is not only consumerism that is demystified for people who allow themselves to be sustained by the biblical narratives; it also forms a rigid and moralistic, overly strained way of living. Many people become twisted and self-absorbed when they strive toward perfection in all matters of life. In the light of the gospel, however, people trust that God has created God's relationship to me, and all living things, as good in itself. This is not an instruction for self-absorption and denial of solidarity with others: gifts exist to be received. Right action is now no longer a question of effortful attention to rules but flows out of this living relationship effortlessly. Self-control and social obligation need to take on forms that are life promoting. Martin Luther, in his *Freiheitsschrift* of 1520, formulates the enduring task of the human subject: attending to the body in discipline and relating to other people[16]—not as a canon of rules to be punctiliously observed but as a flow of life energy and a way of life that cultivates love of self and self-care.

This is not directed, as has repeatedly been asserted in the course of the merciless and murderous history of Christian anti-Semitism, against the "legalism" of the Hebrew Bible. Many Christian churches have finally realized that the Torah is not an oppressive rule for Jews but the foundation for joy and rejoicing. Loving God with one's whole heart, soul, and strength: that, for observant Jews, is a confession that does not signify an uplifting inner disposition but provides a good method for a praxis of life that has as much regard for other life as for one's own. The commandment of love of neighbor is found in the Torah (Lev. 19:18) and is by no means a New Testament "invention." This has been denied for a long time in the Christian history of repression, distortion, and nonrecognition of their Jewish brothers and sisters. Christians can and must learn anew to overcome their centuries-long formation in the separation of pious interiority from everyday life with all its conflicts.

Encountering Difference

Hermeneutical Theology

The Bible is the basis for preaching. But how is it possible for us to have access to the Bible, starting from our own lived experience, in such a way that we will recognize that the biblical writings developed in a historical and social situation fundamentally different from our own? Those situations are not just different; in fact, it has been said that there is a "yawning gap"[17] separating the reality of our lives from the reality presumed by the biblical writings, even though those writings were modified through a process lasting centuries. Since the Enlightenment, historical-critical methods of biblical interpretation have been developed as a means of access to the Bible, and they continue to be further developed today; they have become indispensable.

In our perspective, a historical-critical reading of the Bible remains necessary—not least as a critical counter to "fundamentalist" attitudes that become increasingly attractive—not only within Christianity. When we, in turn, consider that there is a need for a critical extension of historical-critical reading of biblical texts, we will make this no less clear.

Gerhard Ebeling, a German systematic theologian, showed as early as 1950, in an influential essay,[18] that the historical-critical method is not solely a matter of technical applications but also represents a hermeneutical orientation with an enduring relevance for the theologies following the Reformation. It is about an approach to biblical texts that is very close to the Reformation's fundamental conviction, according to which the human encounter with God's revelation takes place *through the word* alone. The unique historical event of God's self-revelation in Jesus Christ must be interpreted, over the long course of history, in terms of its significance for our present time if it is to have meaning for people today. Thus, *hermeneutics* becomes a central feature of Reformation theology. At the same time, the fundamental convictions of the Reformation enable us to see the fragility of the ways by which people had previously attempted to attain contact with God's revelation. This is true for belief in the effectiveness of the sacraments through their mere performance as well as for the mediation of original revelation through an institutional succession manifested in the continuity of the handing on of offices or the attempt to match one's own way of life with the forms of life of the early Christians, for example in monasticism. The word is what does it; the word is the true sacrament: this was the essential insight of the Reformers. The event of salvation is to be conveyed and accepted "through Scripture alone," "for me," "in faith alone."

This is the foundation for a hermeneutical orientation in Protestant theology. The weakness of the alternative position can be easily demonstrated. If biblical texts are regarded as inspired by God and as revelations independent of their historical situation, their application to any particular present time would only be possible through a literal reading. This literal reading has been opposed by another basic theological insight of the Reformation, namely, that the distinction between law and gospel perceives a critical differentiation *in the Sacred Scriptures themselves.* If we were to reckon on a literal, transhistorical validity of biblical texts, the Bible would be limited to its character as law and thus deprived of its essential dimension. The hermeneutical task of theology is directly linked to the critical distinction between law and gospel. The texts of the Bible must be translated, interpreted, and examined for their significance for people today. Therefore, the fundamental conviction of the Reformation is immediately connected to a historical-critical treatment of biblical texts, since contemporary conditions for understanding must be taken seriously if they are to be able to say what God's self-revelation in Jesus Christ means "for me." This, according to Ebeling, includes the compelling perception that a rational approach to the world is unalterably a part of the modern sensibilities about the meaning of life and that everything is regarded as subject to critique if it does not correspond to this shared sense of rationality. This applies, for example, to miracles and metaphysical thought but also to the acceptance of a history of salvation alongside secular history.

Insights from Gestalt Psychology for Preaching

Ebeling's argumentation met with considerable applause, and theological education in Germany has in fact been dominated since the 1950s by a historical-critical hermeneutics, not only in the biblical fields. At the same time, however, critical questions have regularly been voiced about this orientation. We are of the opinion that such questions should especially be posed from a homiletical perspective. Is the image of the modern person, as developed in the 1950s by Ebeling (in a context of discussion that was shared by many: consider only the work of Rudolf Bultmann), really adequate? There are, after all, good reasons to question whether human beings are primarily rational and reasonable in their thinking and acting. We should also ask whether the historical-critical approach to biblical texts focuses too exclusively on the realm of the history of ideas, and thus at the same time constrains the *social* perception and relevance of biblical narratives to the mentality of *specific milieus* in modernity. Moreover, one should ask whether an exclusive focus of the historical-critical approach may also threaten to create a self-historicizing of Christian faith. This would mean that the strangeness of biblical texts will not be attended to and a mentality perceived as modern might become the single criterion, causing us to ignore what here encounters us as other. Finally, we should consider whether Christian faith can realistically be captured in the cognitive dimensions of interpretation, understanding, and self-reflection, or whether the existential attitude that flows from faith does not include as well a felt sense of life, especially the embodied dimensions of life rooted in the power of the holy.

These critical questions do not fundamentally abandon a hermeneutical orientation in theological study and education; rather, they deepen it. Our question—how the Bible can become the basis for preaching to people today—is at the same time the question of the *here and now*, of the *contact* between biblical texts and the people really present here today—and thus adopts a critical stance as it has been developed in *Gestalt theory*. Here we can learn something about the work of preaching.[19] *Gestalt* is a leading concept in a variety of contexts of discourse and action, for example, in the fields of theory of knowledge, therapy, and pedagogy. For homiletics, too, fundamental convictions of Gestalt theory are crucial. When I perceive a gestalt (literally, a shape or a form), I organize what I perceive *here and now for myself*. This is true for all forms of perception. In the context of our discussion, it is important that even in a given biblical text[20] a gestalt emerges as an organizing center of perception, moves into the foreground, and shapes the whole field of perception for the preacher as well as for the congregation. At the same time, it pushes everything that does not belong to this here-and-now contact into the background, though it all remains necessary to the depth of the gestalt.[21]

These gestalt processes illuminate the enduring necessity as well as the limits of historical-critical hermeneutical study of the Bible for preaching. Consideration of historical quest for origins, the original groups of tradents and their interests, and the *Sitz im Leben* of biblical texts are put in their proper dimension by attention to the gestalt, yielding the question: How can I as a preacher make this knowledge relevant and effective here and now for the people now present, to whom I am supposed to convey the promise through my preaching? The insights that I can acquire of a biblical text through historical and exegetical, as well as theological, reflection are by no means irrelevant to this question. Those insights are, however, given a new dimension: namely, they are important and effective as a field, as a background, to the degree that they can give depth to the gestalt that is relevant here and now for the hearers. If we look critically at our own sermons, we realize that this approach is often unsuccessful. If the historical-critical analysis remains dominant in the sermon, it can happen that the biblical text is analytically dissected and becomes a distant text, irrelevant to people living here and now, and from which there is no path leading back to the perception of the Bible as sustaining, *holy* Scripture for people today. "The premise, then, is: It is not we who make the Sacred Scripture valid; rather, it opens up the opportunity to allow life to be ordered and bestowed by God. This requires that we allow Sacred Scripture to make a space in us and with us. That space and the corresponding activity are what I mean by religion."[22]

Practicing Responsory Receptivity

Christian homiletics can learn a great deal from its Jewish sister as regards the intention to allow Scripture to create space in us and with us. This is about a biblical spirituality that augments the critical impulse, which takes the text as an object, analyzes and dissects it, through an attitude of responsory receptivity by which we permit the biblical stories to approach us.[23] This attitude is not simply a technical exercise; rather, it is a performative act of incorporating the gestalt of grace.[24]

The German Jewish homiletician Joseph Wohlgemuth is interested in overcoming the domestication of biblical and Talmudic texts associated with the historically and religiously motivated desire to make them useful. This desire holds them captive and stifles the life within the texts, choking the power of the fire they contain.[25] Against attempts at historical relativization and desacralization, he insists that the divine idea in the Scripture leads its own life, a life that approaches us when it is rightly read: the divine word "laughs and weeps, it rejoices and sighs. It threatens and pleads, it loves and hates."[26] According to Wohlgemuth, the foundation for homiletical work is an exchange in which the text becomes a subject that reads the life stories of believers anew. In this exchange, both the preacher and the hearers become receivers.

Wohlgemuth employs the rabbinic notion of black fire and white fire. Black fire refers to the literal content of the biblical texts, the words placed on paper. It is about what has been written down with black ink on white paper. White fire refers to the intermediate spaces, the spaces between the words, what lies between the lines, to the things that have not been written down in words on paper.[27]

> The fire burns—but it also sends out rays. It kindles—but it also shimmers in a colorful glow. Just as the fire conceals an elementary power within itself that remains entirely hidden from the seeing eye, but wants to exercise it and so customarily dresses it in a visible garment and becomes a flame, so it is with the divine idea. HE, too, the profound one, the indiscoverable, must take on a bodily form, become word, a word with consonants and vowels and grammatical determination. And

as the fire sends forth now a glowing blaze, now a mild shimmer in its beams, plays in all colors, conjures all shadows, so also the divine word.[28]

As Christians, we say that we can perceive the Sacred Scriptures and the world around us bathed in this multifaceted light—seeing them illuminated now in a brilliant glow, now shimmering mildly—and we owe this to the power of the Holy Spirit. We are confident that we are drawn more powerfully into the saving streams of grace overflowing if we give an embodied gestalt to the act of approaching a biblical text. The act of reading opens up the spatial dimension of a text. It is, indeed, always an embodied act, although we might not recognize it this way.

Life is a gift that God gives in abundance; the gift of grace, like a flowing and pulsating stream, makes us present to the tangled, embodied, and interactive world in which we live; Christ dwells in us now so that we can find ourselves in this act of saving decentering of self—all these are not simply disembodied statements. Rather, these sentences strain toward embodiment; they seek to take form as embodied knowledge. We are interested in the embodiment of grace, the gestalt that presses toward forms of expression, in which responsory receptivity can achieve an embodied representation.[29] For these reasons, we appeal for the shaping of a space-time as we prepare to preach, in which the biblical stories can approach us and we can experience ourselves as embodied subjects who, in an attitude of responsory receptivity, can intensify the bodily perception of the text.

In a similar vein, Hans-Günter Heimbrock values the significance of corporeality for homiletics: "The body situated in space is the organizing principle of all sense perception; it is so because the human being in his/her bodily movement (including all sense perceptions) does not merely perform the mechanical acts of an automaton, but lives embodied intentionality, and thus his/her 'being-in-the-world' in a specific way."[30]

During the past thirty years, the bibliodrama movement has shown us many ways in which an embodiment of biblical stories can occur.[31] In bibliodrama, hearing, reading, and the physical reenactment of biblical texts are closely related. Responsory receptivity plays a part because the participants, during the first couple of readings, attend both to the texts and to their bodies. They listen to the movements the reading of a text provokes and "let themselves go" in long or short strides; they run through the room silently or screamingly: unhurriedly or with dignity, in an energetic, purposeful zigzag or sweeping back and forth. Or they simply stand still.

This synaesthetic experience, the combination of movement, hearing, and seeing, allows the text to be listened to and thus heard anew.

This process can be intensified by exercises in perception in which the atmospheres and resonances within the space, arising out of the common act of bodily reading, are named.[32] What lies within the space? What is in the air? What is moving between us?—a weight, a confusion, thunderclouds full of rage, the rigidity of pure disgust, a joyful lightness? Those who learn to listen in on these resonances will also gain a deepened understanding of biblical stories. In bibliodrama, the participants are encouraged to bring these resonances that arise in the reading back to the text, to inquire of it and ask: Where in the text do we find what has been experienced in the play? Can we relate the resonances that the play brought forth back to the text?

Another form of expression in the embodiment of responsory receptivity is the search for words and gestures that evoke memories and that appear in the wake of the first reading process. Here the question is: What is it in you that seeks to be remembered? What wants to come forth, appear on, sweep, or creep to the surface, and let itself be formed into a word, a sound, a gesture? The passive formulations that are used here invite us to give space to the memories that our bodies inhabit in such a way that the resonance of the inner body-space is sensed, perceived, and then can be expressed in words, sounds, movements, gestures, or in stillness. Words and gestures thus discovered can then enter into relationship.

The potential of bibliodrama for the work of preaching lies in the multifaceted processes, through which the biblical text can be transformed into a living word. This takes place in the fluid reciprocity of hearing, reading, and bodily movement, the physical work of remembering that senses the resonances of the word fragments and gives them a gestalt. This also happens through the collective exercises in which people learn to grasp atmospheres that are released from the Scripture readings made fruitful for a deepened interpretation.

Our bodies can be regarded as spaces of memory that have stored up myriad recollections that are partially accessible to us. They are shaped by the way others look at our bodies, by invocations that point us to particular social and cultural locations as gendered, racialized, and social (poor, well-endowed) bodies. The gaze of the others, the normalizing gaze, inscribes itself in our flesh and shapes the way in which we are able to move through the world. These gazes become part of our body memory and thus part of our sense of self.[33]

At the same time, our ability to remember is, from a neurophysiological perspective, a function of the brain. Through complex processes, long-term and working memory exchange information about words, concepts, visual impressions, and motor abilities. Our memory can be seen as a multi-dimensional, compartmentalized structure: *semantic* memory stores facts, concepts, and somewhat abstract connections; our *process* memory preserves the knowledge of habitual practices and abilities from how to ride a bicycle to how to fold our hands at prayer. A third dimension of memory is the *episodic* or *autobiographical* memory, which preserves the recollection of events we have personally experienced and things that have happened to us.[34] All three dimensions of memory are activated, both in the encounter with biblical texts in the process of preparation for preaching and also in listening to the sermon. Intensifying the receptive attitude in the encounter with biblical texts thus also implies deliberately incorporating the body's memory in the body-text dialogue.

Another possibility for practicing responsory receptivity in the body-text dialogue as part of the process of preaching consists in exercises in *focusing*. Silke Leonhard has introduced the concept of focusing in a very meaningful and theoretically persuasive fashion in her study of embodied teaching and learning.[35] A central aim of focusing is to be able to formulate a "felt sense" in a concrete situation located in the here and now by means of sensing one's own body. Leonhard summarizes the position of Eugene Gendlin, the founder of focusing and of pragmatic phenomenology:

> The felt sense is the physical, nonconceptual side of linguistic competency, which marks an "open competency for action" toward something objectively present but bearing the infinite with it. It is about possession of a language different from consciousness: much as with Wittgenstein's goal of clarity in philosophy, Gendlin also emphasizes the back and forth between the conceptual (logical) and the nonconceptual side. "This progressive action, however, demands a constant introspection and a body-soul awareness of one's concrete situation, in order that it may not become a mechanistic routine stuck in tradition."[36]

Those who develop a deeper access to a "felt sense" will be aware that the body knows something, that language is experienced as prior but also somehow "known" by the body, and that words and images simply "come" in a flow experience that goes beyond the linguistic form of words. Focusing practices attentiveness to the physico-spatial form of knowledge.[37]

The dialogue between body and text—whether in focusing or in bibliodrama—describes the most intimate path to a melding of the horizons of life story and biblical narrative. It is interwoven with the broader sphere of the life-world that is shaped by many factors, including the social positions we associate with our being-body-in-the-world. People who are made expendable in the job market, men and women who because of the color of their skin are exposed to racist attacks, and children who have to learn in their preschool years to live a minimal economic existence will bring the sociophysical experiences associated with these things into their deepened understanding of biblical texts if space is made for that to happen. We have found it to be extremely productive to initiate bibliodrama processes in the preparation for preaching, so that the embodied voices of the participants can later find their way into the web of a sermon. The images, metaphors, narrative fragments, and forms of embodiment that move from the bibliodrama process into the sermon then no longer reflect an objectifying perspective; we will no longer speak "about the poor" but instead will be led into the midst of the embodied world of the lives of the "expendables" and how the embodiment of grace finds a gestalt in their lives.

Here is an example:

> A woman who has been jobless for three years takes part in a bibliodrama on the resurrection story in John 20. In the so-called grand play she wraps herself in a cloth and lays herself on the floor, her knees drawn up so that they nearly touch her head. She lies still, on the floor, during the whole play, until at the end she gets involved in a long discussion with another woman who embodies the garden of the resurrection and is sitting next to her on the floor. The garden tells about what is going on inside it: how the sunbeams stream in, as tender as white jasmine blossoms, the enchantingly sweet smell that lies in the air, the hummingbirds that flit here and there through the air, and the great red beech tree in whose shade she found shelter—and with outstretched limbs, not having to shrink herself together. Then she tells how people meet in the garden, of the atmospheres that lie in the air: of an oddly heavy sadness, and then suddenly something like a shock of lightning, and then this overwhelming joy, of the shimmering, living waves that spread and take hold of the whole garden so that everything and everyone suddenly claps hands, with everything available, branches and leaves, roots and wings, and everything is simply carried along, the hummingbirds and the jasmine bushes, the red beech and the shadows. Suddenly the woman in the linen cloth begins to rouse herself until she

rolls completely over. With her right arm she strips off Jesus' linen cloth, which she had slung about her body to find rest and protection. For a moment she lies there, stripped, and takes one, then two deep breaths. Her breast moves slowly up and down. Then she straightens up and begins to free herself from her bent posture—bang! Suddenly there she stands, upright, still swaying a little and with her hair wild: "I want to go to the red beech," she says. "I want to know whether there is a place for me." And then the two stride away, the garden of the resurrection and the woman who had just been wrapped in Jesus' linen cloth. The woman, full of curiosity, takes account of all there is to see in the garden of the resurrection: all the things she could not see before, when she was lying under the cloth.

After the play has come to an initial end she is interviewed by the leader of the bibliodrama and tells of what it was like to be in Jesus' grave cloth: first, she describes the experience of embryonic security and regressive relaxation. The physical position she had first taken had something concealing about it; in her fetal position she was able to protect her vulnerable breast and belly from the outside world. The grave cloth was like a warm blanket over her. She thought of a lot of rainy Saturday afternoons when she had lain, similarly muffled, on her sofa. Then she remembered that when she was a little girl she had often cowered this way in her grandmother's lap; she may have been five or six at the time. But after a while she sensed that while she could still feel secure in this position, she could not breathe very well; her breath stuck in her breast and became shallower. The interruption in the flow of breath produced a feeling of apprehension in her, making her feel heavy and sluggish. "Like being dead" came into her mind, and then she was aware of where she was: in the grave where Jesus was laid after his crucifixion.

The interview ends and the next round shifts and focuses for everybody on what the participants have experienced individually. Now they sit in pairs opposite one another and talk about the connection of the play with their individual life stories. The woman who had been covered by the shroud talks about the moments in her life in which she feels "as if I were dead" because she finds that no one really needs her any more since she has been unemployed. She also describes this ambivalent sense of security that lies in her withdrawal from society. The bodily experience of being able to stretch out and let her breath flow through her whole body while still feeling secure was, for her, the turning point in the play.

Through the journey to the red beech she created a gestalt that included both her longing for security and new life as well as the fear that life could stand still and there would be no more movement, to the point of wishing for death. Her experience in the play in which she wound herself in Jesus' grave cloth opened simultaneously for her both a deepened understanding of the biblical story and of her own life situation. Through the bibliodrama a space was created for her own unique sense in which to develop an articulation of and reflection on the experience in the garden of the resurrection.

The scene just described opens a variety of possibilities for preaching on the resurrection. The sermon could concentrate on the entry into the garden. Since we want to preach about the resurrection of the body, the gestalt movement from the grave cloth to the red beech could serve as an embodied metaphor of how the paschal mystery might touch our lives in the here and now.

We learn from these bibliodrama processes that it is indispensable for the practice of responsory receptivity that we create open spaces in the work of preaching, in which the body-space dimension of biblical texts can be explored in our individual bodies, in community and in the atmospheres that surround us. Giving space to creativity in the course of preparing to preach is of central importance.[38]

Manfred Josuttis reflects on creativity in the context of sermon preparation:[39] "In many cases he [the preacher] must prepare a new sermon every week and every Sunday say something new, interesting, perhaps also exciting in his sermon. It is not only necessary for him to have a mastery of exegetical methods and to know the congregation he is addressing. He also needs inspiration. How does one get inspiration?"[40] Writing a sermon is a creative act. The material, as a rule, is a biblical text, and the goal is a free act of speaking in worship in the presence of the congregation. As an aesthetic event, a sermon is certainly comparable to other production processes of a scientific or artistic nature. There are features explored by psychologists who research the creative activity of human beings that can be applied to the composition of a sermon as well. We can, for instance, distinguish among the phases of the creative process—for example, inspiration and elaboration; or preparation, production, and assessment. Or there may even be five phases: preparation, analysis, production, verification, and reapplication. The psychologist Elisabeth Landau, who explores the phenomenon of creativity, suggests only four phases: "preparation, incubation, illumination, and verification."[41]

The preparatory phase includes the perception of a problem and the gathering of information applicable to the problem. The incubation phase is a time of waiting during which one searches unconsciously. The analogy to medical terms makes this matter rather clear: I have caught a cold; I have been infected, but the illness has not yet erupted. Sometimes an analogy to pregnancy is suggested. In the illumination phase, there is a sudden insight into the solution. In the fourth phase, this solution is given a gestalt as the sermon is developed.

Applied to the sermon, this means for the first phase that the preacher makes herself familiar as early as possible with the text for preaching—ideally on the first day of the week that will conclude with the Sunday on which the sermon is to be delivered. She reads the text out loud every day at a fixed time. In this way, the text for the sermon will be brought into contact with everything that happens during the work week: from confirmation classes to reading the newspaper, from visits to the sick to the mystery play on television in the evening, from pastoral conversations over the garden fence to administrative work in the office. At the same time, there will be space within this phase for gathering information on the exegetical background of the sermon text as well as for theological reflections. Important in this phase is the sensitive perception and openness to new ideas. Many sermons are quite boring; we believe this is due to a constrained perceptive ability in this first phase, a kind of censoring exercised by the preacher over his perceptions and the problems of daily life. The quality of the final form of the sermon is already determined in this beginning phase.

The four different phases do not follow in a clear temporal sequence; they are organized according to the logic of the subject. Thus, there are also no clear boundaries between the preparatory and incubation phases. The major distinction is that the incubation phase proceeds unconsciously. The preacher is not explicitly aware that he is playing with the perceptions and information he has come across. In this phase, he is working on the sermon through other activities—in his work in the congregation, while teaching, but also in his leisure time—circling around ideas, sorting information, weighing it, balancing it. Josuttis writes, following Landau: "This phase, in which the assembled ideas are moving through the unconscious, can be a very restless and frustrating period for the individual, and is often accompanied by feelings of unworthiness; it requires a considerable degree of tolerance for frustration."[42] Those who have attempted to write a poem, compose a piece of music, or put down an academic assignment on paper probably are familiar with this mood.

The next phase, described as "illumination," is the "Aha" experience, or "Eureka!" moment. This is an altogether unwilled instant, a kind of ecstatic moment in which the vague movements of feeling and thought in the previous phase suddenly organize themselves into a meaningful, convincing, and plausible image, a clear, genuine insight, an idea with a power that is at least subjectively persuasive, and sometimes even compelling. This is the phase in which the inspiration for preaching happens. Currents of content and energy flow into it from at least two primary directions: the biblical tradition and the contemporary situation. In this moment of inspiration, the preacher finds the point at which the relevance of the biblical text for the present opens itself both to contact and to contradiction. The inspiration can be a question from the present directed to the text; it can consist of a theme that the text yields for the present time; it can have as its content a symbol or a narrative or an image through which the power of this biblical text for these particular people here and now can be unlocked. In any case, the inspiration is the crystallizing core out of which the next phase, the development or substantiation, emerges: the brief, ecstatic moment of inspiration is now, when the process succeeds, shaped into a good form. Giving enough space for these creative phases in sermon preparation breathes life into the work of the preaching of justification.

We conclude our reflections on practicing responsory receptivity in the act of preparing for preaching with a reflection by Fulbert Steffensky, from his book *Schwarzbrot-Spiritualität* (*Dark Bread Spirituality*).[43] His words take us beyond the homiletical question and sum up what has been said:

> In the practice of prayer, for example, one is always advised to respect the daily dryness of prayer and by no means to give up if one is not inspired, seized, fulfilled, and carried away. You are not the maker of your own wholeness, it is said. . . . It has been said, with Romans 8: "We do not know how to pray as we ought, but [the] Spirit intercedes with sighs too deep for words!" What counts is not being carried away, but being present.
>
> There is a difference between life full of intention and plans and life experienced as a gift. We encounter the gift experience in Paul Gerhardt's song "Go out, my heart." The mystics say something similar: Go out in us! Go out! But not into distant and extraordinary spheres. Be present and you will hear the song of life. "Go out, my heart," Paul Gerhardt sings. Hear the praise of life in the "gardens' beauty," in the song of the lark and the nightingale, in honey, in wheat, and in

wine! . . . What, then, is a spiritual experience? It is not an experience of self-assertion but, rather, self-forgetfulness. Elisabeth [of Bingen] does not focus on self-perception; she reads the eyes of Christ in the eyes of a child. . . . Human pain is no longer only what it appears to be; attentiveness that has been formed over time reads God's pain in the pain of human beings. Happiness is no longer only what it is. It is here that traces of the divine can be discovered. . . . Spirituality is educated attentiveness. The human being lives not only in his/her own interiority and out of his/her good intentions. The human being is not only soul and spirit, but ordinary body. He/she does not have a body, but is a body. The interiority that knows only itself will soon tire.[44]

Example: A Sermon for Fasting[45]

Fasting has always been, in Christianity as well as in other religions, a method for opening oneself utterly to God and preparing to listen. In this sense, fasting can be seen as an exercise in responsory receptivity. What follows is a sermon for fasting that meditates on the prophetic critique in Isaiah 58 in light of current questions about social justice and the contradictions of the culture of wellness regarding the ambivalence of fasting, against the background of overflowing grace for people who are considered superfluous.

Dear people of God, for many of us Protestants, it is unquestionable: social action reflects the gospel and is therefore better than bodily asceticism. The rejection of monasticism and the esteem for worldly professions, especially in their social commitments, are among the store of convictions of the average Protestant. Social justice versus bodily asceticism: Is this the alternative the prophet Isaiah proclaims in the name of God? Or is this the crucial point: false fasting is revealed by the fantasy that God can be impressed by publicly staged abstinence—while at the same time, in the same breath and the same moment, the fundamental rights of other people are being ignored? "Look, you serve your own interest on your fast day, and oppress all your workers."

The demand for justice and turning back to a life that attends to its social obligation is unmistakable. For the prophet, reverence for God's holiness is not compatible with a way of life in which the basic rights of people are trodden underfoot. "Is not this the fast that I choose: . . . to share your bread with the hungry, and bring the homeless poor into your house." I do not hear this as a threat, or a burden, but as a great sigh. To trust in the God who does not demand and oppress but who frees God's people from oppression and desires our liberation.

1. In our culture, fasting is not an explicitly religious practice. Fasting is pretty common in everyday life. Theology students who, like some among us just now, are about to take their Greek exams, will probably not get drunk the night before, and won't stuff themselves at breakfast. Those who are going to participate in sports will abstain from smoking and drinking, and also from eating—well, let's say pig's knuckles and sauerkraut and mashed potatoes. Some of the soccer stars who wanted to win the World Cup this summer had to go without seeing their wives and girlfriends for a few days. And even a modest plan like not letting yourself be overtaken by the street sweepers when you run a half-marathon, while it doesn't demand sexual abstinence, may call for months of training and a controlled intake of food and sweets. Scientific and artistic achievements are incompatible with excessive TV watching or unlimited immersion in the Internet. Presence of mind demands, at least from time to time, some forms of abstinence: from consumption of luxuries and certain foods, from media, from leisure pursuits, and many other things.

Sometimes fasting is really liberating. Anyone who, after several days' celebration of a confirmation, a wedding, or Christmas—consuming cake, meat, and alcohol all day every day—takes an evening off and vows "peace to my liver" will sense the whole body's grateful sigh. Anyone who, after Mardi Gras season, deliberately chooses to join in the "seven weeks' abstinence" very often finds herself or himself closer to God. We are more inclined to assure ourselves of our own independence and determination in terms of things that are no assurance at all—sweets or television, alcohol or the Internet, smoking or strudel. The one who fasts may regain self-assurance and alertness or sense a relaxation of body and soul. There is a well-oiled branch of the economy made up of wellness programs, from mud packs to Reiki, Ayurveda meals to therapeutic teas, massages to fitness exercises, all of them playing with mixed combinations of ideas from the widest variety of philosophical and religious traditions, all of them promising a better life.

Even major developments like the triumph of the capitalist economy would not have been imaginable without daily asceticism: long-term, profit-oriented economizing, doing without consumption that satisfies only for the present in order to reinvest the profit thus accumulated. This form of asceticism has been able to dispense with its religious foundations for quite some time now. And renunciation of consumption means very different things today, depending on which side of the always unequal division of social wealth one occupies. There are managers who receive hundreds of thousands or even millions of dollars per year and have no time to use their wealth in any way that gives them pleasure. And, increasingly in our country and most especially in the poorer regions of the world, there are more and more people who put their hands in front of their faces when they smile, whose front teeth have been reduced to brown stumps because they can't afford to go to the dentist. There are more and more people, among us too, who live in dwellings that stifle every kind of joy in life or creativity and for whom abstinence from a movie or from an evening in a restaurant is anything but a deliberate decision to fast. It is a social scandal that more and more people are forced to restrain themselves with regard to food and education, health care and cultural participation. This is a scandal because there is enough social wealth for all. Worldwide, more and more people are compelled to exist far below the level of their daily needs. They feed the flood of refugees or perish, countless people, each with a unique face: so incalculable a life, often lived and stolen under destructive conditions. Here and in many other cases, abstinence is not a deliberate decision to fast. It is dictated by living conditions that deny access to fulfill basic needs. . . .

2. Fasting thus is a fairly ambivalent matter. When it is healthy and when it is destructive cannot be determined by the act of fasting itself but, rather, by the conditions, including the freedom to decide. Anyone who fasts *for religious reasons* expects that he or she needs to be freed from whatever it is that holds body and soul prisoner—before an encounter with the holy is possible. The Jewish and Christian religions share this conviction with many others. Devotion cannot exist without attentiveness. Spirituality cannot exist without exercising the ability to be free from everyday business and stress.

This kind of attentiveness is about our attitudes to time and money or the use of luxuries, to everyday business and work, and how we deal with power. In religious matters, this sequence is irreversible: separation from and turning toward someone, getting loose and entering into a new relationship, confession of sin and acquittal through forgiveness of sin, being freed from the "old humanity" and putting on the "new humanity." This kind of attentiveness may make it necessary for us to change our lives, but in any case, it demands an interruption of our everyday habits.

The prophet says very clearly that none of this is a matter of public self-presentation. "Is such the fast that I choose? . . . Is it to bow down the head like a bulrush, and to lie in sackcloth and ashes?" (Isa. 58:5). It is something one should do but not in order to seem great to other people. Jesus of Nazareth, too, makes this basic rule very clear: "And whenever you fast, do not look dismal, like the hypocrites. . . . But when you fast, put oil on your head and wash your face, so that your fasting may be seen not by others but by your Father who is in secret" (Matt. 6:16-18). Fasting as a religious exercise is not a matter of self-presentation, and it is not a way to try to influence God, like putting a coin in a slot. The one who fasts does herself or himself something good, first of all. He or she becomes open to an encounter with God, something that *from God's side* is *always* possible, as an invitation and a free gift.

But this is what the prophet is really talking about: this movement of freeing oneself is perverted if it is simply something done for oneself, in body and soul—and does not include attentiveness toward others, and precisely those among us who especially need it—whether they are despised, not respected, poorly paid, made dependent on oneself, or through one's own unchallenged and perhaps also unconscious participation in a certain kind of economy, on political and social structures through which people are robbed of their opportunities for living.

3. In the biblical book that bears the name of the prophet Isaiah, God's holiness and the call for justice go together. If people want to be great before God, without having regard for the rights and the lives of others, they are as mistaken about God as they are about themselves. "Is not this the fast that I choose: to loose the bonds of injustice, to undo the thongs of the yoke, to let the oppressed go free, and to break every yoke?" (Isa. 58:6).

It is pretty clear to whom this demand is addressed. Isaiah does not require the poor to tighten their belts. He challenges those who possess economic resources and social status to stop oppressing others and depriving them of their rights and their very lives. I do not hear this as a hammerhard and unattainable moral demand. Fasting as social justice is, from the prophet's perspective, not an oppressive and unreasonable demand; it is liberation. It is the great sigh that creates disruption and release.

But it is no joke to live in such a way that, because of the way one lives, others are deprived of life's opportunities—and too often even of their lives. We should not imagine that the members of the economic and political elites, then or now, are heartless, thoughtless, and socially irresponsible. The prophet is addressing himself to these very people. His challenge is an invitation: rejoice in the sabbath!

The hope for a great interruption, a great, relaxing sigh breathed forth by all creatures, has a graspable form, a path that can be trodden every week: joy in the Sabbath, the enjoyment of God's day. For Christians: keeping Sunday as a holiday, a day of celebration. Every week anew there is a time for departing from the daily routines and for molding oneself to God's time: "If you honor it, not going your own ways, serving your own interests, or speaking your own empty words; then you shall take delight in the LORD" (Isa. 58:13-14).

The great sigh of not-doing, the liberation of body, soul, and spirit by taking a break: we have to be clear once and for all what a burden it is, how it wears one down, to go on day after day muddling along in a way of life and of doing business that keeps millions of people below the level of their physical and spiritual needs. "Serving your own interests, or speaking your own empty words"—what a relief it would be to stop doing that! What an insult it is to people's intelligence to go on chattering about nothing and even believing it: for example, that economic growth means jobs, when everyone knows that firms with gigantic profits fire people and that full employment would require an annual rate of economic growth of about 32 percent! Or else the unemployed must be forced into the job market, "supply and demand," as if there were already full employment and people who, out of totally incomprehensible laziness, do not seek work and have to be forced into it: ". . . or speaking your own empty words."

What a liberation it would be from this continual tension, this straining not to recognize anything beyond the narrow calculation of profit and loss! This prescribed and self-ordained dullness as regards the happiness of other people and other creatures, and even as regards one's own spontaneous needs! The prophet understands that he can address and can reach his listeners from a perspective of liberation. No exertion for high social achievements, no "heave" that will shake up the whole country, or anything like that, but instead a letting-be, a sigh of relief, a catching of one's breath. Every week, a new joy in the sabbath: at least for one day in the week, letting go of every kind of action or talk that contributes to the subjugation of those who suffer.

What would happen if the churches in our country were to listen to the prophet? Maybe it would set loose creative ideas in the congregations and church institutions, ideas that might even pay greater dividends for church finances than any fundraising program yet devised. For example: a spiritual wellness program. Once a week people from the economic and political elites could come together in beautifully furnished and decorated sanctuaries. They would pay money for this, and it would mainly go to social projects, with a smaller portion devoted to the beauty of these meetings. There would be wonderful things to eat and drink. There would be all kinds of time. Friends, families, couples, and children could be brought along. All cell phones and laptops would be left at home. The only rule would be that everyday affairs, business, and chatter would be interrupted for twenty-four hours. It would be an opportunity for wholeness, holiness, for a thorough letting go, breathing out, and interrupting the normal course of things. A sabbath, a time of God, a holy time, new every week.

What would happen if we were to let ourselves do that? If we were to accept the prophet's invitation: rejoice in the sabbath? One thing is certain: our openness to an awareness of God and people who need it, as well as to ourselves, would increase exponentially. Not through effort, but through becoming free from daily drudgery and the dull effort not to perceive all that is going on. "To let the hungry find your heart." It is a foretaste of the reign of God, new for twenty-four hours every week, the wondrous invitation: rejoice in the sabbath.

"The LORD will guide you continually, and satisfy your needs in parched places, and make your bones strong; and you shall be like a watered garden, like a spring of water, whose waters never fail."

And may the peace of God, who is beyond all our reason, keep our hearts and minds in Christ Jesus. Amen.

Within a Space of Resonance

We describe the event of preaching as the embodiment of grace overflowing as a movement within the resonant space of Sacred Scripture. The appreciation of that space plays a significant role not only in homiletics but also in liturgical deliberations on sacred space.[46] We have already referred to the concept of "atmosphere," introduced by the phenomenologists Hermann Schmitz and Gernot Böhme.[47] Tobias Woydack, in his study *Der räumliche Gott. Was sind Kirchengebäude theologisch?* (*The God of Space: How to Interpret Sanctuaries Theologically*)[48] opens a further practical theological dimension in the understanding of space, namely as—considered from the perspective of divine activity—a *relational space* spanning world and creation, into which individuals and individual congregations can mold their particular, unique relationship with God. Against this background, church buildings are to be understood theologically as "institutionalized" places of spatial relationship with God. This understanding is inspired by Martina Löw's "sociology of space."[49] Löw regards space fundamentally as relational: that is, in terms of human concepts of perception and action—and *not* the reverse, as though a space exists prior to its perception and prior to the actions taking place *in* an *existing* space. That means "that space is constituted by social connections and processes of action, and spaces are not conceived as prior to actions."[50] Against this background, Löw writes: "Space is a relational arrangement of living things and social goods in places."[51] Woydack adapts this insight to a theological understanding of space and applies Löw's idea as follows: "Space is the relational arrangement of living things and the Holy One, that is, God."[52] Church architecture thus gains its fundamental significance as sacred space from the ways human relationship with the divine is expressed in these spaces.

> The human being synthesizes the space of the encounter with God by means of processes of perception, thought, and memory. In traditional terms this is about how one believes. Normally, this act of synthesizing does not take place first through reflection; ordinarily it is done repetitively, automatically. That is the deeper sense of liturgy and ritual.[53]

In our efforts to engage the difference between the text and our embodied experiences in the course of the homiletical process, the *body-space* form of biblical texts comes to light; we have spoken of the body as the space of memory, and we understand the task of preaching as a movement within Sacred Scripture as space of resonance. The following thoughts are intended to apply the concept of space to homiletical reflection.

Hartmut Raguse introduces the ideas of the psychoanalyst Donald W. Winnicott on intermediary spaces into his transdisciplinary reflections on the spatial dimensions of a text.[54] Raguse suggests that an intermediary space in Winnicott's sense is created in the encounter between the reader and the text. In homiletical terms, we might speak of an intermediary space that can arise in the work with a text during the process of sermon preparation. This intermediary space can also unfold between preacher and congregation in the sermon and the preceding Scripture reading within the space of worship. We call these intermediary spaces Scripture's space of resonance.

According to Winnicott, intermediary spaces are created during the infant's process of individuation, as it must begin to deal with the absence of the maternal breast and the associated moments of crisis. The infant reacts to the experience of separation by creating transitional objects in which the absent mother can be made present. These transitional objects can be, for example, the corner of a blanket, a stuffed animal, or a feather, but insubstantial objects such as a hummed note, loud noises, or simple rituals can serve a similar function. In the experience of separation there arises the knowledge that the mother is "not I," and that there is a space between "I" and "not I." This intermediate space can be filled with objects that represent the presence of the mother. Over time, the child can learn how to tolerate the mother's absence and to be alone. Over time, the original objects lose their significance; the intermediary space becomes a cultural space in which a multitude of objects can appear, expand in the intermediate space, and so mediate between the interior psychic reality and the external world. Raguse suggests that biblical texts can also function in this sense: "But Christ is also, according to Christian conviction, absent, and is only present *in* faith and *for* faith. It is this space of the text and the reading in which he, otherwise absent, can become a present event. For me, that is the core of the theology of the Word of God."[55] Raguse insists that the intermediary space is not shaped simply by arbitrary subjective actions in which objects are declared appropriate; rather, there is a third thing at work: "Here one no longer asks whether one has *found* it or *invented* it. *Both* are true."[56]

We believe that both the biblical text and the preaching of grace overflowing for those who are considered "superfluous" can function as an intermediate space in that they can mediate between the internal psychic, conflicted realities that can be associated with the various forms of social and cultural marginalization and the external world, which often appears merciless and in that sense godless. In the construction of this intermediate space, where we tell stories of God's justice as fidelity to community and of grace as an overflowing gift in our lives, a resonant space can be created within which the experience of absence (of grace, justification, etc.) is transformed into presence.[57]

The concept of intermediate space is helpful not only from a psychoanalytic point of view but also in terms of an aesthetic of reception. Intermediate spaces for bodily-spatial forms of expression of grace can be developed especially where the biblical text itself shows gaps. Wolfgang Iser writes about the significance of gaps in his reflections on the interaction between text and reader: "The blank spaces separate the relationships between the perspectives in the text's presentation and thus draw the reader into the text for the purpose of coordinating the perspectives: they effect the controlled activity of the reader in the text."[58] Blank spaces can appear, for example, when sequences of action break off abruptly and are overlaid by a different narrative perspective. They occur when the text says nothing explicitly or gives only the barest indications about feelings and motivations for acting. Iser continues:

> Blank spaces, as omitted connectivity of text segments, are at the same time the condition for the possibility of connection. As such, however, they cannot have any definite content, for they are only able to point to

the required capacity of the text segments to be linked together; they cannot do this themselves. Thus, they can themselves only be described as "pauses in the text," but this "nothingness" inspires an important impulse for the constitution of the reader's activity.[59]

It is especially when the text pauses that it is in need of sensitive intuition, an embodied felt-sense, creative imagination, and obviously also critical reflection, if one is to be able to trace the multiple potentials for interpretation contained in the text itself. The pauses incorporated in the text can furnish the opportunity to create a space of resonance in which to preach the justification of the "expendables." An impressive example of an "inspiring pause" in a biblical text was pointed out by Ernst Lange in the Old Testament book of Jonah.[60] The prophet Jonah receives God's commission to "shout" (literally translated) against the city of Nineveh, the capital of the aggressive and overpowering Assyrian empire, the enemy threatening Israel. This was a politico-military power surrounded by a megacity of a size almost unimaginable in that time. God's commission to Jonah is to "cry" against this city, to proclaim destruction to Nineveh, "for their wickedness has come up before me" (Jonah 1:2). Nineveh is a city in which violence, exploitation, and destruction reign. But of all things, in the prophet's severe proclamation of destruction the people of Nineveh hear a "perhaps." "Who knows? God may relent and change his mind" (Jonah 3:9). From the "man and woman in the street" to the center of power, the people repent. The evil and violent city departs from the context of wicked and violent activity. From the king to the lowest beggar, all social differences are leveled. And God responds to the repentance of the people of Nineveh; God also repents. "When God saw what they did, how they turned from their evil ways, God changed his mind about the calamity that he had said he would bring upon them; and he did not do it" (Jonah 3:10).

In his meditations on the book of Jonah, Lange places the fullest emphasis on a blank space where the narrative invites a pause: at the time it was written, Nineveh, the wicked city, had already been a heap of ruins for many years past. Repentance did not happen; rescue did not take place. The story about the lifesaving repentance of all the people of Nineveh is a narrative contradiction to all that was and is known about social and historical reality. And that is exactly why the story of the rescue of Nineveh had to be told.

The true explosiveness of this biblical narrative lies in this blank space in the text, in what is *not* told: the ruined heap that was Nineveh. Jonah had it just as surely before his eyes as did his contemporaries, and he tells a story *against it*, a story that would have made a better outcome possible.

This huge city, with its 120,000 people who do not know their left hand from their right: it could still have been alive. The opportunity to begin a new, different life was there. That is both promise *and* commandment for the hearers of the biblical book of Jonah, but also for those who hear this biblical text preached today: don't bother to deny the reality—Nineveh is a heap of ruins. The repentance that would have saved it did not happen. The miracle of rescue did not become part of everyday reality. Against that, and because of it, the story of a better outcome continues to be told. The people of the time understood that. They changed their lives. They trusted in God. If the people of the evil city of Nineveh could abandon their unjust actions, then you, the people of God, can certainly do it. Don't stand there staring at the heap of ruins that is your personal, ecclesial, and political history of failures. Live out of the fullness of God's gift; be in solidarity with the deprived, do what life demands, and you can be assured: God will not abandon the work of God's hands.

He Was Hungry . . .

According to many biblical narratives, the relational reality of grace overflowing, grasped in faith and given shape in real life, is directed to all people, above all to those who are especially in need of this gift: the poor, those deprived of their rights, the oppressed, the exploited. The excess of God's grace is first of all for those whom the existing social order has cut out of the distribution of political, economic, and social power, those who have been made "expendable." The Bible is the basis for preaching to the extent that it witnesses to overflowing divine grace poured out onto people who are seen as superfluous. The life situations, the conflicts, and the religious imaginations that animate the biblical narratives largely reflect the perspectives of people who have been made economically poor.

When we say from a homiletical perspective that historical-critical and social-historical studies can help us to create the background against which the gestalt of overflowing grace for people who are considered to be superfluous can be illuminated, it is indispensable to pursue the biblical traces of the experience of poverty and its overcoming. That poverty is a constant social experience is poignantly expressed in Jesus' saying: "You always have the poor with you" (John 12:8). Other biblical texts, such as legal sources, parables, and poetical liturgical pieces, reflect similar sentiments. We will spotlight a few of these to make the point clear.

As the money economy expanded in ancient Israel, there came to be a social polarization between wealth and poverty. We find, in all the bodies of laws in the Hebrew Bible—in the so-called book of the covenant (Exod.

21:1—23:19), in Deuteronomy, and in Leviticus—legal rules attempting at least to moderate the destructive effects of poverty on people. The Israelite law texts, despite their differences owing to the historical situations and theological perspectives, all agree in this: both the book of the covenant and the social laws in Leviticus and Deuteronomy forbid charging interest. Martin Leutzsch concludes:

> These varied explicit motivations show that the prohibition against charging interest is a genuine component of a solidary justice that enables, sustains, and promotes life. This justice grows out of a past experience of liberation (exodus), a present obligation accompanied by blessing (the land of Israel), and a blessed and healthy way of living. It brings nearness to God and life in the fullest sense, as carried out in the close relationship to the underprivileged in the brotherhood and sisterhood required of all Israel for the sake of their lived fulfillment.[61]

The laws for society in the Hebrew Bible forbid the charging of interest (Exod. 22:25; Lev. 25:35-38; Deut. 23:20-21), taking things necessary for life on deposit (Exod. 22:25-26; Deut. 24:6, 10-13, 17), and reaping fields, olive trees, and vineyards to the very verge, thus depriving the poor who are reduced to beggary of what they need to stay alive (Lev. 19:9-10; 23:22; Deut. 24:19-22). The context of these rules is a vicious circle of impoverishment from which the people concerned could not escape. Again and again, small farmers who could not repay loans at staggering rates of interest fell into debt slavery. As a testimony to Israel's enslavement in Egypt, these social laws decree that the poor are not to be oppressed and that every seven years even the fields and vineyards should lie fallow, free from profit-oriented cultivation (Exod. 23:10-11; 25:3-7). It is contrary to God's will for God's people to accept that economic processes are carried on solely for profit and that the working population as well as the natural environment can be made the objects of exploitation to the fullest extent possible.

It is improbable that these social laws really shaped social reality; rather, their existence and constant repetition indicate that the economic and social reality made it necessary for rules of solidarity to be emphasized over and over again. It is possible that this is about a commitment of those who owed their wealth to the labor of others. We could understand the formulas of blessing and curse in Deuteronomy 28 in these terms. If the people keep the laws, God will fill every living being with God's life-giving power. If the law is not kept, God will withdraw God's life-giving power, and all living beings will wither and die. And also—to mention an example from the prophetic writings—the vision of the prophet Isaiah points to the justification of the "expendables." God makes God's covenantal fidelity visible in very concrete things: the rebuilding of the destroyed cities, care for the vineyards, the cultivation of the fields (Isa. 61:4-5). The mission of God's anointed (Isa. 61:1-2), who comes to proclaim good news to the poor, to bind up the wounds of the brokenhearted, and to proclaim liberation to the captives, echoes again in Jesus' first public proclamation (Luke 4:18-19).

The fundamental orientation of the biblical narratives to the poor runs through all the writings of the Old and New Testaments. The gospel is for all people and above all for the poor. The New Testament, too, is full of eschatological imagination of the people in Palestine who, under the Roman occupation, have become part of the "expendable" population and who long for God's coming. In the New Testament, men who want to follow Jesus are challenged to abandon their possessions and to give their money to the needy (Mark 6:10-13; 10:17-22). Eckehard and Wolfgang Stegemann, in their social-historical studies, point out that a majority of the population in Palestine must have been living far below the minimum level of existence.[62] The New Testament speaks of the *ptōchoi*, people who experienced hunger and thirst every day and who had neither adequate clothing nor houses at their disposal. *Ptōchoi* were often day laborers, and widows and orphans must often have been counted among them, as well as small farmers whose subsistence agriculture was scarcely adequate to support life. The larger group were the so-called *penetes*, people who suffered relative poverty and had to expose themselves to unhealthy and overly strenuous work in order to be able to provide the necessities of life for themselves and their families. Some 96 to 98 percent of the population of Palestine belonged to these two groups. Thus, the world of the New Testament largely reflects the world of poor people. For that reason, it is surely no surprise that the coming of God in Jesus Christ is linked with countless stories about food: the *basileia* as a royal banquet; taboo-breaking meals with toll collectors and sinners; the multiplication of bread; a meal at Emmaus, when Jesus' disappointed disciples recognize him in the breaking of bread; the Passover meal he celebrates with his friends in the tradition of the exodus, now applied to himself. Jesus is condemned as a glutton and a drunkard and defends the disciples who plucked heads of grain on the Sabbath because they were hungry.

Eating, drinking, and being satisfied: these are practices that nourish the eschatological imagination that tells of God's coming near. These are such powerful stories because they are told for people whose stomachs are literally growling. In this sense, these stories are probably not immediately accessible to those among us who have not had such or similar experiences of poverty; we cannot easily identify with them. In this sense, it is our task in preaching not only to engage the difference of historical distance but also the difference established by classes and milieus, which lies between the biblical texts and today's middle-class congregations and preachers.

Eschatological imagination is expressed in Mary's Magnificat, in the reversal of circumstances: God has filled the hungry with good things and sends the rich away (Luke 1:51-53). At the heart of the eschatological imagination, the body reappears: empty stomachs are filled. Stories like that of the multiplication of the loaves (e.g., Mark 6:30-44) can be understood as a thorough interpretation of human-divine agency in the midst of poverty and hunger. In the midst of those disastrous experiences, there shimmers the vision of God's economy, of God's just world, the *basileia*, in which people are led to share their little hoards with one another and set aside their fears of scarcity and insufficiency. The New Testament is full of stories woven from the fabric of eschatological imagination that allow us to catch a glimpse of the shimmer of God's just world.[63]

Jesus himself was no stranger to daily poverty. As a carpenter, he belonged to the lower order of the *penetes*.[64] Although he probably did not have to live below the minimum as a rule, he would also have experienced what it meant to be hungry. The narrative of the cursing of the fig tree (Mark 11:12-25) can be read as a story about Jesus' hunger. This strange-sounding story recounts how Jesus, on the way to Jerusalem, saw a fig tree that had no fruit on it. The text mentions that he was hungry and gives us to understand that he behaved irrationally: he looks for food even though it was not yet the season for figs. Jesus curses the fig tree and so makes it barren, even though a few weeks or months later the tree would have been able to bear fruit again. Luise Schottroff writes of the background of the story:

> This story was told by people who followed Jesus. It was important to them. For these people, hunger was a daily reality—as it had been in Jesus' time. In the first century c.e., the Jewish people in Palestine suffered at an escalating rate from famines, debt, and sickness. Extra-biblical sources as well as the gospels narrate these circumstances with intense interest. Only a tiny elite group among the nations within the Roman empire enjoyed hygiene and a good life. The majority experienced increasing poverty. . . . The narrative about Jesus' curse of the

fig tree tells of his hunger because, for Jesus as for most of the people around him, every day was a struggle against hunger. . . . We can see from the story how Jesus is driven by hunger and how disappointed he is (Mark 11:13). He speaks in anger and destroys what he will so desperately need.[65]

With his curse, Jesus portrays in ritual form the destructive effects and consequences of the experience of hunger for body, soul, and social environment: Despair drives people to self-destruction. The future is destroyed. Schottroff compares the story of the cursing of the fig tree to other ancient sources that express a similar despair:

> Happy the man who was never born,
>   Or the child who died at birth.
>   But as for us who are alive, woe to us,
> Because we see the afflictions of Zion,
>   And what has happened to Jerusalem.
> . . . Sow not again, you farmers;
>   And why, earth, should you yield your crops at harvest?
> Keep to yourself your goodly fruits.
> And why any longer, vine, should you produce your wine?
>   For no offering of it will again be made in Zion,
>   Nor again will they offer first-fruits from it.
> . . . And let not the *married* women pray for children,
>   For the barren shall rejoice above all. (2 Baruch 10:6-14)[66]

In the narrative of the judgment of the world in Matthew 25, we find an explicit identification of Christ in personal, interactive, and present terms: what you have done to one of the least of these, you have done to me. Christ is present in the doing of the works of justice. The justice that is spoken of here has a relational character: it applies to those who have been made expendable.

The world of the "expendables" and how God does justice for them and thus demonstrates ṣĕdāqâ, covenant fidelity, is one of the central themes of the biblical writings. It is important to note that this dimension is repeatedly underemphasized or even ignored in many exegetical studies that demonstrate no interest in social-historical questions. In many Protestant milieus, instead, we find the notion that justification is altogether a spiritual-internal matter affecting the relationship of the individual to God. As a result, the fact that the Bible is full of stories about the embodiment of grace, about God's covenant fidelity preserved in the midst of the everyday experiences of the "expendables," is all too frequently ignored in the world of preaching as well.

With regard to research in parables, Luise Schottroff calls our attention to how the theme of poverty is also swept aside. Thus, for example, greed is often interpreted as an individual moral failure; the question of the complicity of the wealthy implied in many texts (e.g., Luke 12:13-21) is not pursued. The gospel of the poor is equated with the giving of alms, leaving the poor in the status of receptive objects instead of seeing them as preachers of the gospel and thus as subjects. This goes hand in hand with the spiritualizing of poverty, incorrectly located in Matthew 5:3. The eschatological call for repentance that sounds again and again in the Bible and is directed to the rich—for example, in the Magnificat—thus goes unheard.[67]

Preachers who seek to enter into the embodiment of grace will not only create spaces where a felt sense of grace might emerge. They will also emphasize social-historical work on the texts, by means of which the fragments of a theology of daily life from the perspective of the "expendables" can be developed and then made useful for proclaiming grace today. Such a program will also incorporate critical analysis of the strategies in exegetical literature, the history of preaching, and the ongoing history of application of the text for neutralizing the theme of poverty.

Throughout the history of Christianity, there have repeatedly been new attempts to give shape to the biblical orientation we have sketched, within particular historical and social situations—from the monastic orders to pietism, from the "common cupboard" of the Reformation period to the work of the Catholic Workers in the United States. Again and again, these initiatives have shattered against the superior power of the given situation. That is not surprising. What is astonishing, however, is that it has never been possible completely to suppress and extinguish this memory. It will be handed on as long as the gospel is preached. Here lies the most important reason for the suggestion that the preaching of the gospel should be affirmed today as a preaching of grace overflowing for people who are considered superfluous.

Those who have adopted the fundamental orientation of the biblical promise to the poor as obligatory for their own lives have always been a minority. Often, they have translated their own precarious life situation into an increasing radicalization of their moral attitudes and demands. Sometimes this happened to the detriment of the preaching of the gospel. For there is always the danger that such preaching may become moralistic, rigid, and legalistic in a bad sense. Such preaching, while it is for the people who have been made expendable, remains subject to what is truly central, what is new, what is the genuine message—namely, the gospel of grace overflowing. The Bible is the basis for preaching because through it the living word of grace overflowing becomes an event in bodies and souls and in the life-worlds people inhabit.

4
PREACHING THAT JUSTIFIES
The Embodiment of Grace as Performative Event

Embodying Grace in Symbol

It is not me from whom I receive my life; it is not me who can preserve, sustain, and save it: this fundamental insight into the ex-centric constitution of human life finds a condensed expression in worship and preaching. This includes above all the insight that, in the course of the liturgy, there is not much we need to invent. Presiding in worship is not primarily about self-presentation of one's own authenticity, since the liturgist can immerse herself into the whole wealth of prayers and songs, the creeds, and above all the biblical narratives. In worship, we mold ourselves, with our own words, into the language of our ancestors, into the exuberantly inclusive communion of saints from all corners of the earth, men and women, adults and children from all cultures, the living and the dead. This includes above all a wealth of symbols and rituals that is always "already there," that we as preachers need not "invent" on our own but that enriches us and empowers us to our own speaking "here and now." We therefore begin this section on the "embodiment of grace as performative event" with some reflections on the power of symbol.

What a symbol is and how it works are questions that are discussed in various contexts: for example, in linguistics and philosophy, psychoanalysis and theology. In some recent publications on the theory of metaphors[1] a *symbol* is considered a "stabilized metaphor." *Metaphors* sustain the moment of the new, the giving of meaning; they have creative power to the extent that they can reveal a new context of meaning and share a "linguistic surplus."[2] Metaphors bring together, in sometimes surprising ways, two spheres of reality, both of which can be seen anew (although what is surprising in a metaphor can be lost through familiarity: for instance, the Johannine "I am" sayings such as "I am the vine, you are the branches"

135

[John 15:5]). "Bizarre predications" open spheres of reality that could not be expressed otherwise.[3]

In contrast to the power of metaphors to create new reality in this interpretive schema, *symbols* have the character of *results*. "Symbols are completed processes. They are history, or better, depictions of what apparently could have been history."[4] What originally can be regarded as metaphor in a text, as "bizarre predication," can be stabilized into symbol as a text is used and handed down over time.

As plausible as this approach may appear at first, it does very little to explain two central phenomena that appear on closer inspection: when children grow up, they move into a world in which all (symbolically mediated) meanings exist already *prior and beyond their individual perception*. Moreover, many experiences, and especially those that are central to life, are first approached and approachable for the subject *as experiences* through symbol. Both these insights indicate that symbols gain their power and significance precisely through the fact that they are present to the human subject that experiences the world both as *prior* and as *other*.

A *psychoanalytical approach* recommends itself for the comprehension of this phenomenon. In our reflections on biblical texts as intermediary spaces, we have already referred to Donald Winnicott's theory of transitional objects.[5] His psychoanalytically oriented ideas are also central as regards the power of symbols. He sees symbols as "transitional objects." Winnicott asserts that the growing child must learn to live with disappointments: "In the simplest case, a normal baby is content with a piece of cloth or a diaper and becomes dependent on it; this happens at the age of perhaps six months to a year or later. Analytic studies of this phenomenon make it possible to speak of the ability to constitute symbols in the form of the use of a transitional object."[6]

On the one hand, children participate in the construction of symbols—by their choices, by associating the chosen object with feelings, and so forth—and on the other hand, they necessarily take as the objects of their choice things that *already exist* outside of and prior to them. Both aspects of symbolic construction, the subjective as well as the objective, are taken seriously in psychoanalytic interpretation of symbols; a central field in which this is being discussed is the growing child's acquisition of language. Here we see a positive evaluation of symbols operating—in contrast to the beginnings of psychoanalytic theory. Sigmund Freud, the founder of psychoanalysis, saw symbols from the negative viewpoint as inadequate, internal psychic protective mechanisms (in dreams, but also in neuroses)—symbolizing (e.g., by a compulsion to wash) suppressed and displaced drives and thus withdrawn from the control of reality by the internal psychic "ego."[7] In more recent discussion, symbols are regarded as necessary for the development of human subjectivity and intersubjectivity.[8] For instance, Alfred Lorenzer speaks of *symbols* in terms of a successful linking between prelanguage forms of interaction and rule-guided language in the life of the growing child. In contrast, for Lorenzer, a *cliché* remains immediately linked to the "scene" that provoked it, without any gain in freedom for the subject; a *sign*, in turn, does not point beyond itself and cannot convey a content-filled contact between language and the particular subjective experience.[9]

In this psychoanalytic view, we can only speak of a symbol when there is successful contact between the intentions, desires, feelings, and so forth of the human subject and some historically and culturally marked forms that are "already there" and stand over against the subject as other. Linguistic and material cultural symbols, but also religious symbols in the narrower sense, are not invented by those who use them but are "already there"—in language acts such as prayer or creeds, in sequences of ritual actions, and in objects placed in sacred spaces.

It is precisely in a central metaphor of the Christian religion—Christ crucified—that an ancient human symbol has been laid claim to: the cross on which Jesus of Nazareth was executed was, in the Roman Empire, an instrument of torture and execution. The reason why the cross was able to become from the fourth century on a central symbol of the Christian religion, however, was not primarily that destructive context (instead, there was debate already in New Testament texts over whether the preaching of the cross should not be understood primarily as a "stumbling block" or "foolishness"—we might say today as "provocation" or "nonsense" [1 Cor 1:18-30]). The cross has power as a symbol also because it is symbolic of life. It is a regularly appearing form common to many cultures and religions and even to prehistoric finds (in connection with the hunt, but also in sacrificial gifts), in which the horizontal and vertical, the cosmos ("heavens") and the microcosm (human bodiliness, e.g., the shoulders and torso) are linked together. Representations of the cross were found through many centuries before the crucifixion of Jesus of Nazareth. The symbol of the cross unites the instrument of execution on which Jesus of Nazareth (like very many of his contemporaries) died and that stands as a concrete historical representation for destruction and suffering with the ancient human sign for power and life. As Peter Biehl writes:

> However, ancient Christianity drew upon religious symbols from antiquity to present the full reality of the eschatological significance of the

story of Jesus. . . . The symbols of the tree of life or world-tree and of the mast stressed the cosmic significance of Jesus' cross. Whenever claim is laid to such religious symbols one must inquire whether they are compatible with the cross of Jesus, *the* Christian symbol. Since biblical-Christian symbols refer to concrete historical experiences, they demand a consistent (social)-historical interpretation within the context of that tradition.[10]

A symbol cannot be fully "transported" through "translation" into other—for instance, existential or rational—conceptual schemata, and above all cannot be made superfluous[11] because, even in modern culture, symbols are part of the spheres of reality occupied by the mythical, the religious, and the scientific, which in the course of history have become separated from one another. Paul Tillich[12] explicitly denies an evolutionary development in the sense that in ancient societies the dominant *mythical* relation to the world was displaced by *religion* and then subsequently by *science*. Certainly, though, there was a separation, in the historical process, between things that at first were one: the elements of the religious (directed to the unconditional), the scientific (directed to the world of things), and the mythical (directed to the objectification of a transcendent, using the views and concepts of empirical reality) increasingly drew apart.

But even in modern society, it is not only religion but also science that uses concepts that transcend reality (Tillich refers, e.g., to the concept of "progress") in order to construct their worldview. Even under the conditions of modernity, symbols participate in the ancient power of myth and can make present once again the lost unity of science and religion. Certainly, in contrast to the experience earlier cultures had of the world, in modernity symbols are only effective as "broken." Their claim to validity stands alongside the rational sphere of science. The reason for symbols' enduring validity lies in their "brokenness": they can no longer be understood literally, word for word, *as such*.

We must assert, with Tillich, that symbols are not subject to representation and can never be replaced by something else—for example, conceptual-rational speech. More precisely than in Tillich's theory of theological symbols, however, we should recall that the symbols of the Christian religion (the biblical narrative tradition, the creeds, the liturgy, and the sacred space but also the constantly renewed ways of being church in historical time) *appeal to people today*. Faith unfolds when people let themselves rely on the word of promise, the word they cannot say for themselves, not even (at first, and certainly not alone) in an interpretation of symbols that point beyond themselves. The courage to live can grow if people set their lives aright in terms of the word of the law and let themselves be gathered in, consoled, and made new by the gospel. Without the whole wealth of symbols this life-creating word cannot be told and retold and heard, cannot be celebrated, cannot be—in the Eucharist—physically enjoyed, and cannot be shared in solidarity with the poor, who are present in every place as the public face of Jesus Christ (Matt. 25:40).

Embodying Grace in Multilayered Subjectivity

It is not me from whom I have my life; it is not me who will preserve it, save it, and sustain it. And yet it is *I* who is present when the event of preaching grace occurs. The insight into the ex-centric constitution of my existence at a particular time as an individual "I" cannot be an adequate answer to the question of how *I* can articulate the divine promise here and now for the people assembled at this place and time. What are the opportunities, what are the boundaries for the "I in the pulpit"? In what follows, we seek to achieve some clarity about this question.

Manfred Josuttis wrote in 1974 a reflection on the "I in the pulpit" that is still helpful.[13] Josuttis first reviews a series of *theological* objections to the ego in the pulpit, especially those presented in discussions between neoorthodox theologians: because the gulf between God and the human being is as limitless as the gulf between heaven and earth, the preacher, in order to speak of God, must in no case speak also of herself. It is not one's own life experience, and certainly not human piety, that is the object of preaching, but knowledge of God. The preacher's ego is banished from the pulpit because God's revelation is something other than human religion. In the background of this theological position is a specific reception of the Reformation's doctrine of justification. In this understanding, the preacher remains also a sinner, and sin consists above all in human ego-centeredness. Since the human being called to preach is also fundamentally a sinner, his "ego" can only obscure an understanding of the gospel. The one who wants to speak of the gospel must be silent about himself. In this view, the preacher is seen in a specific role: as *witness*, like John the Baptizer, who points away from himself and toward Jesus Christ. In witness, the truth of what is attested is separated from the person of the one who witnesses and becomes publicly visible.[14]

But, according to Josuttis, the imposition of a taboo on the ego could have reasons that are not at all theological: it signals the place of the middle-class individual in contemporary society. On the one hand, there is moral pressure not to give clear articulation to individual claims. On the other hand, contemporary society is characterized at its core by the fact that individuals pursue their own interests. The unreasonable demand that one should not say "I" has to be looked at again, in and against the conditions imposed by this context. In the expulsion of the "I" from accepted forms of speaking, we could see the expression of the contradictions in a society that dares not express what it is in order that it may remain what it is.

But the *theological* objection to the "I in the pulpit" must also be critically examined. Josuttis recalls Karl Barth once again: in his doctrine of sin, developed in the context of his Christology, Barth spoke of three fundamental orientations of human sin. The humility of the Son of God corresponds to a particular form of sin on the human side, namely pride. The exaltation of the Son of Man corresponds to human inertia. And the witness of Jesus Christ the mediator is the polar opposite of human falsehood and damnation. Therefore, "sin really has not only the heroic form of pride, but the opposite, corresponding at depth to the utterly unheroic, trivial form of inertia: the form not only of evil deeds, but also of evil omission."[15]

Saying "I" *can* be an expression of human pride, but it is equally true that not saying "I" can be an expression of human *inertia*. The human being serves God not only by renouncing the fulfillment of her own person but also by witnessing *in her own person* to the grace of God. Precisely the "I in the pulpit" stands for a responsible witness that is central in the reflections of neoorthodox theology on the position of the human being in relation to the word of God. In contrast, the "we" in the pulpit is much more exposed to the danger of an unclear and irresponsible discourse, to the extent that it is never clear whether the preacher speaks for himself, or for others, whether he, in the extreme case, accuses the people gathered in the congregation of expressing exactly the ideas or forms of behavior that he, by not saying "I," wants to deny of himself. "The very renunciation of the ego can signify an ideological concealment of one's own interests, whereas the transparent use of the word 'I' always permits the hearer to question whether someone is claiming to speak legitimately in the name of God."[16]

Josuttis suggests that we should distinguish the following *forms* of the "I in the pulpit":

- The *verifying* I: here the statements of a biblical text are verified through one's own pious experiences. Opposing this approach, Josuttis urgently repeats the objection of neoorthodox theology—that too much weight is being given to the preacher's subjectivity: the foundation of faith is grounded in one's own person.

- The *confessional* I: here the preacher speaks of herself not in order to demonstrate the truth of a biblical text through the reality of her own life but in order to show, in one's own person, the fundamental and irresolvable difference between the truth of God's reality and the reality of human life. Here Josuttis sees an altogether legitimate form of ego in the pulpit.

- The *biographical* I: here the preacher presents himself in the context of his life story without trying to legitimate the truth of the biblical text by means of his autobiographical account. For example, the preacher recounts experiences he has had with a biblical word, questions it raised and doubts with which he is still living. The biographical "I" points modestly and soberly to the depth dimensions of human existence.

- The *representative* I: "Why can I not see myself as I am seen? This obscures my own self to me." There appears to be no biographical references here. This is "we" in a concentrated form, representing the preacher not as an individual but as a hearer of the text.

- Close to this form is the *exemplary* I: here it is made explicit that the person of the preacher appears as the first addressee of the biblical text. The preacher speaks of what the text means for her personally in order to tell the hearers what the text also has to say *to them*.

- Finally, there is the *fictive* I: this "I" can appear in narrative, storytelling sermons; for example, in a sermon on Jesus' crucifixion in which the Roman centurion speaks and offers his confession of Jesus as the Son of God in I-form.

Except for the first-named "verifying" I, all the I-forms here listed are acceptable, in Josuttis's sense, and depending on the circumstances they may be meaningful and even required speech-acts by which the preacher brings himself "into play" in his own person. Josuttis's deliberations are situated within German homiletical discourse in the 1970s and '80s, which, in opposition to basic convictions of neoorthodox theology, asserted the right of human subjectivity—not only in preaching but in many spheres of religious life.[17]

The Roman Catholic homiletician Rolf Zerfass has reflected on the "I in the pulpit" from a similar perspective, namely with regard to *preparing* to preach, and considering the question: How do I get inspiration? Zerfass subtitles this section "Drinking from Our Own Wells":[18]

Preaching lives on illuminations. No one can create illuminations, but one can keep oneself open to them. Such openness grows to the extent that we are able to come in contact with ourselves, our experiences and our history. . . . Creating a sermon thus means, really, preparing oneself for an encounter, just as one prepares to visit friends, collecting oneself, thinking about what one can bring, what one will talk about with one's friends, what may be preoccupying them or burdening them at this time.[19]

Regarding the imaginatory phase, Zerfass explains the technique of phrase-thinking: "In preparing to preach I will write down on separate slips of paper all the ideas that occur to me spontaneously, each on its own slip, and move the slips around until the melody of a sermon appears."[20] This technique of phrase-thinking inspires the "imaginatory phase."[21] In the process of creative imagination, the "I" of a person might possibly also come into contact with parts of the self that in everyday consciousness are often hidden or even repressed.

In the last twenty years, there has been a real paradigm shift in practical theology in the assessment of human subjectivity, the individual life story, and thus also the permissibility, indeed the requirement, of saying "I." There is no longer a need to urge that people be permitted to say "I," or even required to do so, as preachers and hearers, as teachers of religion and pastors, or even as participants in life outside the church, for example in the rituals of popular culture from soccer to cinema.[22] This increasingly accepted orientation is evident in reflections on preaching, for example, in the opinion that the preacher must above all show one thing in her or his preaching: namely, *personal authenticity.*

We do not wish to deny either the historical necessity of the new orientation to subjectivity in practical theology in the sense of a gain in freedom (especially from prohibited thoughts) or the opportunities that are linked, for many preachers, to this added freedom. However, we consider it necessary to inquire how the "I" in the pulpit becomes permeable for God's promise. The problem can be illustrated by a common notion that articulates the demand for the preacher to be authentic: "Does the preacher really stand *behind* what she or he is saying?" If we take the metaphor literally, the answer must be: if you are standing behind yourself you can't let anything else through. And is that not precisely the task of the preacher—to become permeable to the flow of God's gifts by means of one's own speech in the pulpit so that the divine promise can reach the hearts and minds of the listeners? Josuttis asks how it can actually happen that the human ego comes into contact not only with its own life story as it is embedded in the unconsciousness but also with the divine, the holy—that is, how the "I" of the preacher of the gospel can be transparent to God's speaking.[23]

Let us return to the question: What do we mean when we say "I"? Considering the question of subjectivity in its multilayered dimension, an interdisciplinary conversation unfolds. As soon as we explore some dimensions of the Western debate from philosophical, pedagogical, or psychoanalytical discussion in the modern era,[24] we find a profound ambivalence regarding the "ego," the "I": Is the ego the locus of the consciousness of life and of cognitive as well as emotional self-assurance? Or is the "I" instead a dependent aspect of a person, by no means always transparent to the human subject? Philosophical as well as psychoanalytical discussions since the beginning of the industrial modern age in Germany have found it *increasingly* questionable whether the human "I" is reflective of its natural environment, its social world, or even its inner nature. Is the human ego in a position of power with respect to everything that is not I—other people but also the natural world? This opinion appears in the ego philosophy of Johann Gottlieb Fichte, which he developed in the context of the anti-Napoleonic freedom movement at the beginning of the nineteenth century and industrial modernity: for the human ego, everything that is not "I" appears as *a challenge to the realization* of the ego itself—without the ego's own self being called into question by its contact with the other.[25] Characteristic of this conception of the "I" is the consistent nonrecognition of the other *as* other. The ego senses other people just like the nature surrounding it, as a challenge: in the case of nature, to subject it to the ego's rule; and in the case of other people, as an obligation to act here and now.

About a century later, the perception was quite different, after decades of industrial and cultural advances in the German empire, which then revealed itself to many contemporaries, in the limitless human sacrifices of the battles of World War I, as fragile and even destructive. In this context, the founder of psychoanalysis, Sigmund Freud, developed a concept of the human ego that is characteristically different from Fichte's a century earlier.[26] The ego is no longer regarded as superior to everything other but is instead assessed more or less according to the formula: no one knows what is in one's own house. The ego—as inner-psychic aspect alongside the id, superego, and ideal ego—becomes, as the "reality principle," the negotiator, the mediator between the social norms that surround the individual and the libidinous and aggressive drives within one's own body. Freud, by means of these ideas, greatly fascinated his contemporaries and also rendered them insecure in the thought that "nature" is not only something outside the surface of the body, outside the boundaries of human bodiliness, but the human in his or her very embodiment is himself/herself "nature."

In the debates after World War II, the profound ambivalence in the perception of the "I" was again alive in different discussions. Did the human ego develop upward—morally, intellectually, religiously—(according to one line of discussion) in the course of a lifetime of maturing, through a series of irreversible stages, until finally, at the highest stage, a moral and religious ability to judge, independent of external forces and models, "guided by principles," could be joined to an open and emphatic perception of the other?[27] Or is the human ego (according to the other opinion) not accessible today in the sense of a closed entity, but only as broken, as a "fragment"—without evidence for continuous improvement? Thus, the psychoanalyst Jacques Lacan, quite differently from Sigmund Freud, did not posit an inner-psychic "ego" in the sense of controlling reality and consciousness or a balancing of drives and the social world.

Lacan sees the joyful, gleeful encounter of the human child with its mirror image—either a mirror in the mechanical sense or the attentive, smiling face of the mother (at about the sixth month of life)—as the crucial foundation for the development of the human ego. Lacan concludes that the formation of the ego in the course of life represents a deeply narcissistic and at the same time an imaginative process.[28] The inner-psychic authority of the ego thus established, because of the way it originates, remains bound up with self-reflection, and it is at first utterly incapable of recognizing or even perceiving an object outside itself.[29] The narcissistic self-referentiality of the subject is disrupted by the child's encounter *with language*. Language—Lacan speaks also about the "Other," with a capital O—grounds and structures the subject's *unconscious*. What for Freud was the self-aware "ego," as the locus of the reality principle, is for Lacan the basis of imaginative self-reflection. What was in the former case seen as an inner nature, an energy-driven aspect of the "id," is here understood as something mediated: the unconscious *is*, in Lacan's lapidary formulation, language, which is always already present outside the developing psychic apparatus of the child. The unconscious, as Lacan somewhat awkwardly says, is the discourse of the Other.[30]

We want to affirm Lacan's insight that the human ego is fundamentally grounded in the Other, in or through others. As regards the preaching of the justification of the "expendables" as a movement within the realm of grace, we have said that we can only speak of a person in the sense of ex-centrist subjectivity. From there, we receive the courage to be attentive to the traces of grace in the face of the Other.

As we seek to understand these things, another important conversation partner is the Jewish philosopher Emmanuel Lévinas. He suggests that it is only the face of the Other that admits of genuine intimacy and personal encounter and at the same time provokes empathy and solidarity; only an "I" that can allow itself to be addressed by the countenance of the Other can become a *human* "I."

Not only in psychoanalysis and philosophy but also in the context of theological discussion, there has been an intensive acknowledgment in recent years that the idea of an "I" which is self-enclosed and uninfluenced by the Other represents a highly problematic and unrealistic notion.[31] "The notion of identity appears *problematic* in the moment when it is no longer used in a critical-regulative sense, but becomes a *normative* model or *achievable* (or to-be-established) identity, and when the concept of ego-identity is attached to ideas of wholeness, completeness, as well as continuity and endurance."[32] The individuality of the human subject is, rather, dependent on the fact that identity is never fully achievable. The complete correspondence of the self-image with the expectations of others can become a totalitarian move. Individuality is only possible because the subject confronts the expectations of others with its own wishes for life, that it does not give up in the face of failures and disruptions in its own life story but proposes new possibilities: in a word, accepts life's limitations as an opportunity to live its own life. Identity is always fragmentary: this is the consequence, not to be overcome in any wholesome way, of human mortality.[33]

For theological reflection on the "I" today, but also for a way of life in the church that is supportive of the human "I"—in terms of a courage to live, a sense of human agency and openness to others—it seems very important to us that the destructive narcissistic compulsions are not simply to be religiously imitated. The courage to live and a sense of human agency and openness to others are necessary achievements for people today, especially in view of the global destruction of basic resources on which human life and the survival of the planet relies. The church of Jesus Christ can contribute something indispensable by handing on the biblical-narrative tradition of God's demanding and liberating covenant of friendship with the whole divine creation as the Other, as the partner that is necessary for human self-reflection. Since the great flood, God's covenant embraces all living beings, and Christians have been taken into that covenant in the Jew Jesus of Nazareth.

Biblical narratives can rouse our imagination and build up internal images with regard to human subjectivity. They help us not to allow ourselves to be cowed by any political and economic power or internal threat, and to be aware both of the joy of being alive and of the injustice in the distribution of life's social and ecological resources today, an injustice that cries out to heaven. Internal images are only effective if they are socially embedded and can be carried out in our lives. That is why it is so important that the church of Jesus Christ in every place—when it worships in solidarity with the people and creatures of a planet under peril—is continually renewed as a space in which community can be experienced and lived: not as a cramping kind of stagecraft but as an opportunity given.

The question of the "I in the pulpit," as proposed by Josuttis, should be reformulated today: How can I become an "I" who, as preacher of the gospel, *is transparent* to God's grace? In pointing to the question about the human ego that takes seriously not only its psychological and cognitive but also its spiritual, dimension, we need to ask: How can *we* preach, and how can *I* preach? This is, in our view, not primarily a question about technical skills but about the search for a fundamental *attitude* that goes beyond all individual knowledge, capabilities, and skills, that expresses itself in one's own embodied sense of self in the world. The ability to spread the gospel depends on a specific attitude of embodied attentiveness that is usually discussed under the label of "spirituality." This has nothing particular to do with "inwardness" but primarily with openness to perception of the whole of lived reality, especially where human beings are being deprived of their lives' potential. Especially with regard to the preaching of the justification of the "expendables," we have described this attitude as responsory receptivity.

To ask about the appropriate attitude for preaching the gospel is to raise the question of basic formation.[34] A comparison suggests itself: those who study music must not only learn music as an academic discipline. They must be able to play the piano. They have to learn all sorts of things: historical and systematic knowledge about the development of different musical styles, important musicians and their works. They have to get some idea of music in a general sense—the "grammatical" rules of harmonic and rhythmic form in particular. But they also have to acquire knowledge and skills for their *particular, individual* articulation of the general, including skills of improvisation. But above all, it is necessary for the music student to learn *to play the piano.* A body-oriented praxis must be acquired and practiced again and again in such a way that it is not merely "known" and "reflected" but also brought to light as a mental *and* corporeal expression. We think that preachers of the gospel need to learn something similar. They, too, need historical and theological knowledge. Above all, they need to learn to read the Bible. But they must learn one thing above all, translated into the forms of reflection and articulation that belong to a *theological* education: they have to learn to play the piano. They need an ability in which achievements in knowledge and reflection are conveyed in bodily presence and articulation as a specific *attitude*. They should practice a specific form of *presence*, of *contact* with oneself, with other people, with God, a presence that is other and more than the sum of what is known and what is thought.

It has become increasingly clear to us in the course of our theological education that the question of the basic practices of life cannot be answered without a practice of *spiritual discipline*. Acquiring an attitude of presence and contact requires, in our lives and in our work, above all a *prayerful* attitude exercised in a set rhythm. Prayer, practiced repeatedly, will establish a trusted-trusting form of space-time without being rigid. The rule of *social unobtrusiveness* (Matt. 6:5) avoids a too-swift external identification with specific milieus within the church whose attitude breathes too little of the freedom of the Christian. On the other hand, with regard to the power of prayer within a globalized Christianity, there is much to be learned, for example, from African Christians, beyond the bounds of Lutheranism and extending into Pentecostal Christianity.[35] The prayers may be brief and should be oriented to physical movement that follows the rhythm of breathing in and out, and they find their focus in a doxological formula. *Some* daily practice of a kind of flow in which, in the name of the triune God, I am freed from the destructive claims of power and drawn into God's healing presence is a precondition for my being able likewise to do this *with and for others*: in worship and preaching, in pastoral care and religious education, in social work, but also in political and cultural presence and participation.

In *Schwarzbrot-Spiritualität* (*Dark Bread Spirituality*), Fulbert Steffensky sets forth a short list of rules that those who want to practice this kind of attentiveness should take to heart.[36] We will recall them here, at the conclusion of our reflections:

> Decide on a modest plan for your path to prayer! . . . One such modest step could be to pray a psalm quietly in the morning or the evening, to set aside a few minutes for reading. . . . If that is not possible, it is not because of the hectic pace or excessive burden of our job, but because we are living falsely. . . . Set a fixed time for your plan! Don't just pray when you feel like it, but when it is time for it. Regularly scheduled times are rhythms; rhythms are time schedules. It is only scheduled times that are sustainable. . . . Set a fixed place for your plan! Places speak to and build on our inwardness. . . . Be stern with yourself! Don't make your

mood and your momentary needs the rulers of your actions! Moods and immediate needs are ambivalent. Observing times, places, and methods purifies the heart. . . . Don't expect your plan to be a bath for the soul! It is work! labor!—sometimes beautiful and fulfilling, often boring and dry. The feeling of inner fulfillment does not justify the thing, and the feeling of inner emptiness does not condemn it. Meditation, prayer, reading are educational processes. Education is a long-term undertaking. . . . Don't strive for fulfillment, but instead be thankful for getting halfway there! There are compulsions to completeness that cripple our actions and depress us. . . . Prayer and meditation are not reflection. They are places of intense passivity. One sees the images in a psalm or a Bible verse and allows them to remain gently present. Meditation and prayer mean freedom from searching, intention, and grasping. One desires nothing but to let come what will. . . . Don't begin just anywhere in your attempt, but build for yourself a little repetitive liturgy. Begin, for example, with a formula ("Lord, open my lips"), a gesture (the sign of the cross on the lips), and follow it with one or more psalms! Read part of the Bible! Keep a time of silence! Finish with the Our Father or a concluding formula. The psalms and readings should be chosen before your meditation. That is, don't start searching during the exercise! . . . Learn formulas and brief sentences from the treasure of prayers and images in the tradition by heart (psalm verses, Bible verses . . .)! Repeated formulas rock you in the spirit of the images. They help us to achieve passivity. They are also an emergency language when life robs us of words. . . . If there are times when you can't pray, let it go! But keep the place free for prayer; that is, don't just do something else, but stay quiet in some other way! Read; sit quietly! Don't lose track of your place and time! . . . Don't be violent toward yourself! Don't force yourself to be focused! Like almost everything we do, this little thing is fragile, too; we shouldn't lose our sense of humor about the things that go wrong.[37]

The Efficacy of the Word in Luther's *Invocavit* Sermons

In this section, we will examine more closely Luther's theology of the word, because it establishes the connection among body, word, and performativity.[38] We particularly want to examine the idea of the power of the word, which means turning away from a destructive exercise of power to a perception of power in the framework of flow of energy.[39] The preaching of the gospel is not a lecture on the justification of the "expendables" but the embodied word as performative event in which justification happens. Luther develops this idea in many places, especially in his *Invocavit* Sermons.

According to Luther, God reveals God's self as *deus praedicatus* in the *verbum externum*: God acts in the present—through the gospel as the famous "good shout."[40] Luther's theology of preaching is pneumatologically based. Through the preached word, God gives the Spirit and does so by means of the external word. In *the good shout of the gospel,* the Holy Spirit binds herself to the preached word. Luther underscores the *orality* of preaching as the word of God. By means of the living voice, the biblical text becomes the *viva vox evangelii*.[41] So he laments: "That people, however, had to write books already does great harm and is an affliction to the Spirit; [but] necessity has compelled it and it is not the way of the New Testament."[42]

Of the human voice, Luther says that it is among the poorest of all creatures; it is nothing more than a breath of wind.[43] The minute the mouth stops speaking, the sound of the voice ceases. Consequently, there is nothing more vulnerable and ephemeral than the human voice. But at the same time, it is so *powerful* that with it one can rule a whole country.[44] The preached word thus sounds through the human voice, which represents both power and vulnerability. This insight has been maintained to the present time in education for liturgical presence. The actor Thomas Kabel calls the voice the "fingerprint of faith in body-language."[45]

Let us consider Luther's *Invocavit* Sermons from 1522.[46] By means of these sermons, Luther is able within a very short time to soothe the situation in the Wittenberg congregation—after some troubled months that had even included iconoclasm but also the closing of the bars and brothels in the city. A central moment in his *Invocavit* Sermons is the concentration on the word. How can we understand Luther's sole focus on the *word*?[47] Is this an intellectualist contraction of the life of faith? Does it represent a lack of concentration on and interest in the *social* form and life of the congregation? Does this narrowing in itself throw open the door to the later influence of the secular authorities on the social form of church life?

These questions cannot be answered without looking at the content of Luther's *Invocavit* Sermons. His rejection of efforts to accomplish the Reformation by means of forceful action, even when necessary through violence, by no means indicates his readiness to associate himself with the interests of the forces oriented to the status quo. His assessment of the limitations of human action—including its limited ability to translate Christian freedom effectively—is, rather, a realistic and healthy conclusion from insight into the power even of the word of God as preached.

Whoever reads Luther's *Invocavit* Sermons will be captivated by the unheard-of exaltation of the word we encounter here. *Everything* depends on the word, "for God's word cannot exist without God's people, and in turn God's people cannot exist without God's word."[48] How, then, will the preached word that creates faith and builds up the congregation be described in the *Invocavit* Sermons? Luther did not have in mind any special word altogether different from everyday speech. No, preaching is not a sacred, set-apart language. We are talking about the commonly understood, publicly presented language of everyday speech. The word of *God*, Luther says, is not uttered in some special, holy language, and not in a special internal word that can be understood only by people with a particular, interior faith but in the form of the "external" word, as Luther calls it. God acts in the present through the "shout" of the gospel. God acts through the word of preaching and does not give the Spirit apart from this external word. The Holy Spirit is not revealed in ecstatic experiences, in visions or things heard, in speaking in tongues; rather, the Holy Spirit is effective in relation to the external word. That also says something about God that is real and present in preaching: God is not in a mysterious place "afar off," someone who can only be known through secret knowledge, but God is present for human beings in the form God has chosen to reveal in the word preached and in a way that is accessible and healing.

Only through the word—the speaking and the hearing of the gospel—does a Christian become a Christian; according to Luther:

> If you take away the tongue and ears, there remains no notable difference between the kingdom of Christ and the world. For a Christian lives an external life like an unbeliever: he builds, farms, plows just like others, does no work or deed that is special, neither eating, drinking, working, sleeping, or anything else. It is only those two features that make a difference between Christians and non-Christians: that a Christian speaks and hears differently.[49]

Luther highlights three aspects in his interpretation of the word:

1. The preaching of the word of God has power; it is more powerful than any other action.
2. Preaching is a form of action that includes turning away from the *destructive forms of power.*
3. The power and effectiveness of the word can be understood in terms of flow of energy.

As to the first point: in some works on Luther's homiletics, his emphasis on the external, the world of everyday language, is construed as his concern with conceptually clear teaching and the appropriate interpretation and intelligible handing on of what a Christian needs to know. We, on the other hand, question whether the power of the preaching event is adequately understood if it is seen exclusively as an act of intellectual comprehension and intellectual communication.

The question of the effectiveness of the preached word is Luther's central issue in the *Invocavit* Sermons as such. "I have pushed, preached, and written nothing but God's word, and nothing else have I done."[50] The word "set free" in this way has acted of its own power, and it has done more "to counter the power of the pope than any act of princes or kings had previously been able to accomplish."[51]

The preached word works, in this sense, analogously to God's creating word; indeed, it *becomes* a creative word through which God accomplishes all things. "*Verbo creat omnia.* He needs nothing more than a word. That is what a master can do. When the prince says something about anything, *nulli sunt qui faciunt.*"[52] Besides this focus on the creating power of the word, there is also a christological characterization of the *power* of the preached word: "I think that I now speak German and that my word is no longer mine, but Christ's." The words have a grand power that is more effective than any other form of action, because what happens through it is that the human heart is captured and moved. "If I pursue God's word alone, preach the gospel, and say, 'dear lords and priests, depart from the Mass, it is not right, you are sinning thereby.'"[53] Through this preaching, the hearts of the hearers are changed; "but no weapon can be any help against it, than the word of God alone, the sword of the Spirit."[54]

Regarding the second point: Luther sees the sermon as a turning away from the destructive forms of power. "*Natura enim verbi est audiri.*"[55] The nature of the word is to cause hearing, to bring people to hearing, *and nothing else*. With this frequently repeated phrase, "and nothing else," Luther also states a specific *limitation* of the act of preaching. The "dynamics of the word," as Luther also frequently describes it, is a form of effective action "that happens without compulsion and without violence."[56] "*Summa summarum* will I preach, will I say, will I write. But force, compel with violence will I none, for faith wills to be put on willingly and without necessity."[57] This distinguishes the form in which the word acts from every other form of effective action, which always tends to become violent. "If I had wanted to act with hardness I would have poured all Germany into a giant kettle."[58]

Luther's sharp distinction of the preached word from the violent forms of effective action is grounded in a trust in the power of the word that is *not* founded on *human* language and likewise is not at the disposition of human language. This insight also contains a possibility of accepting the limitation and restriction of one's own, human ability to act. Luther frequently said in his Table Talk that he could sit quietly during an evening with his friends, drinking beer, because it is the word itself that "is pregnant," creates faith, and advances the new order of the church's life. Human efforts at communication need not be limitless and endless; human consultation can take a break sometimes, because the power of the word of God is not dependent on human speech, either in correct dogmatic formulations and knowledge or in successful communicative action.

Insight into one's own limitations makes it possible to regain a realistic perspective on human opportunities for action: "For the word created heaven and earth and all things; that must it do, and not we poor sinners."[59]

Regarding the third point: the power of the word can be understood in terms of flow and exchange of energy. The word of God is active, and its effects are not ultimately under human control. The word of God has a power that is hard to classify in the familiar models of linguistics. So, for example, there have been attempts to apply model theories of speech-acts to explain this understanding of the word. In that connection, there is often reference to the effects of performative utterances—that is, utterances that do not refer to a reality outside themselves but themselves create what they utter. The usual example given is that of a promise: I promise you that I will do this. The promise is a speech-act that founds a relationship and establishes a reality that is not real outside the speech-act itself but, rather, is created by it. Declarations of love are similar instances.[60]

But the speech-act theory cannot capture crucial features of Luther's understanding of the word. It is true that God's word makes use of human speech-acts, but it is still effective when those break off and fall silent. Luther's idea that the word continues and is still effective even when he is sitting down with a beer on the Wartburg decouples the power of the word of God from face-to-face communication: human speech can cease, communication can come to an end or be unsuccessful, and still, Luther thinks, the word of God continues its powerful and salvific work.

It seems that ideas about space and effectiveness in terms of flow of energy are best suited to clarify the way Luther imagines the power of the word of God.[61] This is rather difficult to follow if one claims Luther as a pioneer of "modern" subjectivity, since such an understanding of the word has as much, but certainly not more, to do with successful communication and self-reflection as with magical ideas about language that, from a modern point of view, ought to be relegated to a grim past.

The word of God creates a space in which people can live safely. Such safe space is built up in common public prayer. This is the reason why Luther advocated daily worship services in which the word of God could be heard as read and interpreted. It should spread through the land like a river, like a wind, like a vibrant energy that opens a life-giving space.

For our notion of language, which usually shifts understanding and agreement to the center, this is an idea that is hard to grasp. But as regards the spread of the word, Luther was not interested in hard-to-understand holy utterances but in speech in everyday language, something that could be followed and publicly articulated. He was not concerned with the functional or normative meaning of the words, however, or the contribution of words to a successful personal or comprehensive communication. Rather, his focus was on the specific character of sound: words are spoken, they fill the space, they spread through human beings. The people who live within the sphere of this powerful word-space are renewed in their entire lives, freed from death and the devil, justified by God, and can live their lives as Christians under the conditions of the old world. Luther writes: if God has "poured out all his good things on us," we live now in a "glowing oven full of love that reaches from earth to heaven."[62] We live in a realm shaped by God—a space free of human domination. This is a space in which the human being "disappears into God," that is, is lost and rises up in God. The preached word spreads, grasps more and more people, and changes reality. In order that such a sounding space can come to be, a space in which the congregation can live, it must happen—as is usual in oral cultures—that "first the sounded word . . . is released." The exhalation, the breath that fills the space, is the bearer of the potency concealed in the spoken word. "But you must put aside sense and reason and think that what a Christian does is something different, and you hear nothing more of it than the breathing and sighing. You hear the voice, follow and believe. . . . Those are the Holy Spirit's voice, his sighing and whistling."[63]

When we reflect on the relationship between Christian faith and language as regards preaching as a speech-act, we should note that our understanding of "word" in the theological sense, that is, as "the word of God," is always only partially equivalent to what human communication means by language—although the two are mutually related.[64]

Embodying Grace amid Energy Exchanges

Martin Luther provides a theological approach to the development of the efficacy of the word. Luther's ideas about the preached word as an energy-filled space in which human beings can get lost, that radiates with love like a glowing oven and in which the word can spread itself as a healing energy, will be brought into conversation with a particular theory of energy exchange, namely the *primal pattern theory*.[65] We want to consider what it means to speak of the embodiment of grace in preaching in the context of this theoretical framework.[66] We seek to understand the extent to which the embodiment of grace implies a felt knowledge or "felt sense" nourished by the everyday experience of the energies of our bodies.[67] Pondering the performative dimension of preaching invites further exploration in the embodiment of the word.[68] A performative homiletics is interested in reflecting the interwoven fabric of form and content and thus holding together the questions of how and what.[69] The dimensions that affect the presentation of the sermon should not be regarded merely as a matter of technique. Rather, we will ask what it means to see body, voice, rhythm, sound, and energy as integral components of the sermon as delivered—in performative, aesthetic, and theological perspectives. The performative dimension of the preaching of justification is thus part of the overarching question of theological content.

A performative homiletics[70] will thus seek an intensive grounding of the corporality of the word and thus place themes such as voice,[71] rhythm,[72] sound,[73] and energy[74] in conversation with performance studies. It will ask what the effects of particular energy forms in preaching are.

Primal pattern theory is based on neurophysiological and social-psychological studies that attempt to demonstrate that there are four basic patterns of energy that move our bodies.[75] In everyday life, in worship, and in the pulpit, our bodies are at home in all four dimensions of energy. These four basal energy patterns are: *thrust, shape, hang,* and *swing.* Within these patterns of energy, which work in our bodies in a constantly flowing exchange, we move through the world. However, certain patterns of energy are dominant because of our physiological composition, the *habitus* associated with our corporeal movement-presence, and the sociocultural disciplining of our bodies. These patterns of energy move our bodies: in terms of their specific character, we move through the world and apprehend everyday scenes in particular ways. They effect a type of somatic integration within which bodily knowledge can develop. But they also shape our sense of the holy; they shape kinesthetic God images. These energy patterns form the basis for our moral judgments and the options we develop in our everyday doings. They shape our experience in worship: for example, in the catalytic, forward-pressing thrust energy with which a song of blessing sends us out into the world, or in the strongly "formalized" and structured gestures, sustained by shape energy, with which the pastor makes the sign of the cross when she or he speaks the words of institution in the Eucharist and that convey to us a feeling of tradition. To be distinguished from these is swing energy, which spreads through the space when the members of the congregation are invited to leave their own seats in the pews and move back and forth through the church to greet strangers and acquaintances. Hang energy is disseminated in the space when people let themselves fall into the sphere of silence and stillness, or when meditative chants are sung, sustained like a mantra by the repetition of words and rhythm and the constant breathing, within which the participants can enter into almost trancelike states.[76]

These energy patterns hold ambivalent potential, depending on the contexts in which they are developed. They can evoke a mood of confidence and at-homeness in worship but also feelings of alienation and unease.

Thrust preachers can raise enthusiasm and convey confidence and trust. A thrust preacher evokes plain reactions, the clear and affirmative response of the congregation: Yes, we are living in the reality of justification! We believe! In times of depression, they enliven spirits. The ethical implications associated with thrust images of God depend on the particular context.

But an excess of thrust energy can also appear authoritarian. It admits of no middle ground, no contradiction. Since the preaching of the justification of the "expendables" stands in diametrical opposition to so many values, maxims for action, and social experiences, there can be too little space for dissonance in a preaching dominated by thrust energy. Honest expression of ambivalence might be constrained when there is too much thrust energy present. Thrust energy is often supported by a rhetoric of either-or that can have a demagogic effect. Introverted, doubtful, or wounded people quickly feel overwhelmed by this energy, which breaks over them like a mighty wave. Too much thrust energy has a crippling effect on them; it freezes and silences them. Sermons that build on works-righteousness or speak out of an unrealistic view of human agency are often dominated by the forward-driving power of thrust energy.

Hang energy offers the opportunity to open oneself to the attitude of responsory receptivity. The openness to perceive the gift of life and the love of God can be enabled in energy spaces that are not aiming at forward-leaning activity but at sensitizing oneself for one's own be-ing before God: God's presence and covenant fidelity are omnipresent and surround us;

God's *ṣĕdāqâ* takes form all around us; what is at stake in worship and preaching is that we allow ourselves to be drawn into this faith reality, leave ourselves open, listen eagerly, let ourselves fall: the divine creative process is already working at full speed. Preaching should help us to open ourselves to this process in a paradoxical attitude: to be attentive through defocusing.

People who find their home in hang energy do not need directive, frontal, liturgical direction. For preaching, this means that at best there should be no sermon at all. If there must be one, then ideally poetic, meditative forms should be used. Hangers have the gift to open themselves to ambivalences, images, multiple meanings, and question marks; they love open thoughts and not closed systems.

But hang energy is also an ambivalent phenomenon. If it is overpowering in worship and preaching, it can happen that the hearers feel disoriented after a while; they feel an absence of clarity or a definite orientation. The impulses to shaping one's life and anticipatory vision, to prophetic disruption that can work with the preaching of the justification of the "expendables," are probably too quickly dissipated when hang energy is dominant. Whereas in *shape* energy, trust in the creative power of the Holy Spirit can be lost and the sermon threatens to get stuck in legalism, overpowering *swing* energy can produce the contrary effect.

A performative homiletics that tries to explore the embodiment of grace in preaching will therefore ask to what extent worship participants develop and express experiences of God both energetically and kinesthetically.[77] It will strive to understand the significance of particular images and metaphors for God when they are not thought of as words on paper but are perceived as performed, energetically moved words that are impelled by *hang, swing, thrust*, and *shape* dynamics. A performative homiletics will consider the body-energy form of the dynamic of law and gospel. Preachers ought to make themselves at home in all the energy dynamics, for it seems to us that it is only in a balance of energy patterns that the embodiment of grace in preaching can happen.

Embodying Grace in Speech-Acts

Even though, in looking at Luther's understanding of the effective power of the word, we noted that speech-act theory is inadequate for a full expression of what is at stake here, it still seems to us helpful to adduce some insights of speech-act theory and the pragmatics of speech for the purposes of reflecting on the performative dimension of preaching.[78] Our focal point is the question of how the intent and the effect of the sermon are related in the communication of particular speech-acts. There are frequent dissonances here, as we described in the example of the theology student in our introductory chapter.[79] Frank M. Lütze speaks about this problematic situation:

> At the end of sermons that proclaim God's grace I am often, paradoxically, overcome by a guilty conscience. The sermon has spoken of undeserved grace, of a gift and an acceptance, of justification and the overcoming of works-righteousness, formulated in sentences of convincing theological correctness such as might be found in every theological textbook. But in spite of all the semantic abundance of grace, I retain a diffuse impression that without my own contribution, grace would fall by the wayside. . . . Even now Christ will become a human being among us, but that seems to depend on our cooperation; even now the Holy Spirit wants to transform us—if we only let it.[80]

Speech-act theory is interested in the action character of spoken sentences. The speaking of words that are put together in sentences is an action that effects something. As regards the question of the performativity of the word, it is especially the writings of John L. Austin[81] and his student John R. Searle,[82] and then the modification of speech-act theory by Jürgen Habermas,[83] that are relevant to homiletics. Speech-act theory has been prominent since the 1980s; it seeks to explain the extent to which spoken words are efficacious actions.[84] It regards speech as a form of behavior. A preacher who uses the medium of speech behaves in a certain way; her or his words effect something as she or he, through the sermon, enters into relationship with the congregation. Speech-act theory distinguishes locution—that is, the phonetically realized expression of a subject in a particular field (proposition)—from the illocutionary act in which the sound of what is spoken is accompanied by a particular intention. Illocution expresses itself in the mode of speech (e.g., as question, request, praise, or curse), but also in the tone and the use of the voice.[85] Searle distinguishes five classes of speech-acts in which illocutionary action can express itself: assertive or representative speech-acts, in which something is stated or established: I think, I assert, I take it as given. The second category includes speech-acts in which emotions are expressed: I apologize, I feel sorry for your loss. The third class includes appeals such as petition, urging, commanding. The fourth genre of illocutionary acts is that of commissive speech-acts, which can extend from threats through announcements to promises. The last group Searle identifies is that of public declarations that create a certain institutional reality: I baptize you in the name of the Father, the Son, and the Holy Spirit; or, I dub you knight.

In addition to proposition and illocution, speech-act theory identifies a third aspect of speech, namely perlocution. It describes the effects of speech on the communication partner.

In homiletic debates, speech-act theory has been applied to the analysis of sermons. Hans-Werner Dannowski has studied prevailing speech-acts in sermons and discovered that assertive discourse is strongly dominant. Questions, hopes, laments, and confessions, by contrast, are speech-acts seldom used.[86]

In addition, there has been an intense debate in homiletics about failed speech-acts in connection with the analysis of sermons: in such cases, there is incongruence between the preacher's intention and the effect on the hearers, with the result that some sermons become incomprehensible. Special attention has been given to the discrepancies, contradictions, and tensions between the propositional, illocutionary, and perlocutory dimensions of the sermon. Speech-act theory makes it possible not to separate questions of social construction, truth, content, intention, and effect but, instead, to understand them as constitutive for the understanding of speech-acts.[87] Lütze has shown, however, that speech-act theory has only limited application in the analysis of sermons. In particular, early speech-act theory neglected so-called indirect speech-acts, which accomplish a different speech-action than was actually intended. So, in his analysis of sermons, he shows that, especially in sermons whose content addresses the message of justification, there is often an indicative formulation, but what is intended is an appeal, something along the lines of: "You may trust God."[88]

Another weakness of speech-act theory is that it primarily assumes the perspective of the speaker; the viewpoint of the hearers remains obscure. In addition, it looks only at sentence units. But the speech-acts carried out in preaching should be analyzed within larger units if the conventionalization of certain models of action is to be identified. Lütze presents a helpful analysis as regards the preaching of justification, working out models of interruptive and expansive action. These models apply to the ways in which the sermon speaks about sin and *incurvatio*, to appellative models with regard to being able to/having to/being allowed to believe, to models of action for personal and representative confession with regard to the event of justification, to anticipatory preaching that moves within the free space of grace, and to the demystification of sin in sermons on justification by which the way we talk about sin is reframed in order that we may speak of its disempowerment.

Embodiment and Performance

In homiletics as a scholarly reflection on the practice of preaching, the aspect of performativity is central.[89] What is at stake here is the performed sermon. Preaching exists only in the moment of its performance.[90] It cannot be understood apart from corporeal forms of expression. As text, it is only a manuscript. Preaching is a verbal, somatic action in which something is said by means of the modulation of the voice and the movement of the body. Thus, preaching always produces an embodiment of the word. In physical speaking, information is conveyed—but not only information; also metaphors, images, poesy, through which we say things about God and the world that can only be said in this way, and not otherwise. In embodied speaking, both information and the metaphorical are conveyed. "With language, or in language, we actualize a certain order out of the plenitude of the possible; we accomplish the differentiation and complex interweaving to which we make reference as to our world."[91] Johannes Anderegg offers a helpful distinction between instrumental and medial uses of language.[92] Instrumental use of language in daily life is a tool for designating what is given; it fixes and describes available circumstances, the world of "naked" facts. In medial use of language, we move within the realm of lament, the language of hope, of longing for what is unavailable to us or can only be known in its potentiality. Preachers struggle within a world that, in public discourse, grants primacy to the instrumental realm of speech, on behalf of the space of medial language; they shape hopes for the coming of God and the resurrection of the flesh in concrete narratives; they pour confidence in the justification of the "expendables" into narrative and poetic forms; they articulate the lament for unredeemed creation and in doing so also give speech to the world of naked facts. In embodied speaking, atmospheres are also set free through the presentation of states of feeling and moods, through sense apprehensions such as smelling, seeing, hearing, and tasting, through the development of sound-spaces and rhythms, and through the flow of currents of energy.[93]

It will be helpful, as we seek a better description for the relationship between text and sermon in regard to the dimension of performativity, to introduce a comparison with music performance. Alessandro Barrico writes of music:

> This is what is unique and out of the ordinary about music: Its transmission and interpretation are one and the same process. We can preserve books and pictures in libraries or museums; we can also interpret them, but that is a different and separate process that has nothing to do with

their mere preservation. It is different with music. Music is sound; it only exists in the moment in which it sounds—and in the moment when one causes it to sound, one unavoidably interprets it. The process of its preservation, its transmission, is always "marked" by the infinite possibilities of variation that making music brings with it. As a result of this state of things, the musical world suffers from a guilt complex that is foreign to the other arts: the constant fear of betraying the original, because as a result it could be lost. It would be like burning a book or destroying a cathedral. The indignation of a music lover at a somewhat more daring interpretation, expressed in a classic "but that's not Beethoven!" is like the outcry over the burglary of a museum. One feels oneself robbed.[94]

Just as music only exists in the moment in which it sounds, so also the sermon only exists in the moment in which it is spoken. As impossible as it is to copy the original Beethoven, so is it impossible—and not even desirable—to copy this or that biblical text with the greatest possible fidelity to the original. Preaching, then, is not about the imitation of a fictitious original but about the performance of a new text.

While Barrico sees fear of betraying the original as an impulse that destroys the pleasure of the interpretation, we see this fear in the context of the narrative acts in worship as a creative impulse for the dialogue with Scripture in preaching.

The aspect of performativity of the word can be developed in several directions: biblically, theologically, and from a practical-theological viewpoint. From a theological point of view, performative homiletics assumes that the sermon is word in motion.[95] And this is so because God moves the words that *we* stammer out. It is grounded in the promise that God will be heard in and through the preacher's voice—that is, within the corporeal determinations of human existence—but without being fully exhausted in the process.

In what follows, we will take up some ideas from performance and theater studies in speaking about the performative quality of the staged word.[96] In a performative perspective, we begin with the perception that a sermon is a dramatization which sets words in the scene by means of the body. It is a part of a larger sequence of actions, namely the liturgy. David Plüss has developed the concept of dramatization in fundamental fashion in his performative aesthetics of worship in conversation with theater studies.[97] His reflections are also helpful for the development of a performative homiletics. Plüss begins with the mechanical dimension, in which he describes dramatization as production, in which a dramaturgy of different sequences of actions is developed by means of various "media such as space (structure, light, materials, decoration, color), roles, movements, voices, sounds, and music."[98] "Dramatizations are sensory processes deliberately produced or introduced . . . and thus are *intentionally created events*."[99] Dramatizations set effects of denotation and presence free. The culture of denotation is developed in a dramatization through the audience's interpretation of what is presented; this is about the decoding of meanings in what is re-presented. The culture of presence is about making present, about experiences of being touched, and about existing in a state of self-discovery beyond the interpretive act. The culture of denotation and presence can be found in every dramatization, therefore also in worship and in preaching. Plüss quotes Hans Ulrich Gumbrecht: "What aesthetic experience ultimately discovers are situations of tension and oscillation between perception and denotation, between the dimension of presence and that of absence."[100] In addition, when Gumbrecht speaks of the production of presence, he concludes that this cannot ultimately be done deliberately. Presence occurs in encounter, as an uncontrollable action.

Preaching, too, can be described as a deliberately introduced or accomplished sensual process, in which a biblical text is staged against the background of the world of experience of the "expendables," so that a realm of possibility can be opened in which God's faithfulness is made present in audible and sensual form. As regards preaching, we can describe the effects of presence as those moments within the congregation in which the lagging knowledge of God's righteousness can be "inhaled," with a deep "yes," a recognition that illuminates and is not merely the conclusion of theological argument.

Peter Brook speaks of the soulful and mysterious character of theatrical dramatizations: the stage is for Brook the place "where the invisible can appear."[101] Ultimately, a dramatization should not be about the audience's ability to remember the beauty of the gesture with which the actor pointed to the moon but, rather, that they will really have seen the moon.[102]

Plüss also emphasizes the importance of the body in dramatization: in the play, a body shows itself to other persons physically present; this showing contains a basic form of communication that implies a mimetic structure and is prior to verbal and sensual culture:

> Mimetic action is *neither* identical repetition of something already given *nor* altogether original. . . . It is characterized by *having recourse* to what is known and familiar and *adapting* it to the new situation. This

> adaptation takes place as a *staging adequate to the situation*, or *re-staging*. The current action is like whatever functions as a model without being identical with it.[103]

Mimetic action is always likewise bodily action produced by the corporeal form and perceptions of the body and its surface, by *habitus* and gestures, and interpreted by those present within the space. We can describe as mimetic acts the preacher's walk to the pulpit, how she or he creates a space after arriving there, how through gestures she or he engages the upper body and with these gestures, eye contact, and the sound of her or his voice seeks contact with the congregation; in these mimetic acts, things familiar to those present are always incorporated and at the same time modified to a degree.

If the preacher leaves the pulpit and walks through the nave during the sermon, or speaks from some place in the church where she or he is invisible, this would be seen in some congregations as a disturbance in the order of things. A change in the dramaturgy of the sermon leads to new sensory and presence effects.

Michael Meyer-Blanck's introduction of the concept of dramatizing the gospel is helpful as an approach to tracing the interweaving of human word and divine word:

> God's (katabatic) action is carried out (anabatically) as human art. Is the worship service then only a dramatization? No, not *only*, but rather, dogmatically speaking it is not less than the dramatization of the gospel. It is not the telling of the gospel—that took place once for all in the history of Jesus Christ. It is the dramatization, the presentation of this reality that has already come into effect, using the possibilities of human communication and presentation. Those who talk about dramatization can no longer posit an opposition between God's word and human communication.[104]

It is of central importance for us to differentiate between putting into effect and dramatizing; it makes possible the movements of critical distinction and reference that are fundamental to the preaching of justification.[105] It can be read as a performative version of comprehension as discovery or, in Magdalene Frettlöh's sense, as a wondering and wounded knowledge.[106]

Meyer-Blanck deepens the concept of dramatization by means of the categories of dramaturgy and presence.[107] The question of the dramaturgy of a sermon or a worship service points to the dimension of practical form:

"It asks about the experiential connection of the individual parts of the liturgy for the dialogue with God."[108] Just as we can inquire about the dramaturgy of an entire worship service, so we can also ask about the dramaturgy of a sermon.

In addition to dramaturgy, Meyer-Blanck points to a third dimension that is of central importance for the dramatization of the gospel, namely, presence: "Presence is the authenticity broken by the awareness that something is staged. . . . 'Presence' describes the actors' role-related, role-conscious, and yet communication-directed soul-body presence on the stage."[109]

Meyer-Blanck focuses the concept of presence differently from what has been described above, concentrating on the actors, the preacher, and the liturgists.[110] All of them are persons who interact bodily in the performance and who must find a balance between their role and their own self. Unlike in the theater, however, liturgical presence is about the participation of the whole congregation, and there is only a limited comparison between the division of stage and auditorium, on the one hand, and the way the worship space relates the preacher and the congregation, on the other. From the perspective of an aesthetics of reception, the presentation of the sermon reaches its high point in the reception by the audience and their response.

> Good actors and liturgists are present in their roles. What liturgy demands is a presence that gives strength to hold out through many presentations: It is about a devotedness in staging. Still, the necessity of staging cannot be avoided for the sake of a supposedly achievable real ("genuine," "true") authenticity, which then easily declines into a public pretense of intimacy. That would in itself be a lie, because one would be denying one's own role while actually playing it before the eyes of all.[111]

If we now turn from the theories of dramatization we have been considering to biblical-theological ideas, we may find that the biblical writings offer us an abundance of metaphors in which the living word, in its performative quality as event, assumes a powerful corporeal form. This is true, for example, of biblical ideas of God's voice, which is creative power turned toward the universe and the earth. Thus, the psalmist utters praise: "By the word of the LORD the heavens were made, and all their host by the breath of his mouth. . . . For he spoke, and it came to be; he commanded, and it stood firm" (Ps. 33:6, 9). God's voice sounds over the waters; it thunders, goes out with power, breaks cedars, flashes flames of fire, makes the wilderness shake, causes oaks to whirl, and strips the forest bare (Psalm 29). God's voice is creative in that, by separating, it causes something new to come forth out of the waters of chaos.[112]

God's voice creates relationship: it promises and creates the covenant with Israel (Gen. 17:2). The saving voice is encountered in the voice of the angels: in the wilderness, Hagar hears the saving voice, and Mary hears one that is deeply disturbing. The voice of the angels lets these women break free. And according to the Gospel of John, the word became flesh and dwells among us. Jesus' words (and his accompanying touch) heal lepers: *Be clean!* And the leper is clean (Matt. 8:1-4).[113] Many biblical stories testify to the performativity of the divine word as a corporeal experience: it effects what it says; it saves and heals, destroys and disturbs, helps people to enter into freedom and gives birth to new creation. When, in the process of preaching, we get in touch with this biblical wisdom and dive into it, the sermon can be a participation in the performative quality of the word.

Example: The *Romaria da Terra*

We conclude our reflections on preaching the justification of the "expendables" with a rather long account by the Brazilian theologian Julio Cézar Adam of the *romaria da terra*,[114] a special form of procession in which Brazil's "expendables" protest the wounding of the earth, the soil, and their own damaged environments and celebrate in praise and thanksgiving a foretaste of the resurrection of the body. As in the example from the Tenderloin in San Francisco, the justification of the "expendables" is here set on its feet; it is surely not sufficient for a single individual to preach.

This example is not meant to take the place of a final conclusion. Rather, we use it to open a window into the world of the globalized economy beyond the German and North American context, a world in which the "expendables" are lifting up their voices.

What is *romaria da terra*?

∽◉〜

The *romaria da terra* arose in the years of Brazilian dictatorship (1964–1985) in the southern regions of Brazil, and was directly connected to liberation theology, which at that time was in its early phase, as a movement of protest directed against social injustice in the rural areas. The support of the poor people of the land—Indians, agricultural workers, tenants and land users, small farmers, the landless, and those affected by the building of dams and water-power works—this marked the birth of the *romaria*. From the beginning it was a mixture of elements of traditional religious pilgrimage and political protest marches.

In the earliest phase the Rural Pastoral Commission (CPT) of the Catholic Church took responsibility for future *romarias da terra*. The CPT originated as a church service for the organization of resistance by agricultural workers and tenants driven from the land. It offered pastoral, theological, methodological, legal, political, and sociological advice and education. From the beginning, local CPTs saw their work as ecumenical: other churches and religious communities as well as nonchurch organizations took part as well. The practical work of the CPT was done essentially by laypersons (pastoral workers), even though the pastoral work was broadly shaped by the church's support and theological advice provided by priests and pastors.

The liturgical structure of the *romarias da terra* is very similar throughout Brazil. In general, it can be divided into three major parts or liturgical phases: (1) gathering and opening phase (greeting and opening, greetings to Mother Earth, reception of the symbols of the *romaria*, procession with the Bible, procession with the *romaria* cross, memorials), (2) the pilgrimage or procession proper, or the "way" as such (with stations for protest, music and songs, speeches and prayers), and (3) the concluding feast at the end of the way (feast, action, blessing, sending forth). The whole liturgical action is in the hands of laity; it is planned, developed, prepared for, led, and evaluated by teams composed of lay pastoral workers, some theologians, and the participants themselves.

The *romarias da terra*, like traditional pilgrimages and processions, attract a great number of people who are motivated by the work of the CPT: groups of landless people, organizations of small farmers (tenants, agricultural workers, groups of family farmers or other agricultural organizations, rural labor unions), Indian peoples, rural base communities, groups of Afro-Brazilians and women's groups, or simply people who identify with the church of the poor as well as base communities from the cities, groups involved in pastoral care of workers and youth, political parties and nongovernmental organizations, and so on. Altogether they comprise about five thousand to seven thousand people.

The participants organize themselves for the *romaria* in groups or communities. Many spend months in preparation with the material distributed by the CPT on the theme selected for the planned *romaria*. The theme of a *romaria* is always related to the reality of the region in which the *romaria* is taking place. Such a theme could be agrarian reform, assistance for the development of small businesses, the lack of schools, or the expulsion of a group from their land or the building of a dam and the resulting destruction of the land by flooding.

The length of a *romaria* varies from place to place. Normally it lasts a day, but there have been places in which they have gone on for three to seven days, or even three weeks.

The horizon of those participating in a *romaria* constitutes a clear sociopolitical project: an agrarian model as alternative to capitalist-globalized agriculture. In this case the alternatives have much more to do with concrete experiences within agrarian organizations than with political ideology. It is true that the backdrop is the idea of a model society, but the model grows out of concrete, everyday experience. Mystical-utopian elements are also part of it, as well as an explicit theology of the earth. Both are represented in the *romarias da terra*: the earth belongs to the Creator God, and concentration of its ownership in the hands of a few does not correspond to God's will. As in the biblical witness—from the exodus through the prophets to Jesus Christ—God takes the part of the little ones, identifies with them, and is present in their stories and their struggles. In the *romaria*, too, God is underway with the people. Consciousness raising as a method of organization in view of the unjust situation and this contextual theology of a partisan God play a very important part in the context of the quest for a space to live.

❧

The liturgy of the *romaria da terra* in Paraná is constantly in process. Currently we can structure the *romaria* in three basic parts: (1) Opening, (2) *Caminhada* (movement on the way), and (3) Concluding Celebration.

1. *Opening*: The pilgrims come in caravans from throughout the state. They gather in a public plaza that has a historical significance for the theme of the *romaria*. Some are still eating breakfast while listening to music from truckbeds equipped with loudspeakers. There are songs and battle cries. Then the celebration officially begins. Priests, pastors, bishops, leaders of the CPT, local officials, and people from the local community greet the pilgrims and the *romaria* as a whole. The groups and caravans are named, interspersed with choral shouts of the *romaria* motto, and the *romaria* is begun in the name of the triune God. Prayers and songs are interspersed throughout.

A lane in which the opening rituals will be performed is opened through the crowd. The first ritual is a greeting to the earth. Since the eleventh *romaria da terra* this greeting, frequently addressed to *Mother Earth*, has become an important feature. In my opinion this can be seen as a creation ritual; usually it is enacted by women, children, and in some of the most recent *romarias da terra*, even babies. Then the central symbol of this particular *romaria*, always pertinent to the theme, is borne from the back of the crowd to the front, to the truckbed stage. It could be a cross made from the fenceposts of a landed magnate, a truck used every day to transport day laborers (*bóias-frias*), a cow as metaphor for a family's chance of survival through milk production, an oxcart or horsecart, and so forth. This symbol of the particular *romaria* has acquired more and more space and relevance in the course of the years. What at the beginning (in the third *romaria da terra*) was a simple cart without hand-painted sides or a maté plant, was later transformed into a great procession of about forty horse-drawn carts and the families that owned them (e.g., in the fourteenth *romaria da terra*). . . .

Each *romaria* has its cross, which remains afterward as an emblem for the neighborhood. Until the tenth *romaria da terra* the cross was always related to the theme of that particular *romaria*. A good example is the cross of the twelfth *romaria da terra*. Because that *romaria* took place in a camp belonging to the landless movement, the organizers built a cross out of pieces of wood from the fence of the estate being occupied by the landless. The Bible is also borne in symbolic procession into the *romaria* and is met and then read from. Sometimes the Bible is carried through the lane, together with the symbol of the *romaria*, for example on an oxcart (twelfth *romaria*).

The procession with the cross normally contains a moment of protest. Here expression is given, at the place where the *romaria* begins, to the particular complaints and protests connected with the theme of this *romaria da terra*. In the course of years the place where the opening phase takes place has acquired a significance symbolic of the terrible experiences in the history of the country's poor. Thus, the fourteenth *romaria da terra* opened at the place where the train station in the town of Rebouça formerly stood. The station was understood in the *romaria da terra* as a reminder of the building of the railway system; for its construction thousands of farmers were driven from their lands and it provoked the war of *Contestado*. Songs are sung throughout, and the history of the place is told; theatrical scenes depicting the struggle for land in the region are presented. The liturgy is structured in such a way that the pilgrims can really participate: through songs, responses, dance, gestures, liturgical antiphons, common readings, and so on.

2. *On the way*: The common movement in procession is the most politically relevant part of the *romaria*. The pilgrims march with their flags, placards, and banners from the place of the opening phase to a new, significant locus. Both the symbol of the *romaria* and the Bible and cross are carried at the fore. The truck with the loudspeakers is driven in the middle of the procession; from it the whole march is coordinated and the songs are led. At different points on the common march the procession halts. The history of the place and symbols of protest are staged as in a theater. At one point during the procession of the fourteenth *romaria da terra* huge placards bearing the trademarks of chemical weedkillers were burned. It is the usual thing that in the course of the common procession the cross of the *romaria* is planted in the ground in front of a church—for example, in the thirteenth *romaria da terra* at a Lutheran church. There is much common singing and the Our Father is prayed often. The people of the place who do not join in the march stand on the sidewalks to greet the pilgrims or offer them water. It takes about two hours to complete the course of about four kilometers. Pilgrims of all ages laugh and talk with each other. Many of them have to carry their personal belongings as well as their lunch, babies, and small children.

3. *Concluding celebration*: After the common procession it is time for a break. When the blessing for the common meal has been spoken from the stage on the truck bed, small groups of people share and eat their lunch. During the meal, and afterward, there is a time for an *open stage*. Everyone can make use of the stage to say something, to give thanks, to ask for something, or to present something: a musical number, a dance, a play.

In many places in Brazil the closing celebration of the *romaria* is in the form of a Mass or an ecumenical worship service. Nowadays in Paraná the celebration is marked by a special ritual for the distribution of the food, similar to an agape feast, or it is combined with a celebration of a good harvest or the success of an agrarian project. Fruit, other foods, and regional dishes are set out in sufficient quantity on tables in the midst of the crowd and then eaten. Almost always the food and drink are prepared and served by inhabitants of the place itself.

One very special moment is that of concrete action. Sometimes it is nothing more than calling to mind the struggle for the land. At other times it is something with concrete consequences, such as an educational project for day laborers and especially for illiterate land-users following the ninth *romaria da terra* in Pinhão. At the end of this part the blessing is said and the participants are sent home with an explicit dismissal, to participate in the ongoing struggle for the possession of the land or for the sake of the earth. During the blessing and dismissal the participants receive a memorial object to take home with them. It could be a corn kernel or a piece of sugar cane.

∞⊚◠

Not only is the political struggle for land given a religious foundation and dramatization during a *romaria*; one's own particular piece of earth is visualized as an element of nature, praised as the means of production that sustains life, or blessed as an important place in history. The earth is celebrated in multiple rituals—touching the earth or kneeling on it, dancing to greet Mother Earth, the distribution of sacks of dirt as memorials for the pilgrims. Sometimes one gets the impression that the concept of land or earth is almost interchangeable with the idea of *God*. During the *romaria* at Paraná, *God* was frequently called upon and named as *God of land and life*. At the beginning of the celebration the pilgrims and frequently Mother Earth are greeted simultaneously.

Relationship to earth, land, and the elements of the earth has become an increasingly important aspect of the *romaria* celebration. Here we can sense a clear rediscovery of the significance of the earth in Indian and African piety. The CPT has for years observed the intimate relationship between small farmers and the land and cycles of nature. It seems that just now, with the last creation rituals, this relationship has attained its solemn expression.

For the Inca, Maya, Aztecs, and Guarani, the earth is a sacred place, a privileged place for the encounter between humans and God. Good Mother Earth (*Pachamama*) brings human beings into the world, cares for and nourishes her children, gives mountains and rivers, fields and solid ground. This is the place where the ancestors rest: the roots of Indian economy, culture, and spirituality (*Peuch*).

∞⊚◠

The Bible is present as the word of God in which the history of God's justice with the poor of the earth is recounted. The Bible, decorated with flowers or bright cloths, is often carried in a special procession and greeted by the pilgrims with praise, songs, dance, waving, and clapping. From the Bible are read the texts about creation, the exodus, the prophets' struggle for justice, Jesus as the beginning and example of the reign of God. The stories of the pilgrimage of the people of God are also frequently read, or simply recounted as the founding stories of the *romaria da terra*. The book as such, even when it remains closed, is itself an occasion for songs of praise. As a reflection of Catholic piety, people dance with the Bible in their arms, or it is kissed and passed through the crowd from hand to hand.

It is difficult to draw a precise boundary between the liturgical and political elements of the *romaria da terra*. . . . Likewise, the question of the boundaries between sacred and profane, religion and politics is very important and has many layers. One could probably say that the entire celebration of the *romaria* is shaped by an interplay between religio-liturgical and politico-social elements. . . . A *romaria* represents a large public mass manifestation of a particular class or group within society that takes place outside in a street or plaza and is also deliberately presented as a kind of political event. The flags, the placards, the banners with sayings, the combative tone of the speeches, the march—all are elements that point strongly to a link with the political demonstrations of the landless movement, unions, or social protest marches. We will show later how this politics of the *romaria* differs from politics as partisan civil engagement.

At the same time, the people draw a clear distinction between a *romaria* and a demonstration: ordinarily, in a political demonstration by the landless movement one sees a lot of Labor Party flags. Although many of these same people come to a *romaria*, one seldom sees party flags here. Speeches by politicians are also given only limited time and the distribution of party propaganda material is forbidden. On the other hand, the flags—for example, of the landless movement, which is not organized as a closed political party but is nevertheless very much oriented to political parties—are present in both *romarias* and demonstrations.

Inspired by traditional pilgrimages and political demonstrations, the *romarias* have developed around the experience of pilgrimage as walking together. The religious common movement of many people together has enormous symbolic power, and many know or remember that political powers have been and can be shaken by such—for example, by Gandhi's hunger marches in his pacifist struggle against British colonialism.

The pilgrims of the *romaria da terra* have already experienced walking together, either in a religious context, that is, in pilgrimages, or in political marches. Especially familiar are the long marches of some three hundred kilometers, sometimes lasting more than two weeks, undertaken by farmers, the landless, and Indians from their homes to the particular seats of power of the political institutions in their regions. Although those political marches have had no religious foundation or occasion, they have been imbued with clearly religious elements: a cross borne ahead; flags; silent or barefoot walking; the dimension of common sacrifice; the pacifist element of nonviolence.

∼❧∼

The work of remembering in the *romaria da terra* serves to elevate the stories of the people and to link them to the Christ story, which permeates hope for the future. The special culture of feast and celebration that marks a *romaria* is a form of anticipation of the future through and in hope. Although the lives of those belonging to the CPT are often marked by severe conflicts, poverty, and death, the people who participate in the *romaria* have a special love for festivals and celebrations, because it is precisely through these that the *romaria* is applied to their whole life.

∼❧∼

"Here, in the heart of the city, where the rusty gears of power turn, we carry the blood, the pain, and the resistance of the workers of our state. Certainly, the government would like to ignore this suffering. Our little, forgotten communities in the interior of Paraná do not exist in the geography of power. But we are here today to say that we exist, we resist, we demand a life of dignity. We are here to lament over the debts of society. . . . They ought to be paid by the state and the elite in society, on the basis of fundamental political, ethical, and evangelical principles, so that there may be life and resurrection. Like a great Way of the Cross, we traveled through unknown places. In these fourteen years we have celebrated with the pain and the victory of the workers. In order that this *romaria* may be a station of the resurrection, the debts must be forgiven. Only when there is human dignity and peace can there be life and resurrection. Here, into the heart of the city, we want to bring the holy earth of these forgotten places. The earth itself is the lament of oppression. It is the splinter in the eye of repressive and deadly power. . . . From the land we draw life, sustenance, and hope. Whoever plants a seed, believes in the future. . . . The land is the basis for a life project. It is the real mortar and cement of the new world. Therefore these fourteen samples of earth are memory, agreement, and hope. They are fourteen cries of the people, fourteen groans of fear, fourteen years on the way. . . .

"The wheelbarrows symbolize the building of the city. They are remembrance of all the builders, the men and women who built but cannot live here." . . .

"I come from afar; I am from the Sertão. I am Pedro, I am Paulo, I am the nation. I build the cities, but I remain a stranger; I fight for the Fatherland and yet all I gained was servitude. And now say, all of you, whether I, I too, do not have rights as a citizen; I am a creature of God. I am the nation, and yet I am also a brother! I am the people of God and yet I am left out. I know only hunger and thirst and pain; for me there is nothing but work and yet I am worth nothing. I build the cities, but I dwell in misery. I plant and harvest, but others eat. I come from the land, but it is not mine; I can only labor and I go away empty." This song not only summarized the theme of the fifteenth *romaria da terra* and the critique of Curitiba very well; it also recalled the creation of humanity from the opening prayer in which a refrain questioned: "And now say, all of you, whether I, I too, do not have rights as a citizen; I am a creature of God."

"We bring the sacred earth of Guaíra and recall the first *romaria da terra* at Paraná in the year 1985. The earth of the islanders, flooded by the waterpower works at Itaipú. This earth bewails the cultural and anthropological debts under which the people of Brazil suffer. The inhabitants of the islands were culturally divided; they were shut out of their own places, where they had created their stories, their faith, their symbols, their myths, their songs, their foods. This earth holds the cry of all that our Brazilian identity and culture are to be respected."

"We are a nation under the command of the International Monetary Fund, the World Bank, and the capitalist empires. Foreign debt is the great cross laid on the Brazilian people. It is the cross of hunger, of pain, the lack of land, of education, of dignity. . . . Therefore the cross of the *romaria da terra* from Paraná is the cross of a crucified land awaiting the resurrection. It is the cross of suffering and pain of a stolen land and a betrayed people. It is the cross of a flag bound with the barbed wire of landed estates." . . .

⊷

"God of the massacred, the excluded, those oppressed by foreign debt and social debts, Lord of the jubilee year of the land and of justice, You alone have the word of life and hope. Deliver us from the evil of hunger, of hatred, of greed, and of subjection. For yours is the true kingdom, yours is the power that shows itself through the hands of the people, and yours is the glory forever that requires no elevated throne at the centers of power." . . .

⊷

"The word of God is the word of life. It is a seed and a kernel. Word of life and word of hope. Therefore we have brought earth with us from the center of Paraná. Out of this earth will be born the hope for a new project, the society we desire. Out of the earth appear the alternatives of life and liberation of the people of God. . . . Out of the earth springs the people's resistance as they search for a form of education for the people who live on the land, an education that accepts their identity and their lives as farmers and through which their experiences can be processed and understood. It is a sign of the presence of countless alternative educational projects on the land, such as APEART, the *Projeto Vida na Roça* ("Project Life on the Land"), and the educational projects in the camps of the landless movement."

⊷

It was an explosion of joy and festival, as if the place—the center of power—had no more barriers to hold back the masses. The social debts in the country had to be lamented on the way through the city. Pointing out successes makes the debts still more unbearable. The successes really affect the crowds like a resurrection of the people because they strengthen utopia and hope. The good news of the alternatives in the country for a new society must be proclaimed in the streets, and they must be celebrated. The feast of the resurrection makes the resurrection of life tangible.[115]

NOTES

Preface to the German Edition

1. Rudolph Bohren, *Predigtlehre*, 6th ed. (Gütersloh: Kaiser, 1993), 17.

Chapter 1

1. Christoph Türcke, *Kassensturz. Zur Lage der Theologie* (Frankfurt: Fischer-Taschenbuch, 1992), 114–15.

2. Elsa Tamez, *The Amnesty of Grace: Justification by Faith from a Latin American Perspective*, trans. Sharon H. Ringe (Nashville: Abingdon, 1993), 14.

3. In what follows we prefer the use of the term God's *justice* instead of *righteousness* since it carries more explicitly the economic dimension that we seek to introduce into the theological debate about God's justice and justification.

4. See also for homiletical reflections on the performative dimension of preaching, Clayton Schmidt and Jana Childers, eds., *Performance in Preaching: Bringing the Sermon to Life* (Grand Rapids: Baker Academic, 2008).

5. See Wilfried Härle, *Menschsein in Beziehungen. Studien zur Rechtfertigungslehre und Anthropologie* (Tübingen: Mohr Siebeck, 2005), 7.

6. The Latin original of this text is found in *Weimar Ausgabe* 54, 185, 23–37 (hereafter *WA*). This English translation is by Andrew Thornton, OSB, for the St. Anselm College Humanities Program, © 1983 by St. Anselm Abbey and available for use through Project Wittenberg at http://www.iclnet.org/pub/resources/text/wittenberg/luther/tower.txt, accessed November 18, 2009.

7. Härle, *Menschsein in Beziehungen*, 10.

8. Ibid., 11.

9. Ibid., 13.

10. For both the common and the philosophical uses, see also Michael Moxter, "Rechtfertigung und Anerkennung. Zur kulturellen Bedeutung der Unterscheidung zwischen Person und Werk," in Hans Martin Dober and Dagmar Mensink, eds., *Die Lehre von der Rechtfertigung des Gottlosen im kulturellen Kontext der Gegenwart. Beiträge im Horizont des christlich-jüdischen Gesprächs* (Stuttgart: Akademie der Diözese Rottenburg-Stuttgart, 2002), 22–26, as well as Eberhard Jüngel, *Das Evangelium von der Rechtfertigung des Gottlosen als Zentrum des christlichen Glaubens*, 4th rev. ed. (Tübingen: Mohr Siebeck, 2004), 4–6.

11. Moxter, "Rechtfertigung," 23–24.

12. Our critical remarks are directed against the *exclusive* usage of a forensic interpretation. We want to emphasize at the same time that the idea of God's judgment is

necessary in light of the question of divine justice and, in eschatological perspective, for the healing of the effects of human destruction.

13. See Frank M. Lütze, *Absicht und Wirkung der Predigt. Eine Untersuchung zur homiletischen Pragmatik* (Leipzig: Evangelische Verlagsanstalt, 2006), 45–50.

14. Ibid., 47.

15. Ibid., 48.

16. For example, in Luther's *Small Catechism,* the concept of salvation is of central importance.

17. See, e.g., *WA* 5, 144, 20–21, and Wilfried Joest, *Dogmatik,* vol. 2, *Der Weg Gottes mit dem Menschen* (Göttingen: Vandenhoeck & Ruprecht, 1986), 439ff.

18. Tamez, *Amnesty of Grace,* 42.

19. OECD Annual Report 2009, http://www.oecd.org/LongAbstract/0,3425,en_2 649_34489_43125524_119687_1_1_1,00.html, accessed on January 2nd, 2010, 43.

20. See *Growing Unequal? Income Distribution and Poverty in OECD Countries,* http://www.oecd.org/LongAbstract/0,3425,en_2649_34637_42255286_1_1_1_1,00 .html, accessed January 3, 2010.

21. Wilhelm Heitmeyer and Sandra Hüpping, "Auf dem Weg in eine inhumane Gesellschaft," *Die Süddeutsche* (21–22 October 2006): 13.

22. *Die Zeit* (12 August 2004): 19.

23. All information from ibid., 20–21. The Hartz IV concept is named for the Volkswagen personnel director Peter Hartz, who chaired a commission of the German Bundestag that developed new social regulations intended to offer a reform of the labor market. The changes put into place on 1 January 2003 were geared especially toward welfare and unemployment regulations. At the core of the reform was the fusion of the former unemployment benefits for the long-term unemployed (*Arbeitslosenhilfe*) with welfare benefits (*Sozialhilfe*), leaving both at approximately the lower level of the former *Sozialhilfe*. This fusion has drastically shortened the time span for receiving unemployment compensation as well as the amount of money unemployed persons receive from the state. So far as we can see, one of the effects of Hartz IV that causes greatest concern is the increase of child poverty in Germany.

24. Thus states the German journalist Ulrike Hermann, "Sein und Haben. Die deutsche Wirstchaft boomt, doch die große Mehrheit der Bevölkerung profitiert nicht mehr von ihren Wachstumsgewinnen," *taz* (3 May 2007): 11.

25. Barbara Dribbusch, "Wenn Kellnern nicht für die Familie langt," *taz* (28 August 2007).

26. Ibid.

27. Not only measurable data but also people's expectations have changed dramatically in contrast to previous decades. Fear of downward social mobility has, in the meantime, arrived at the center of society, and, parallel to the massive social shifts and uncertainties about the possibilities of maintaining one's own perspective on one's life, the threat to democratic culture in Germany is increasing. This has led to an explosion of violence from the radical right.

28. More and more children and youth in Germany are living in poverty. According to Klaus Hurrelmann, there are now almost 1.2 million youth below the age of

eighteen receiving social assistance. As early as 1997, 40 percent of the 2.8 million who received social assistance were from the coming generation. Children represented a risk of poverty for their parents because only about 60 percent of the financial expenses of children were covered by child payments and tax deductions. See *taz* (22 September 1997).

29. Ibid.

30. Olaf Groh-Samberg and Matthias Grundmann, "Soziale Ungleichheit im Kindes- und Jugendalter. Bundeszentrale für politische Bildung," *Aus Politik und Zeitgeschichte* 26 (2006).

31. At the beginning of the unified German state, in the early 1990s, 4.2 million persons were dependent on social assistance, and of those, 54.5 percent were women and 45.5 percent were men. In all of Germany, women are more affected by dependence on social assistance than are men. This information and what follows are taken from Ernst-Ulrich Huster's study *Neuer Reichtum und alte Armut* (Düsseldorf: Patmos, 1993), 29–30. For the unequal distribution of child and dependent care in the family, see, for example, Hans Bertram, *Familien leben. Neue Wege zur flexiblen Gestaltung von Lebenszeit, Arbeitszeit und Familienzeit* (Gütersloh: Verlag Bertelsmann-Stiftung, 1997).

32. See Huster, *Neuer Reichtum und alte Armut,* 35–36.

33. Wolfgang Glatzer and Werner Hübinger, "Lebenslagen und Armut," in *Armut im Wohlstand,* ed. Diether Döring et al. (Frankfurt am Main: Suhrkamp, 1990), 31–55.

34. See ibid., 34ff.

35. See Huster, *Neuer Reichtum,* 9ff.

36. The scenes from the 1990s that Huster describes reveal a situation that has significantly expanded in the new decade, especially since the introduction of "second-stage unemployment assistance." In social-science discussions, but also in the tabloids, there is talk of the creation of a "precariate," a rapidly growing poor population that is enduringly excluded from the social safety nets and also from the opportunities for production, consumption, and participation in our society.

37. We owe this reference to Jürgen Ebach, "Biblisch-ethische Überlegungen zur Armut," in idem, . . . *und behutsam mitgehen mit deinem Gott* (Bochum: SWB, 1995), 215.

38. The saying is from Bertolt Brecht, "Ballade über die Frage: Wovon lebt der Mensch?" in his *Die Dreigroschenoper,* 40th ed. (Frankfurt am Main: Suhrkamp, 1968).

39. Tamez, *Amnesty of Grace,* 42–43.

40. The social, cultural, and religiously pluralized conditions of life in Germany are only gradually being recognized by academic practical theology as a context for preaching the gospel. A good introduction to this issue is presented by Albrecht Grözinger, *Toleranz und Leidenschaft. Über das Predigen in einer pluralistischen Gesellschaft* (Gütersloh: Gütersloher, 2004). For several years now, the academy for mission in Hamburg, in conjunction with the faculty of Protestant theology, has offered theological continuing education for African pastors and congregational leaders in Hamburg and other cities: "African Theological Training in Germany" (ATTIG), in which Hans-Martin Gutmann participates. It was in this context that contact was made with African communities in Hamburg and with Pastor Okeke.

41. Pastor Ossai Okeke, in an e-mail to Hans-Martin Gutmann from May 2007.

42. Pastor Ossai Okeke, "The Message to the Poor," unpublished sermon, trans. Andrea Bieler. The male God-language of the sermon has not been modified in this translation.

43. In the 1980s, it seemed that the subject of work in particular had taken on increased significance for practical theology: see, for example, in homiletics Helmut Barié, *Predigt und Arbeitswelt. Analyse und praktische Anregungen* (Stuttgart: Calwer, 1989); Horst Albrecht, *Arbeiter und Symbol. Soziale Homiletik im Zeitalter des Fernsehens* (Munich: Kaiser, 1982); Michael Schibilsky, *Alltagswelt und Sonntagskirche. Sozialethisch orientierte Gemeindearbeit im Industriegebiet* (Munich: Kaiser, 1983). For more recent North American homiletical discussion, see, e.g., André Resner, ed., *Just Preaching: Prophetic Voices for Economic Justice* (St. Louis: Chalice, 2003); Marvin A. McMickle, *Where Have All the Prophets Gone? Reclaiming Prophetic Preaching in America* (Cleveland: Pilgrim, 2006).

44. See, for example, the work of Kristina Augst, *Religion in der Lebenswelt junger Frauen aus sozialen Unterschichten* (Stuttgart: Kohlhammer, 2000). In this book, Kristina Augst examines how young women interpret their lives after leaving school. She asks how reality is perceived and interpreted by these women and how the implicit points of contact for religious interpretation can be identified. Sibylle Tobler proposes a counseling model that supports dealing with unemployment in her book *Arbeitslose beraten unter Perspektiven der Hoffnung. Lösungsorientierte Kurzberatung in beruflichen Übergangsprozessen* (Stuttgart: Kohlhammer, 2004). In addition, we need to mention Susanna Kempin's dissertation, which deals with the theme of unemployment and to which we will refer below; cf. *Leben ohne Arbeit? Wege der Bewältigung im pastoralpsychologischen und theologischen Deutungshorizont* (Münster: Lit, 2001). For the British discussion, cf. Malcolm Brown and Peter Sedgwick, *Putting Theology to Work: A Theological Symposium on Unemployment and the Future of Work* (London: CCBI, 1998). In North American practical theology, the theme of poverty is only marginal; cf., for example, Pamela Couture, *Seeing Children, Seeing God: A Practical Theology of Children and Poverty* (Nashville: Abingdon, 2000); idem, *Blessed Are the Poor? Women's Poverty, Family Policy and Practical Theology* (Nashville: Abingdon, in cooperation with the Churches' Center for Theology and Public Policy, Washington, D.C., 1991).

45. See Norbert Mette and Hermann Steinkamp, eds., *Anstiftung zur Solidarität. Praktische Beispiele der Sozialpastoral* (Mainz: Matthias-Grünewald, 1997).

46. Norbert Mette, "Anstiftung zur Solidarität—zur not-wendenden Aufgabe der christlichen Gemeinde heute," in idem, *Praktisch-theologische Erkundungen 2* (Berlin and Münster: Lit Verlag, 2007), 325–36, at 334.

47. See Wolfgang Huber, Johannes Friedrich, and Peter Steinacker, eds., *Kirche in der Vielfalt der Lebensbezüge. Die vierte EKD-Erhebung über Kirchenmitgliedschaft* (Gütersloh: Gütersloher, 2006).

48. In the section "Die sozialkulturelle Verortung der Kirchenmitglieder," we find a brief nod to economic integration: "Of members strongly tied to the church and having a high degree of religious devotion, 23.1 percent are strongly integrated; in the membership type with the greatest distance it is 48.6 percent. The religious members with greater distance from the church (Type 2) are, at 36.2 percent, more economically integrated than in the contrary case, the third type, who number 23.9 percent" (ibid., 157).

49. See Elisabeth Gräb-Schmidt, "'Die Kirche ist kein Unternehmen!' Die Rede

vom 'Unternehmen Kirche' in ekklesiologischer Sicht," in Joachim Fetzer et al., eds., *Kirche in der Marktgesellschaft* (Gütersloh: Kaiser, Gütersloher, 1999), 65. Barrenstein is the head of the consulting firm McKinsey & Co. in Munich.

50. See Uta Pohl-Patalong, *Ortsgemeinde und übergemeindliche Arbeit im Konflikt. Eine Analyse der Argumentationen und ein alternatives Modell* (Göttingen: Vandenhoeck & Ruprecht, 2003).

51. See Mette and Steinkamp, *Anstiftung*; Mette, *Praktisch-Theologische Erkundungen*.

52. Fulbert Steffensky, *Der alltägliche Charme des Glaubens* (Würzburg: Echter Verlag, 2002).

53. Ibid., 98.

54. See the works of Wolfgang Grünberg, especially his *Die Sprache der Stadt. Skizzen zur Großstadtkirche* (Leipzig: Evangelische Verlagsanstalt, 2004).

55. See, for example, Ingrid Breckner and Andrea Kirchmair, eds., *Innovative Handlungsansätze im Wohnbereich—Informationen über Projekte, Träger und Initiativen* (Dortmund: Dortmunder Vertrieb für Bau- und Planungsliteratur, 1995).

56. See Manfred Josuttis, "Seelsorge im energetischen Netzwerk der Ortsgemeinde," in idem et al., eds., *Auf dem Weg zu einer seelsorgerlichen Kirche. Theologische Bausteine* (Göttingen: Vandenhoeck & Ruprecht, 2000), 117–26; idem, "Seelsorge in der Gemeinde," *Pastoraltheologie* 90 (2001): 400–408.

57. See Grünberg, *Die Sprache der Stadt*.

58. Waldemar Sidorow, *Gemeinden geben Raum für andere: Am Beispiel von Aids-Betroffenen in Hamburg und Obdachlosen in Berlin* (Schenefeld: EB-Verlag, 2005).

59. Ibid., 17, 52–55.

60. See Kempin, *Leben ohne Arbeit*, xiii.

61. See ibid., 48.

62. See ibid., 42.

63. Ibid., 68–69.

64. Ibid., 42.

65. Ibid., 56.

66. Ibid., 57.

67. Ibid., 97.

68. Ibid., 106.

69. Ibid., 98.

70. Ulrich Beck, "Die uneindeutige Sozialstruktur. Was heißt Armut, was heißt Reichtum in der Selbstkultur?" in idem and Peter Sopp, *Individualisierung und Integration. Neue Konfliktlinien und neuer Integrationsmodus?* (Opladen: Leske & Budrich, 1997), 192.

71. See Kempin, *Leben ohne Arbeit*, 108.

72. Ibid., 117.

73. Ibid., 164.

74. *WA* Tr. 2, no. 2408b.

75. These questions will receive further attention in chapter 2.

76. On this, cf. Hans-Martin Gutmann, *Ich bin's nicht. Die Praktische Theologie vor der Frage nach dem Subjekt des Glaubens* (Neukirchen-Vluyn: Neukirchener Verlag, 1999); and idem, *Über Liebe und Herrschaft. Luthers Verständnis von Intimität und Autorität im Kontext des Zivilisationsprozesses* (Göttingen: Vandenhoeck & Ruprecht, 1991), 109ff.

77. On this, see below, 71–73.

78. As a classic example from the current debate, see Hans Martin Müller, *Homiletik. Eine evangelische Predigtlehre* (Berlin and New York: de Gruyter, 1996).

79. A classic definition of this relationship between divine and human speech comes from the Zürich Reformer Heinrich Bullinger, himself the successor to Zwingli: *praedicatio verbi divini est verbum divinum*. Karl Barth reformulated Bullinger's phrase by analogy to the christological doctrine of two natures, although with the distinction that the identity between divine and human word is not permanent but through the power of divine promise happens over and over again. Barth thus modifies the assertion of the early phase of "dialectical theology" that it is impossible for human beings to speak of God and explains the difference thus described between the divine and the human word in his *Church Dogmatics*, in the doctrine of the "threefold form" of the word of God: namely as an irreversible difference between Jesus Christ, as the one Word of God, the Sacred Scriptures as witness to him, and preaching as the word of God attesting to him here and now. See Karl Barth, *Homiletik. Wesen und Vorbereitung der Predigt* (Zürich: EVZ, 1966), 30.

80. This understanding was applied to Christian preaching by Gert Otto, *Predigt als Rede. Über die Wechselwirkungen von Homiletik und Rhetorik* (Stuttgart: Kohlhammer, 1976).

81. See Manfred Josuttis, "Über den Predigteinfall," in idem, *Rhetorik und Theologie in der Predigtarbeit*. Homiletische Studien 1 (Munich: Kaiser, 1985), 70–86.

82. See idem, "Offene Geheimnisse. Ein homiletischer Essay," in idem, *Offene Geheimnisse. Predigten* (Gütersloh: Kaiser/Gütersloher, 1999), 7–15.

83. See idem, "Die Predigt des Evangeliums nach Luther," in idem, *Gesetz und Evangelium in der Predigtarbeit*. Homiletische Studien 2 (Gütersloh: Kaiser, 1995), 42–65.

84. See Gerhard Marcel Martin, "Predigt als 'offenes Kunstwerk,' " *Evangelische Theologie* 44 (1984): 46–58.

85. Wilfried Engemann, "Predigen und Zeichen setzen," in Uta Pohl-Patalong and Frank Muchlinsky, eds., *Predigen im Plural: Homiletische Perspektiven* (Hamburg: EB-Verlag, 2001), 7–24.

86. Ibid., 8.

87. Fred B. Craddock makes a similar point in *As One Without Authority*, 4th ed. (St. Louis: Chalice, 2001).

88. See Martin Nicol, *Einander ins Bild setzen. Dramaturgische Homiletik* (Göttingen: Vandenhoeck & Ruprecht, 2002).

89. Martin Nicol, "To Make Things Happen," in Pohl-Patalong and Muchlinsky, eds., *Predigen im Plural*, 50. The conceptual structure originates with David Buttrick, *Homiletic: Moves and Structures* (Philadelphia: Fortress Press, 1987).

90. See Eduard Thurneysen, "Die Aufgabe der Predigt" (1921), in Gert Hummel, ed., *Aufgabe der Predigt* (Darmstadt: Wissenschaftliche Buchgesellschaft, 1971), 105ff.

Chapter 2

1. We will be looking especially at the German-language debates of the last two generations, using the positions of some selected figures as examples.

2. For what follows, we rely on Magdalene Frettlöh's discussion of the controversy between Cremer and Barth; see her book *Gott Gewicht geben. Bausteine einer geschlechtergerechten Gotteslehre* (Neukirchen: Neukirchener, 2006), 77ff.

3. August Hermann Cremer, *Die christliche Lehre von den Eigenschaften Gottes* (Gütersloh, 1897), 22.

4. Ibid., 18.

5. Karl Barth, *Kirchliche Dogmatik* II/1, *Die Lehre von Gott. Erster Halbband*, 3d ed. (Zollikon-Zürich: Evangelischer, 1948), 292.

6. Ibid., 315.

7. Frettlöh, *Gott Gewicht geben*, 94.

8. Karl Barth, *Homiletik. Wesen und Vorbereitung der Predigt*, 3d ed. (Zürich: EVZ-Verlag, 1986); for this interpretative figure, see also Barth, *Kirchliche Dogmatik* I/1, 89–128.

9. Barth, *Homiletik*, 42.

10. Ibid., 47.

11. Manfred Josuttis, "Die Predigt des Evangeliums nach Luther," in *Gesetz und Evangelium in der Predigtarbeit*. Homiletische Studien 2 (Gütersloh: Kaiser, 1995), 42–65.

12. Ibid., 52.

13. Ibid., 60.

14. *WA* 7, 38.

15. See *WA* 5, 144, 3–4 and 144, 20–21.

16. For a reflection on the difference and reciprocity with and between God's self-communication and human subjectivity in theological reflection in the sermon, see below, 79–83.

17. On this, see Eberhard Jüngel, *Das Evangelium von der Rechtfertigung des Gottlosen als Zentrum des christlichen Glaubens*, 4th rev. ed. (Tübingen: Mohr Siebeck, 2004).

18. The concept of spheres of freedom is inspired by Christoph Dinkel, *Freiheitssphären—Vertrauensräume. Predigten* (Stuttgart: Betulius, 2005).

19. We borrow the concept of *comprehension as discovery* from Jüngel, *Das Evangelium von der Rechtfertigung*, 205: "The *yes* that we are to understand faith to be is the *comprehending discovery* by the human being of the divine decision about the human being." Jüngel, following 1 Thess. 5:5, describes this yes of faith as the recognition of one aroused from sleep that he/she has been awakened; it is the comprehension that one's own heart must first be conquered in order to be able in the first place to be freed to say yes.

20. See Martin Luther, "Römerbriefvorlesung" 15, 15/16, *WA* 56, 356, 5–6.

21. Wilfried Joest, *Ontologie der Person bei Luther* (Göttingen: Vandenhoeck & Ruprecht, 1963), 224.

22. See also Andrea Bieler, "Das Denken der Zweigeschlechtlichkeit in der Praktischen Theologie," *Pastoraltheologie* 7 (1999): 274–88.

23. Luise Schottroff, "Die Schreckensherrschaft der Sünde und die Befreiung durch Christus nach dem Römerbrief des Paulus," in idem, *Befreiungserfahrungen. Studien zur Sozialgeschichte des Neuen Testaments* (Gütersloh: Gerd Mohn, 1990), 57–72, at 62.

24. Ibid., 59.

25. See in detail, Klaus Wengst, *Pax Romana. Anspruch und Wirklichkeit: Erfahrungen und Wahrnehmungen des Friedens bei Jesus und im Urchristentum* (Munich: Kaiser, 1968).

26. Michel Foucault, *Von der Subversion des Wissens*, trans. from French by Walter Seitter (Frankfurt am Main: Fischer, 1987), 14.

27. Hans-Martin Barth has pointed out that this conversation must concern itself both with a variety of theoretical presuppositions in anthropology. See idem, "Rechtfertigung und Identität," *Pastoraltheologie* 86 (1997): 88–102.

28. The problem of narcissism is a controversial subject in psychoanalysis; we can recognize a multidimensional understanding of it already in Freud. He used the concept in multiple ways, applying it, on the one hand, to the libidinous expansion of the drive for self-preservation into egoism, and, on the other hand, using it to describe behavior resulting from a withdrawal of the libido from the world outside. Freud attempts to use his concept of narcissism to explain four phenomena: (1) a type of choice of objects, (2) a mode of relation to objects, (3) various aspects of the ego's construction of an ideal, and (4) an early stage of psychic development preceding the oedipal phase. Other authors who choose as a point of entry the concept of the self refer to narcissism as a libidinous preoccupation of the self aimed at self-fulfillment through engagement with objects. See further Berthold Rothschild, "Der neue Narzißmus—Theorie oder Ideologie?" in Psychoanalytisches Seminar Zürich, ed., *Die neuen Narzißmustheorien: Zurück ins Paradies?* (Frankfurt am Main: Syndikat, 1993), 31–68.

29. Michael Roth sees this expressed in several of Augustine's writings. At the same time, though, he perceives another theological view in Augustine: "*Augustine*, however, also assigns a positive value to self-love, for—according to Augustine—there are four things that the well-ordered human being must love: God, oneself, one's neighbor, and one's own body." Michael Roth, "*Homo incurvatus in se ipsum*—Der sich selbst verachtende Mensch. Narzißmustheorie und theologische Hamartiologie," *Praktische Theologie* 33 (1998): 14–33, at 15.

30. See in detail Christiane Tietz, *Freiheit zu sich selbst. Entfaltung eines christlichen Begriffs der Selbstannahme* (Göttingen: Vandenhoeck & Ruprecht, 2005).

31. Roth, "*Homo incurvatus*," 18.

32. Ibid., 26.

33. See, e.g., Christopher Lasch, *The Culture of Narcissism: American Life in an Age of Diminishing Expectations* (New York: Warner, 1979).

34. See 33–34 above.

35. Ulrich Beck, *Risikogesellschaft. Auf dem Weg in eine andere Moderne* (Frankfurt am Main: Suhrkamp, 1986), 158.

36. See also Isolde Karle, *"Da ist nicht mehr Mann noch Frau . . ." Theologie jenseits der Geschlechterdifferenz* (Gütersloh: Gütersloher, 2006), esp. ch. 4: "Reale Mütter und der Muttermythos," 121–60.

37. See Joachim Hohl, "Zum Symptomwandel neurotischer Störungen: Sozial-historische und sozialpsychologische Aspekte," in Heiner Keupp and Helga Bilden, eds., *Verunsicherungen. Das Subjekt im gesellschaftlichen Wandel.* Münchener Beiträge zur Sozialpsychologie. Münchener Universitätsschriften. Psychologie und Pädagogik (Göttingen: C. J. Hogrefe, 1989), 103–24, at 120.

38. See ibid., 104–5.

39. See Lasch, *Culture of Narcissism,* 7.

40. Ibid.

41. See Donald Capps, *The Depleted Self: Sin in a Narcissistic Age* (Minneapolis: Fortress Press, 1993), 32–33.

42. Richard Sennett, *The Fall of Public Man* (New York: Norton, 1992), 259.

43. See Tilman Walther-Sollich, *Festpraxis und Alltagserfahrung. Sozialpsychologische Predigtanalysen zum Bedeutungswandel des Osterfestes im 20. Jahrhundert* (Stuttgart: Kohlhammer, 1996).

44. Ibid., 233.

45. See ibid., 230ff.

46. Ibid., 231.

47. See also Andrea Bieler, "Ich habe Angst—Die Predigt vom Kreuz im narzißtischen Zeitalter," in Benita Joswig and Claudia Janssen, eds., *Aufstehen und Errinern. Antworten auf Kreuzestheologien* (Mainz: Matthias Grünewald, 2000), 132–49.

48. Frank M. Lütze also suggests that the preaching of justification should be staged as a creative event in terms of the disruption of experiences of diminishment. See Lütze, *Absicht und Wirkung der Predigt,* 45–66.

49. See 124–25 below on the concept of texts as intermediary spaces, following Donald W. Winnicott.

50. Martin Luther, "Third Disputation against the Antinomians" (1538), *WA* 39/1, 508, 2–8.

51. Michael Moxter, "Rechtfertigung und Anerkennung. Zur kulturellen Bedeutung der Unterscheidung zwischen Person und Werk," in Hans Martin Dober and Dagmar Mensink, eds., *Die Lehre von der Rechtfertigung des Gottlosen im kulturellen Kontext der Gegenwart. Beiträge im Horizont des christlich-jüdischen Gesprächs* (Stuttgart: Kohlhammer, 2002), 20–42, at 40. See also idem, *Kultur als Lebenswelt. Studien zum Problem einer Kulturtheologie* (Tübingen: Mohr Siebeck, 2000).

52. Jörg Lauster, *Gott und das Glück. Das Schicksal des guten Lebens im Christentum* (Gütersloh: Gütersloher, 2004), 151ff.

53. Ibid., 151.

54. Ibid., 153.

55. Wilhelm Schmid, *Schönes Leben? Eine Einführung in die Lebenskunst* (Frankfurt am Main: Suhrkamp, 2000), 169.

56. Ibid., 168.

57. See Rolf Zerfass, *Grundkurs Predigt,* vol. 1: *Spruchpredigt,* 2nd ed. (Düsseldorf: Patmos, 1989), 64.

58. Ibid., 67.

59. See Mihaly Csikszentmihalyi, *Flow: Studies of Enjoyment* (Chicago: University of Chicago Press, 1974), as well as the reception of the concept in Victor Turner, *From Ritual to Theatre: The Human Seriousness of Play* (New York: Performing Arts Journal Publications, 1982), and especially the essay in that collection titled "Liminal to Liminoid, in Play, Flow, and Ritual," 20–60. A basic introduction to these concepts is provided by Harald Schroeter-Wittke, "Übergang statt Untergang. Victor Turners Bedeutung für eine kulturtheologische Praxistheorie," *Theologische Literaturzeitung* 128 (2003): 575–88.

60. Csikszentmihalyi, *Flow*, quoted by Victor Turner in *From Ritual to Theatre*.

61. Mary Catherine Hilkert, a Roman Catholic homiletician, has presented a theological treatment of the theme of imagination in preaching. Following David Tracy's distinction between dialectical and sacramental imagination, she understands the act of preaching as the art of giving form and naming divine grace. She follows the path of sacramental imagination, founded in an incarnational Christology. See Hilkert, *Naming Grace: Preaching and the Sacramental Imagination* (New York: Continuum, 1997). We deviate from her position insofar as we attempt to see the dialectical and sacramental imaginations as interrelated and not as two alternative means to homiletical and theological reflection.

62. For the concept of disruption in relation to the context of prophetic and pastoral preaching from a homiletical perspective, see also Mary Donovan Turner, "Disrupting a Ruptured World," in Jana Childers, ed., *Purposes of Preaching* (St. Louis: Chalice, 2004), 131–40.

63. On this, see Susanna Kempin, *Leben ohne Arbeit? Wege der Bewältigung im pastoralpsychologischen und theologischen Deutungshorizont* (Münster: Lit, 2001); and Hannah Arendt, *Vita activa oder vom tätigen Leben*, 8th ed. (Munich: Piper, 1996). On 76–79, we will explain in more detail the extent to which the concept of the *vita contemplativa* is important for the preaching of justification within the resonance of the liturgy.

64. Jüngel, *Das Evangelium von der Rechtfertigung*, 226.

65. Moxter, "Rechtfertigung und Anerkennung," 41.

66. See Regina Becker-Schmidt, "Identitätslogik und Gewalt. Zum Verhältnis von Kritischer Theorie und Feminismus," *beiträge zur feministischen theorie und praxis* 12/24 (1989): 51–64, at 53.

67. See, e.g., Heiner Keupp, "Auf der Suche nach der verlorenen Identität," in idem, *Riskante Chancen. Das Subjekt zwischen Psychokultur und Selbstorganisation. Sozialpsychologische Studien* (Heidelberg: Asanger, 1988), 131–51.

68. Judith Butler, "Contingent Foundations: Feminism and the Question of 'Postmodernism,'" in Seyla Benhabib et al., eds., *Feminist Contentions: A Philosophical Exchange* (New York: Routledge, 1995), 35–58.

69. See Gunther Wenz, *Einführung in die evangelische Sakramentenlehre* (Darmstadt: Wissenschaftliche Buchgesellschaft, 1988), 73ff.

70. Ibid., 80.

71. See also Hans-Martin Gutmann, *Ich bin's nicht. Die Praktische Theologie vor der Frage nach dem Subjekt des Glaubens* (Neukirchen-Vluyn: Neukirchener, 1999).

72. Wayne A. Meeks, "The Image of the Androgyne: Some Uses of a Symbol in Earliest Christianity," *History of Religions* 13 (1974): 165–208, at 182.

73. For the eschatological imagination, see also Andrea Bieler and Luise Schottroff, *Eucharist: Bodies, Bread, and Resurrection* (Minneapolis: Fortress Press, 2007), 15–48.

74. Zerfass, *Gundkurs Predigt* (Düsseldorf: Patmos, 1992), 2:14.

75. Ibid.

76. Ibid., 17.

77. Ibid., 18.

78. *WA* 7, 20ff.

79. See Ingrid Schoberth, "Aufmerksamkeit für die Spur des Anderen: zum Alltag der Seelsorge," in Heinz-Dieter Neef, *Theologie und Gemeinde: Beiträge zu Bibel, Gottesdienst, Predigt und Seelsorge* (Stuttgart: Calwer, 2006), 264–74.

80. Ibid., 267.

81. John S. McClure, *Other-Wise Preaching: A Postmodern Ethic for Homiletics* (St. Louis: Chalice, 2001), 9.

82. See Helga Kuhlmann, "Abschied von der Perfektion. Überlegungen zu einer 'frauengerechten' Rechtfertigungstheologie," in Irene Dingel, ed., *Feministische Theologie und Gender-Forschung: Bilanz, Perspektiven, Akzente* (Leipzig: Evangelische Verlagsanstalt, 2003), 97–122.

83. Ibid., 99.

84. Ibid., 112–13.

85. Ibid., 114.

86. San Francisco Network Ministries can be found on the Internet at http://www .SFnetworkministries.org, accessed November 23, 2009. Since 1972, the network has been working to improve the living conditions of people in the Tenderloin. It offers computer courses for the unemployed and works to promote public housing programs. Childcare is offered, and pastoral counseling for people with HIV and AIDS. The Safe-House Initiative helps women prostitutes to leave this life and develop new careers and outlooks on life. Several times a week, funerals and memorial services are held for the poor and homeless, in which it is proclaimed that in the eyes of God every individual life is precious. In addition, other political activities are organized to put religious and social work in a larger structural context. Temenos Catholic Worker concentrates on work with homeless youth in the Tenderloin; see its Web site at http://www.temenos .org, accessed November 23, 2009.

87. What follows is an extract—the first four stations—from a Good Friday procession in the Tenderloin in 2006, designed by Pastor Glenda Hope, who works for San Francisco Network Ministries, and Father River Sims. We are especially grateful to Glenda Hope for making this unpublished text available to us.

88. Eugene H. Peterson, *The Message: The Bible in Contemporary Language* (Colorado Springs: NavPress, 2002).

89. For responsory receptivity, see below, 109–18.

90. Peter Cornehl in particular, in the first volume of his work on liturgics, points out that preaching and worship should no longer be understood as separate objects of practical-theological reflection; rather, the two should be more closely related. The

liturgy of divine worship in many liturgical traditions situates the sermon, along with the Lord's Supper, as one of the two outstanding moments of the liturgical journey. By far the majority of Protestant sermons are not delivered as spontaneous actions of day-to-day communication or as events staged for their own sake but are part of a worship service. Reflection on the sermon and the worship service belong together. Homiletics and liturgics should be seen as closely related disciplines of practical theology, in many respects directed at the same problems. On this, see Peter Cornehl, *Der Evangelische Gottesdienst. Biblische Konturen und neuzeitliche Wirklichkeit* (Stuttgart: Kohlhammer, 2006), 1:21ff.

91. Marjorie Hewitt Suchocki, *In God's Presence: Theological Reflections on Prayer* (St. Louis: Chalice, 1996), 47.

92. Ibid., 52.

93. For this example, see also Andrea Bieler, "'Wenn der ganze Haufen miteinander betet.' Über die Brüchigkeit und die Unverzichtbarkeit des liturgischen Wir," *Zeitschrift für Gottesdienst und Predigt* 3 (2001): 11–12.

94. Matthew Boulton, "Forsaking God: A Theological Argument for Christian Lamentation," *Scottish Journal of Theology* 55, no. 1 (2002): 58–78, at 59.

95. Barth, *Homiletik,* 30.

96. See Friedrich D. E. Schleiermacher, *Die praktische Theologie nach den Grundsätzen der evangelischen Kirche im Zusammenhange dargestellt*, ed. Jacob Frerichs, in *Schleiermachers sämmtliche Werke*, Part 1, Vol. 13 (Berlin: Reimer, 1850).

97. See Alexander Schweizer, *Homiletik der evangelisch-protestantischen Kirche systematisch dargestellt* (Leipzig: Weidmann, 1848). See also Friedrich Wintzer, *Die Homiletik seit Schleiermacher bis in die Anfänge der "dialektischen Theologie" in Grundzügen* (Göttingen: Vandenhoeck & Ruprecht, 1968), 75ff.

98. See ibid., 75ff.

99. See Friedrich Niebergall, *Wie predigen wir dem modernen Menschen?* 3 parts (Tübingen: Mohr, 1905–1921), and see the partial revision of this proposal in idem, *Die moderne Predigt: kulturgeschichtliche und theologische Grundlage, Geschichte und Ertrag* (Tübingen: Mohr, 1929).

100. See Otto Baumgarten, *Predigt-Probleme. Hauptfragen der heutigen Evangeliumsverkündigung* (Tübingen: Mohr, 1905).

101. See Paul Drews, *Die Predigt im 19. Jahrhundert. Kritische Bemerkungen und Praktische Winke* (Gießen: J. Ricker, 1903).

102. See Karl Barth, "Das Wort Gottes als Aufgabe der Theologie," in idem, *Das Wort Gottes und die Theologie. Gesammelte Vorträge* (Munich: Kaiser, 1924), 1:156–78.

103. Eduard Thurneysen, "Die Aufgabe der Predigt" (1921), in Gerd Hummel, ed., *Aufgabe der Predigt* (Darmstadt: Wissenschaftliche Buchgesellschaft, 1971), 105–19.

104. See Ernst Lange, "Zur Theorie und Praxis der Predigtarbeit," in idem, *Predigen als Beruf* (Stuttgart and Berlin: Kreuz, 1976).

105. See Manfred Josuttis, "Der Prediger in der Predigt—sündiger Mensch oder mündiger Zeuge?" in idem, *Praxis des Evangeliums zwischen Politik und Religion. Grundprobleme der Praktischen Theologie*, 3rd ed. (Munich: Kaiser, 1983), 70–94.

106. See Josuttis, *Praxis des Evangeliums.*

107. See Rudolf Bohren, *Predigtlehre*, 6th ed. (Gütersloh: Kaiser, 1993).

108. Fulbert Steffensky, *Schwarzbrot-Spiritualität* (Stuttgart: Radius, 2005), 13–14.

109. See *WA* 57, 222, 3ff.

110. See also Helga Kuhlmann, *Leib-Leben theologisch denken. Reflexionen zur theologischen Anthropologie* (Münster: Lit, 2004); and Silke Leonhard, *Leiblich lernen und lehren. Ein religionsdidaktischer Diskurs* (Stuttgart: Kohlhammer, 2006).

111. Christoph Bizer has spoken repeatedly along these lines; see, for example, his "Liturgie und Didaktik," *Jahrbuch der Religionspädagogik* 5 (1988): 83–115.

112. This distillation of the idea of eschatological time was worked out by Hermann Schmitz. See his *System der Philosophie*, vol. 1: *Die Gegenwart* (Bonn: Bouvier, 1964), 460ff. See also Hans-Martin Gutmann, "Die Wahrnehmung der Gegenwart," in idem et al., eds., *Theologisches geschenkt. Festschrift für Manfred Josuttis* (Bovenden: Foedus, 1996), 94–107.

113. On this, see also Jochen Cornelius-Bundschuh, *Die Kirche des Wortes. Zum evangelischen Predigt- und Gemeindeverständnis* (Göttingen: Vandenhoeck & Ruprecht, 2001), 292ff.

114. See, e.g., *WA* 57, 156, 19ff. See also Hans-Martin Gutmann, *Über Liebe und Herrschaft. Luthers Verständnis von Intimität und Autorität im Kontext des Zivilisationsprozesses* (Göttingen: Vandenhoeck & Ruprecht, 1991), 109ff.

115. See *WA* 7, 52, 25ff.

116. See *WA* 7, 52, 37ff.

117. *WA* 7, 54–55.

118. See *WA* 7, 55, 1ff.

119. *WA* 7, 55, 8ff.

120. It will become clear, however, in what follows that this idea, as regards its view of the relationship of the sexes, tends to be heterosexist.

121. *WA* 7, 55, 1ff.

122. *WA* 7, 55, 8ff.

123. From *Der Große Katechismus deutsch*, in *Bekenntnisschriften der evangelisch-lutherischen Kirche*, 12th ed. (Göttingen: Vandenhoeck & Ruprecht, 1998), 561, 8ff. English translation from Martin Luther, *The Large Catechism*, trans. F. Bente and W. H. T. Dau, in *Triglot Concordia: The Symbolical Books of the Ev. Lutheran Church*. (St. Louis: Concordia, 1921), accessible online at http://www.iclnet.org/pub/resources/text/wittenberg/luther/catechism/web/cat-03.html, accessed November 23, 2009.

124. On this, see Marcel Mauss, *Die Gabe. Form und Funktion des Austausches in archaischen Gesellschaften*, quoted in idem, *Soziologie und Anthropologie*, vol. 2, ed. Wolf Lepenies et al. (Frankfurt: Ullstein, 1978); for the theological significance of the theory of gift exchange, see also Bieler and Schottroff, *Eucharist*, 91–96.

125. See also Hans-Martin Gutmann, "Der gute und der schlechte Tausch. Das Heilige und das Geld—gegensätzliche ökonomische Beziehungen?" in Jürgen Ebach et al., eds., *"Leget Anmut in das Geben." Zum Verhältnis von Theologie und Ökonomie. Jabboq* (Gütersloh: Kaiser, 2001), 1:162–225.

126. Georges Bataille, *Das theoretische Werk*, vol. 1: *Die Aufhebung der Ökonomie* (Munich: Rogner & Bernhard, 1975), 45.

127. See Thomas Ruster, "Geld," in Norbert Mette et al., eds., *Lexikon der Religionspädagogik* (Neukirchen-Vluyn: Neukirchener, 2001), 670–75.

128. We emphasize that the distinction between law and gospel is about the description of a fundamental religious logic. If law is here simply identified with Torah, or with so-called Jewish law or the Old Testament, the door is opened wide for anti-Jewish patterns of argumentation. For the debate about law and gospel in homiletics, see the fundamental treatment by Eberhard Hauschildt, "'Gesetz' und 'Evangelium'—eine homiletische Kategorie? Überlegungen zur wechselvollen Geschichte eines lutherischen Schemas der Predigtlehre," *Pastoraltheologie* 80 (1991): 262–87. See further, for a fundamental confrontation with the problem of anti-Judaism in regard to this topic, Evelina Volkmann, "'Gesetz' und 'Evangelium' in der Predigt," in Hans Martin Dober and Dagmar Mensink, eds., *Die Lehre von der Rechtfertigung des Gottlosen im kulturellen Kontext der Gegenwart. Beiträge im Horizont des christlich-jüdischen Gesprächs* (Stuttgart: Akademie der Diözese Rottenburg-Stuttgart et al., 2002), 106–23.

129. See further on the interruption of the logic of reception Theodor Ahrens, *gegebenheiten. Missionswissenschaftliche Studien* (Frankfurt am Main: Lembeck, 2005).

130. Emanuel Hirsch, *Die gegenwärtige geistige Lage im Spiegel philosophischer und theologischer Besinnung. Akademische Vorlesungen zum Verständnis des deutschen Jahres 1933* (Göttingen: Vandenhoeck & Ruprecht, 1934), 142–43.

131. Emanuel Hirsch, "Gottes Offenbarung in Gesetz und Evangelium," in idem, *Christliche Freiheit und politische Bindung* (Göttingen: Vandenhoeck & Ruprecht, 1934), 76ff.

132. Ibid., 77.

133. Ibid., 79.

134. Karl Barth, "Evangelium und Gesetz," *Theologische Existenz heute* (1935), repr. in Ernst Kinder and Klaus Haendler, eds., *Gesetz und Evangelium. Beiträge zur gegenwärtigen theologischen Diskussion* (Darmstadt: Wissenschaftliche Buchgesellschaft, 1968), 129.

135. See ibid., 4.

136. "You will believe! You who have other gods beside me . . . who take my name in vain . . . you will, against these sins of yours . . . fear and love God!" Ibid., 11.

Chapter 3

1. See Manfred Josuttis, "Die Bibel als Basis der Predigt," in Andreas Baudis et al., eds., *Richte unsere Füße auf den Weg des Friedens. Helmut Gollwitzer zum 70. Geburtstag* (Munich: Kaiser, 1978), 385–93. Since Josuttis wrote this essay, the German-speaking discussion about the place of the Bible in preaching has been further developed in the "dramaturgical homiletics"; see Martin Nicol, *Einander ins Bild setzen. Dramaturgische Homiletik* (Göttingen: Vandenhoeck & Ruprecht, 2002); and idem and Alexander Deeg, *Im Wechselschritt zur Kanzel. Praxisbuch Dramaturgische Homiletik* (Göttingen: Vandenhoeck & Ruprecht, 2005). There are also advances among those who speak of preaching in terms of conversation and entertainment: cf. Harald Schroeter-Wittke, *Unterhaltung. Praktisch-theologische Exkursionen zum homiletischen und kulturellen Bibelgebrauch im 19. und 20. Jahrhundert anhand der Figur Elia* (Frankfurt am Main: Peter

Lang, 2000); and Susanne Wolf-Withöft, *Predigen lernen. Homiletische Konturen einer praktisch-theologischen Spieltheorie* (Stuttgart: Kohlhammer, 2002). Homiletical traditions are also discussed in Josuttis's own proposal. Here we may recall especially Rudolf Bohren's pneumatological and aesthetic orientation in homiletics. See especially his *Predigtlehre*, 6th ed. (Gütersloh: Kaiser, 1993), and his *Daß Gott schön werde. Praktische Theologie als theologische Ästhetik* (Munich: Kaiser, 1975).

2. Hans van der Geest, "Von Himmel und Erde. Glaube an Gott aus einer individuellen Sicht," unpublished text kindly provided to us by the author. See also idem, *Das Wort geschieht. Wege zur seelsorgerlichen Predigt* (Zürich: Theologischer Verlag, 1991).

3. Geest, "Von Himmel und Erde." We did not change the male God language in this quote.

4. The New Testament scholar Mary Ann Tolbert has also concerned herself with the question of the authority of biblical texts for readers today. Following Max Weber, she distinguishes the *narrative or existential authority* of biblical texts, which gives orientation for the personal religious search for meaning; *formative authority*, which applies to the building of the collective identity of a group; and, third, the *dogmatic or juridical authority* of texts by which a religious institution legitimizes its power. These several dimensions are related and have different weight according to the context. See Mary Ann Tolbert, "Reading the Bible with Authority: Feminist Interrogation of the Canon," in Harold C. Washington, Susan Lochrie Graham, and Pamela Thimmes, eds., *Escaping Eden: New Feminist Perspectives on the Bible* (Sheffield: Sheffield Academic Press, 1998), 141–62.

5. Josuttis, "Die Bibel als Basis der Predigt," 385ff.

6. See also the debate over the authority of texts, preachers, and sermons against the background of the questioning of authority in the postmodern context: Ronald J. Allen, *Theology for Preaching: Authority, Truth, and Knowledge of God in a Postmodern Ethos* (Nashville: Abingdon, 1997), as well as Arthur van Seters, "To What Do Preachers Appeal?" in idem, *Preaching and Ethics* (St. Louis: Chalice, 2004), 99–118.

7. See previously Ernst Lange, "Zur Theorie und Praxis der Predigtarbeit," in idem, *Predigen als Beruf* (Stuttgart and Berlin: Kreuz, 1976), 9–52. The problem named here by Josuttis was also central to Emanuel Hirsch's homiletical reflections: cf. Wilhelm Gräb, *Predigt als Mitteilung des Glaubens. Studien zu einer prinzipiellen Homiletik in praktischer Absicht* (Gütersloh: Gütesloher Verlagshaus Gerd Mohn, 1988).

8. For the establishment of liturgical authority in worship, see further Andrea Bieler, "This Is My Body—This Is My Blood: Inventing Authority in Liturgical Discourse and Practice," *Yearbook of the European Society of Women in Theological Research* (Leuven: Peeters, 2005), 143–54.

9. For what follows, see also Hans-Martin Gutmann, "Warum leben?—Keine Frage! Bemerkungen aus theologischer Besorgnis," in Regula Venske, ed., *Warum leben? Ein Lesebuch* (Munich: Scherz, 2001), 34ff.

10. *Die Bekenntnisschriften der evangelisch-lutherischen Kirche*, 12th ed. (Göttingen: Vandenhoeck & Ruprecht, 1998), 560.

11. See also the reflections on the religion of the *homo economicus* in Andrea Bieler and Luise Schottroff, *Eucharist: Bodies, Bread, and Resurrection* (Minneapolis: Fortress Press, 2007), 84–91.

12. For the connection between the idea of redemption and economic concepts and mythologies, see also Marion Grau, *Of Divine Economy: Refinancing Redemption* (New York: T&T Clark, 2004).

13. Jürgen Ebach has repeatedly developed this connection in his exegeses and political speeches. See his ". . . *und behutsam mitgehen mit deinem Gott.*" *Theologische Reden 3* (Bochum: SWB, 1995).

14. See *Mechiltha. Ein tannaitischer Midrasch zu Exodus.* Erstmalig ins Deutsche übersetzt und erläutert von Jakob Winter und August Wünsche (Leipzig: Hinrichs, 1909), 116. In the Mekhilta, the midrash on Exodus, alongside a number of statements on Exodus 15 in which God is blessed for his saving action on behalf of God's people Israel (e.g., "and it was not only the Israelites who uttered their song before God, but also the serving angels, as it says [Ps. 8:2]: 'O LORD our Sovereign, how majestic is your name in all the earth! You have set your glory above the heavens,'" cf. ibid., 116), there are also individual voices that show sympathy for the death of the Egyptian forces. So it says: "And why is this thanksgiving different from all (other) thanksgivings in Scripture; for in all the thanksgivings in Scripture we read: 'Give thanks to the Eternal, for it is good (*tob*, joyous)' but in this thanksgiving it does not say: 'for it is good'? Only, if one may say so, that there was no joy before him over the destruction of the wicked" (cf. ibid., 113–14). In the perspective here adopted of seeing the other and feeling with his or her perspective on life we have learned much especially from Emmanuel Lévinas. See his *Vier Talmud-Lesungen* (Orig.: *Quatre lectures talmudiques*, Paris, 1968; Frankfurt am Main: Verlag Neue Kritik, 2003).

15. See Christoph Bizer, "Verheißung als religionspädagogische Kategorie," *Wissenschaft und Praxis in Kirche und Gesellschaft* 68, no. 9 (1979): 347–58.

16. *WA* 7, 60, 3ff.; 64, 15ff.; 66:25ff., "that he should rule his own body and have intercourse with men."

17. This notion was introduced by Gotthold Ephraim Lessing, in his pamphlet "Über den Beweis des Geistes und der Kraft," in idem, *Werke*, vol. 8, *Theologiekritische Schriften*, ed. Herbert G. Göpfert (Munich: Hanser, 1979), 9–14, at 13.

18. See Gerhard Ebeling, "Die Bedeutung der historisch-kritischen Methode für die protestantische Theologie und Kirche," *Zeitschrift für Theologie und Kirche* 47 (1950): 1–46.

19. See Christoph Bizer, "Die Schule hier—die Bibel dort. Gestaltpädagogische Elemente in der Religionspädagogik," in idem, *Kirchgänge im Religionsunterricht und anderswo. Zur Gestaltwerdung von Religion* (Göttingen: Vandenhoeck & Ruprecht, 1995), 31–49.

20. For example, a biblical narrative, a psalm, a prophetic text, a New Testament passion account.

21. See ibid., 41.

22. Ibid., 49. See also Ingrid Neumann, "Gestalttherapie und Predigtarbeit," in Franz Kamphaus and Rolf Zerfass, eds., *Ethische Predigt und Alltagsverhalten* (Munich: Kaiser; Mainz: Matthias Grünewald, 1986), 118–28.

23. For a fundamental orientation to biblical spirituality, see the important work of Sandra Schneiders, *The Revelatory Text: Interpreting the New Testament as Sacred Scripture*, 2nd ed. (Collegeville, Minn.: Liturgical, 1999).

24. See our remarks on responsory receptivity above, 76.

25. See further on Wohlgemuth's homiletical theory: Andrea Bieler, *Die Sehnsucht nach dem verlorenen Himmel. Jüdische und christliche Reflexionen zu Gottesdienstreform und Predigtkultur im 19. Jahrhundert* (Stuttgart: Kohlhammer, 2003), 120–22, and more generally on the conversation with Jewish homiletics, the outstanding work of Alexander Deeg, *Predigt und Derascha. Homiletische Textlektüre im Dialog mit dem Judentum* (Göttingen: Vandenhoeck & Ruprecht, 2006).

26. Joseph Wohlgemuth, *Beiträge zu einer jüdischen Homiletik. Jahresbericht des Rabbiner-Seminars zu Berlin für 1903/1904 (5664)* (Berlin: H. Itzkowski, 1904), 1–107, at 31.

27. For the meaning of white fire in midrash, cf. Tim Schramm, "Schwarzes und weißes Feuer," in Friedemann Green et al., eds., *Um der Hoffnung willen. Praktische Theologie mit Leidenschaft. FS für Wolfgang Grünberg* (Hamburg: EB-Verlag, 2000), 231–39, at 232. Uta Pohl-Patalong also works with this concept in her homiletical project on the "bibliologue," which is about setting in motion an imaginative and participatory preaching process in which the whole congregation joins in preaching. See her "Das schwarze Feuer achten, das weiße Feuer schüren. Inspirationen und Reflexionen zu einem Predigen mit der ganzen Gemeinde," in Michael Krug et al., eds., *Beim Wort nehmen—die Schrift als Zentrum für kirchliches Reden und Gestalten. Friedrich Mildenberger zum 75. Geburtstag* (Stuttgart: Kohlhammer, 2004), 354–64, as well as her *Bibliolog. Gemeinsam die Bibel entdecken im Gottesdienst—in der Gemeinde—in der Schule* (Stuttgart: Kohlhammer, 2005).

28. Wohlgemuth, *Beiträge*, 29. See also Marc-Alain Ouaknin, *Das verbrannte Buch. Den Talmud lesen* (Weinheim: Quadriga, 1990).

29. For the bodily dimension, see also above, 83–85.

30. Hans-Günter Heimbrock, *Spuren Gottes wahrnehmen. Phänomenologisch inspirierte Predigten und Texte zum Gottesdienst* (Stuttgart: Kohlhammer, 2003), 194.

31. Bibliodrama has become an established movement in religious education, liturgy, homiletics, and other aesthetic processes and has been developed in Germany by, among others, Heidemarie Langer, Samuel Laeuchli, Natalie Warns, Ellen Kubitza, Tim Schramm, and Gerhard Marcel Martin. See, e.g., Gerhard Marcel Martin, *Sachbuch Bibliodrama. Praxis und Theorie* (Stuttgart: Kohlhammer 1995), as well as Tim Schramm, *Die Bibel ins Leben ziehen. Bewährte "alte" und faszinierende "neue" Methoden lebendiger Bibelarbeit* (Stuttgart: Kohlhammer, 2003).

32. The concept of atmosphere, as developed by the philosopher Hermann Schmitz, has frequently been adopted in practical-theological discussions in a phenomenological context. It is also useful in this context. Schmitz is concerned, among other things, with criticizing the theory of introjection in the development of feelings: "i.e., the inclination to regard feelings as subjective, private conditions of the individual human soul rather than as arousing, stirring powers that act on their own and come over people—not just individuals, but also crowds and groups—without needing to be lodged in a subject and being merely the invention, content, or characteristic of the subject." See his *System der Philosophie*, vol. 1: *Die Gegenwart* (Bonn: Bouvier, 1964), x. For more on Schmitz's critique of the theory of introjection and his phenomenology of embodiment, see the instructive summary by Julia Koll, *Körper beten. Religiöse Praxis und Körpererleben* (Stuttgart: Kohlhammer, 2007), 25–49.

33. For the theme of bodily memory from a deconstructivist and neurophysiological perspective, see also Bieler and Schottroff, *Eucharist*, 157–78.

34. See ibid., 175–76. "It is clear, therefore, that memory is not a single, isolated function of the brain; rather, it is multifaceted. We engage not only socially but also physiologically in a process of reconstruction when we remember. That is why it is crucial for us to reflect on anamnesis in an embodied and holistic way that takes into account all these various dimensions of memory. Likewise, our memory practice in worship also encompasses all these dimensions: the cognition of facts and concepts, our acquired ritual knowledge, as well as the personal biographical memories we put together in memory sequences. Because all these dimensions are present when we worship we must ask whether we engage them purposefully in our ritual practices."

35. See Silke Leonhard, *Leiblich lernen und lehren. Ein religionsdidaktischer Diskurs* (Stuttgart: Kohlhammer, 2006), and see the reception of *focusing* for pastoral care, e.g., in Hans-Martin Gutmann, *Und erlöse uns von dem Bösen. Die Chance der Seelsorge in Zeiten der Krise* (Gütersloh: Gütersloher, 2005), 269ff.

36. Leonhard, *Leiblich lernen*, 191.

37. For the method of focusing, see ibid., 139–42. For the philosophical background of pragmatic phenomenology, see ibid., 151–68.

38. For the significance of the creative process in the work of preaching, cf. also Jana Childers, *Birthing the Sermon: Women Preachers on the Creative Process* (St. Louis: Chalice, 2001); Wilfried Engemann, "On Man's Re-Entry into His Future: The Sermon as a Creative Act," in Gerrit Immink and Ciska Stark, eds., *Preaching: Creating Perspective* (Utrecht: Societas Homiletica, 2002), 25–49.

39. Manfred Josuttis, "Über den Predigteinfall," in idem, *Rhetorik und Theologie in der Predigtarbeit*, Homiletische Studien 1 (Munich: Kaiser, 1985), 70–86.

40. Ibid., 70.

41. Ibid., 71. Josuttis refers to Elisabeth Landau, *Psychologie der Kreativität* (Munich et al.: Reinhardt, 1969).

42. Josuttis, "Über den Predigteinfall," 73.

43. Fulbert Steffensky, *Schwarzbrot-Spiritualität* (Stuttgart: Radius, 2005), 13–14.

44. Ibid., 13–14, 18ff.

45. Sermon on Isaiah 58:1-14, worship service at the University of Hamburg, 5 November 2006, by Hans-Martin Gutmann.

46. For the connection between space and preaching, see Michael Meyer-Blanck, "Die Predigt in Raum und Ritual," *Praktische Theologie* 34 (1999): 163–78; and Thomas Klie, "Wort—Ereignis—Raum. Kirchenpädagogische Überlegungen zur Predigt," *Praktische Theologie* 35 (2000): 251–63.

47. See, for example, Gernot Böhme, *Atmosphäre. Essays zur neuen Ästhetik* (Frankfurt am Main: Suhrkamp, 1995).

48. Tobias Woydack, *Der räumliche Gott. Was sind Kirchengebäude theologisch?* (Hamburg: Schenefeld EB-Verlag, 2005).

49. Martina Löw, *Raumsoziologie* (Frankfurt am Main: Surhkamp, 2001).

50. Ibid., 113.

51. Ibid., 271.

52. Woydack, *Der räumliche Gott*, 176.

53. Ibid.

54. See Hartmut Raguse, *Der Raum des Textes. Elemente einer transdisziplinären theologischen Hermeneutik* (Stuttgart: Kohlhammer, 1994), as well as Donald W. Winnicott, *Vom Spiel zur Kreativität*, 9th ed. (Stuttgart: Klett-Cotta, 1997) [English original: *Playing and Reality* (New York: Routledge, 1971)]. For the significance of Winnicott's theory of intermediary space for the analysis of religious experiences, see also Ann Belford Ulanov, *Finding Space: Winnicott, God, and Psychic Reality* (Louisville: Westminster John Knox, 2001).

55. Raguse, *Der Raum des Textes*, 10.

56. Ibid.

57. For more on the concept of intermediate space, see Andrea Bieler, *Gottesdienst interkulturell. Predigen und Gottesdienst feiern im Zwischenraum* (Stuttgart: Kohlhammer, 2008).

58. Wolfgang Iser, *Der Akt des Lesens. Theorie ästhetischer Wirkung*, 4th ed. (Munich: Fink, 1994), 267.

59. Ibid., 302.

60. Ernst Lange, *Die verbesserliche Welt. Möglichkeiten christlicher Rede erprobt an der Geschichte des Propheten Jona* (Stuttgart: Kreuz, 1968). On this, see Wolfgang Grünberg, "Die Stadt—Laboratorium der Zukunft," in Barbara Deml-Groth et al., eds., *Ernst Lange weiterdenken, Impulse für die Kirche des 21. Jahrhunderts* (Berlin: Wichern, 2007), 9–33.

61. Martin Leutzsch, "Das biblische Zinsverbot," in Rainer Kessler and Eva Loos, eds., *Eigentum: Freiheit und Fluch. Ökonomische und biblische Entwürfe* (Gütersloh: Kaiser, 2000), 107–44, at 121–22. See also in the same volume Frank Crüsemann, "Gottes Fürsorge und menschliche Arbeit. Ökonomie und soziale Gerechtigkeit in biblischer Sicht," 43–63, and Rainer Kessler, "Armut, Eigentum und Freiheit. Die Frage des Grundeigentums in der Endgestalt der Prophetenbücher," 64–88.

62. Eckehard W. Stegemann and Wolfgang Stegemann, *Urchristliche Sozialgeschichte* (Stuttgart: Kohlhammer, 1997), 89.

63. On this, see also Bieler and Schottroff, *Eucharist*, 74–84.

64. See Stegemann and Stegemann, *Sozialgeschichte*, 178.

65. Bieler and Schottroff, *Eucharist*, 75.

66. Translation in H. F. D. Sparks, *The Apocryphal Old Testament* (Oxford: Clarendon, 1984), 845–46.

67. For these strategies of neutralizing the gospel of the poor, see Luise Schottroff, *The Parables of Jesus* (Minneapolis: Fortress Press, 2006), 86–89.

Chapter 4

1. On this, see, e.g., Philip Wheelwright, "Semantik und Ontologie," in Anselm Haverkamp, ed., *Theorie der Metapher*, 2nd ed. (Darmstadt: Wissenschaftliche Buchgesellschaft, 1996), 106–19; Enno Rudolph, "Metapher oder Symbol. Zum Streit um die schönste Form der Wahrheit. Anmerkungen zu einem möglichen Dialog zwischen Hans Blumenberg und Ernst Cassirer," in Reinhold Bernhardt and Ulrike Link-Wieczorek,

eds., *Metapher und Wirklichkeit. Die Logik der Bildhaftigkeit im Reden von Gott, Mensch und Natur, FS Dietrich Ritschl* (Göttingen: Vandenhoeck & Ruprecht, 1999), 320–28; see esp. also Silke Petersen, *Brot, Licht und Weinstock. Intertextuelle Analysen johanneischer Ich-bin-Worte* (Leiden: Brill, 2008). For what follows, see also Hans-Martin Gutmann, "Kreuz," in Wilhelm Gräb and Birgit Weyel, eds., *Handbuch Praktische Theologie* (Gütersloh: Gütersloher, 2007), 322ff.; and idem, "Symbol," in Friedrich Wilhelm Horn and Friederike Nüssel, eds., *Taschenlexikon Religion und Theologie*, 5th ed. (Göttingen: Vandenhoeck & Ruprecht, 2008), 1139–44.

2. See Eberhard Jüngel, "Metaphorische Wahrheit. Erwägungen zur theologischen Relevanz der Metapher als Beitrag zur Hermeneutik einer narrativen Theologie," in idem and Paul Ricoeur, eds., *Metapher. Zur Hermeneutik religiöser Sprache* (Munich: Kaiser, 1974), 71–122.

3. See Paul Ricoeur, *Die lebendige Metapher* (Munich: Kaiser, 1988).

4. Rudolph, "Metapher oder Symbol," 327.

5. On this, see above, 124–25.

6. Donald W. Winnicott, *Reifungsprozesse und fördernde Umwelt. Studien zur Theorie der emotionalen Entwicklung* (Munich: Kindler, 1974).

7. See, for example, Sigmund Freud, "Der Traum," in idem, *Vorlesungen zur Einführung in die Psychoanalyse* (1916/17) (Frankfurt am Main: Fischer, 1980).

8. Alfred Lorenzer, *Das Konzil der Buchhalter. Die Zerstörung der Sinnlichkeit. Eine Religionskritik* (Frankfurt am Main: Europäische Verlagsanstalt, 1988), 85ff., 109ff., 152ff.

9. See ibid., 93.

10. Peter Biehl, *Symbole geben zu lernen. Einführung in die Symboldidaktik anhand der Symbole Hand, Haus und Weg* (Neukirchen-Vluyn: Neukirchener Verlag, 1989), 59.

11. See Paul Tillich, "Das religiöse Symbol" (1928), in *Gesammelte Werke* (Stuttgart: Evangelisches Verlagswerk, 1959), 5:196ff.

12. For what follows, see also Hans-Martin Gutmann, *Symbole zwischen Macht und Spiel* (Göttingen: Vandenhoeck & Ruprecht, 1996), 51ff.

13. See Manfred Josuttis, "Der Prediger in der Predigt. Sündiger Mensch oder mündiger Zeuge?" in idem, *Praxis des Evangeliums zwischen Politik und Religion* (Munich: Kaiser, 1974), 70ff.; for his current view of the ego problem, see, for example, "Von der Identität zur Konversion," in idem, *Segenskräfte. Potentiale einer energetischen Seelsorge* (Gütersloh: Kaiser, Gütersloher, 2000), 65–78.

14. Karl Barth, "Der Christ als Zeuge," *Theologische Existenz* 12 (Munich, 1934), reprinted in idem, *Theologische Fragen und Antworten. Gesammelte Vorträge*, 2nd ed. (Zürich: Evangelischer, 1986), 185–96.

15. Karl Barth, *Kirchliche Dogmatik* IV/2, 453.

16. Josuttis, "Der Prediger in der Predigt," 85.

17. In the North American homiletical debate, it was especially Fred B. Craddock who linked the question of the "I" in the pulpit with the question of foundations for the preacher's authority. He noted the profound crisis of an institutionally dependent concept of authority in Christian religion and asserted the need to preach without external legitimation, "as one without authority." The crisis of Christianity and the doubt being

expressed within it were to be interpreted positively; where presuppositions that had been taken for granted were dissolving, faith could be born. This should be welcomed by preachers. "Unless there is room to say no, there is no room for a genuine yes. And yet it is apparent that the new situation in which preaching occurs is critical, and unless recognized by the minister and met with a new format, sermons will at best seem museum pieces." Fred B. Craddock, *As One without Authority*, rev. and with new sermons, 4th ed. (St. Louis: Chalice, 2001), 14.

18. See Rolf Zerfass, *Gundkurs Predigt*, vol. 1: *Spruchpredigt*, 2nd ed. (Düsseldorf: Patmos, 1989), 62ff.

19. Ibid., 62.

20. Ibid.

21. Ibid., 66.

22. Wilhelm Gräb has repeatedly addressed this point. See, e.g., *Predigt als Mitteilung des Glaubens. Studien zu einer prinzipiellen Homiletik in praktischer Absicht* (Gütersloh: Gütersloher Verlagshaus Gerd Mohn, 1988), and his more recent publication, *Religion als Deutung des Lebens. Perspektiven einer Praktischen Theologie gelebter Religion* (Gütersloh: Gütersloher, 2006). See also the discourse on subjectivity in Henning Luther, *Religion und Alltag. Bausteine zu einer Praktischen Theologie des Subjekts* (Stuttgart: Radius, 1992). In general theological perspective, see Ulrich Barth and Wilhelm Gräb, eds., *Gott im Selbstbewusstsein der Moderne. Zum neuzeitlichen Begriff der Religion* (Gütersloh: Gütersloher Verlagshaus Mohn, 1993), as well as Jörg Dierken, *Selbstbewusstsein individueller Freiheit. Religionstheoretische Erkundungen in protestantischer Perspektive* (Tübingen: Mohr Siebeck, 2005).

23. Josuttis, *Segenskräfte*, 65ff. In all these considerations, what is intended is a challenge of theological convictions, which in individual cases may include a highly painful personal learning process. At the end of this path, however, lies the inner vitality of faith and its external openness for the sake of communication with other people.

24. We are limiting ourselves here to the industrial era since the beginning of the nineteenth century.

25. See Johann Gottlieb Fichte, "Über den Grund des Glaubens an eine göttliche Weltregierung" (1798), in I. H. Fichte, ed., *Johann Gottlieb Fichte Werke* (Berlin: Veit, 1845–46; repr. Berlin: de Gruyter, 1971), vol. 5; also idem, *Die Wissenschaftslehre. Zweite Vorlesung im Jahr 1804*, Philosophische Bibliothek 284 (Hamburg: Meiner, 1986). The human "I" reveals its vitality and power by its expansion and pushing of boundaries with respect to everything that does not belong to the ego itself. In this idea, Fichte joins the rational activity of the *empirical* ego with *governance*. It maintains itself as technical reason in taking charge and subjecting the other, intentionally in the *negation* of the not-I ("nature"). And as moral reason, it maintains itself in the act of accepting *obligation*. The individual absorbs the irrefutable feeling that, through an accidental encounter with a section of the whole of the social-historical process of life, he or she encounters *his/her obligation*, through the acceptance of which he or she for the first time becomes a *human I*.

26. A good overview of Freud's important writings on this subject is found in his *Kulturtheoretische Schriften* (Frankfurt am Main: Fischer, 1974).

27. See Lawrence Kohlberg, *Collected Papers on Moral Development and Moral Education* (Cambridge, Mass.: Harvard University Press, 1973); for the religious development

of the ego, see James W. Fowler, *Becoming Adult, Becoming Christian: Adult Development and Christian Faith* (San Francisco: Harper & Row, 1984).

28. Jacques Lacan, *Schriften*, vol. 1 (1966) (Weinheim and Berlin: Quadriga, 1973), 64.

29. Ibid., 69.

30. See ibid., 119.

31. Henning Luther, "Ich ist ein Anderer. Zur Subjektfrage in der Praktischen Theologie," in idem, *Religion und Alltag. Bausteine zu einer Praktischen Theologie des Subjekts* (Stuttgart: Radius, 1992).

32. Henning Luther, "Umstrittene Identität. Zum Leitbild der Bildung," in ibid., 155.

33. Henning Luther, "Identität und Fragment. Praktisch-theologische Überlegungen zur Unabschließbarkeit von Bildungsprozessen," in ibid., 168.

34. For what follows, see also Hans-Martin Gutmann, "Praktische Theologie im neuen Jahrhundert—nichts Neues?" in Eberhard Hauschildt and Ulrich Schwab, eds., *Praktische Theologie für das 21. Jahrhundert* (Stuttgart: Kohlhammer, 2002), 67ff.

35. Here Hans-Martin Gutmann has learned especially from contacts with African pastors and congregational leaders who were continuing their theological education in the ATTIC program of the Missionsakademie Hamburg. Andrea Bieler, through her worship experiences in the United States, has gathered impressions of common, Spirit-filled, ecstatic prayer from both Asian American and African-American Pentecostal congregations.

36. Fulbert Steffensky, *Schwarzbrot-Spiritualität* (Stuttgart: Radius, 2005), 20ff.

37. Ibid.

38. See in general on the Reformation's understanding of the word of God, the instructive overview by Ulrich H. J. Körtner, *Theologie des Wortes Gottes. Positionen— Probleme—Perspektiven* (Göttingen: Vandenhoeck & Ruprecht, 2001), 72–93.

39. For the energy dimension, see also below, 154–56.

40. Martin Luther speaks in his prologue to the New Testament of the gospel's good shout (or cry): "*Evangelion* is a Greek word and means in German also: good news, good tidings [story], good, new times [news], good shout [tidings, proclamation], about which one sings, speaks, and is joyful" (*WA* DB 6, 2, 23–24). In this context, see also Dorothee Sölle, *Mystik und Widerstand. "Du stilles Geschrei,"* 5th ed. (Hamburg: Hoffmann und Campe, 1999).

41. For the *viva vox*, see, e.g., *WA* 43, 94, 12.

42. *WA* 10, I/1, 627, 1–3 (*Kirchenpostille*, 1522). This does not mean, however, that Luther did not ultimately value the written word. In his conflict with the "Schwärmer," he emphasized the significance of the written word. On this, see Oswald Bayer, "Was macht die Bibel zur Heiligen Schrift? Luthers Verständnis der Schriftautorität," in Michael Krug, Ruth Lödel, and Johannes Rehm, eds., *Beim Wort nehmen. Die Schrift als Zentrum für kirchliches Reden und Gestalten. Friedrich Mildenberger zum 75. Geburtstag* (Stuttgart: Kohlhammer, 2004), 24–41, at 31–33.

43. For more on Luther's ideas regarding the effectiveness of the word in terms of energy flow, e.g., the pregnancy of the word, the fluidity of the word, the word as a space of sound and light, see Jochen Cornelius-Bundschuh, *Die Kirche des Wortes. Zum*

evangelischen Predigt- und Gemeindeverständnis (Göttingen: Vandenhoeck & Ruprecht, 2001), 188–92.

44. For the ambivalence of the voice metaphor, see also Mary Lin Hudson and Mary Donovan Turner, *Saved from Silence: Finding Women's Voice in Preaching* (St. Louis: Chalice, 1999).

45. Thomas Kabel, *Handbuch Liturgische Präsenz. Zur praktischen Inszenierung des Gottesdienstes* (Gütersloh: Gütersloher, 2002), esp. 1:79–109. See also Thomas Hirsch-Hüffell, *Gottesdienst verstehen und selbst gestalten* (Göttingen: Vandenhoeck & Ruprecht, 2002).

46. The original form of Luther's *Invocavit* Sermons of 1522 is somewhat unclear. We have only notes written afterward; we also do know scarcely anything about Luther's preaching style and performance. In what follows, we were inspired primarily by Cornelius-Bundschuh's interesting interpretations of Luther's *Invocavit* Sermons.

47. For what follows, see Cornelius-Bundschuh, *Die Kirche*, 175ff.

48. *WA* 50, 629, 34-35.

49. *WA* 37, 513, 20–26.

50. *Studienausgabe* 2, 537, 6–8.

51. Ibid.

52. *WA* 31, I, 545, 19–21.

53. *Studienausgabe* 2, 536, 7–9.

54. *WA* 10, II, 22, 15–16.

55. *WA* 4, 9, 18–19.

56. Cornelius-Bundshuh, *Die Kirche*, 181.

57. *Studienausgabe* 2, 537, 2–5.

58. *Studienausgabe* 2, 537, 12–13.

59. *Studienausgabe* 2, 537, 1–2.

60. Regarding the significance of speech-act theory for the construction of homiletical theory, see the instructive overview by Wilfried Engemann, *Einführung in die Homiletik* (Tübingen: Mohr Siebeck, 2002), 330–44.

61. See Cornelius-Bundschuh, *Die Kirche*, 294ff.

62. *Studienausgabe* 2, 555, 2–3.

63. *WA* 47, 29, 29–31; 30, 36–37.

64. See also the interpretation of Bullinger's *praedicatio verbi divini est verbum divinum* in above, 37.

65. For what follows, see the outstanding work of Marcia McFee, *Primal Patterns: Ritual Dynamics, Ritual Resonance, Polyrhythmic Strategies and the Formation of Christian Disciples*, unpublished dissertation, Graduate Theological Union, Berkeley, 2005. Primal pattern theory was first developed by Josephine Rathborne, Valerie Hunt, and Sally Fitt, who studied sequences of movement and patterns of energy, as well as by Betsy Wetzig, a teacher of dance and improvisation.

66. Andrea Bieler has referred to primal pattern theory as applied to the development of a performative homiletics: see her "Das bewegte Wort. Auf dem Weg zu einer performativen Homiletik," *Pastoraltheologie* 7 (2006): 268–83.

67. For the question of the extent to which ritual knowledge is to be understood as body-knowledge, see also Andrea Bieler, "Embodied Knowing: Understanding Religious Experience in Ritual," in Hans Günter Heimbrock and Christopher Scholtz, eds., *The Immediacy of Experience and the Mediacy of Empirical Research in Religion* (Göttingen: Vandenhoeck & Ruprecht, 2007), 39–60.

68. For the North American discussion on the performative dimension of preaching, see Clayton Schmidt and Jana Childers, eds., *Performance in Preaching: Bringing the Sermon to Life* (Grand Rapids: Baker Academic, 2008).

69. On this, see our reflections above in "The Homiletical Perspective: Interweaving Content and Form," 37–43.

70. On this, see also Jana Childers's reflections on a performative homiletics based on resources from drama and theater: *Performing the Word: Preaching as Theatre* (Nashville: Abingdon, 1998).

71. For the theme of voice in the context of theology, see Stephen H. Webb, *The Divine Voice: Christian Proclamation and the Theology of Sound* (Grand Rapids: Brazos, 2004); from a homiletical perspective, see Hudson and Turner, *Saved from Silence*.

72. A theological reflection on the theme of rhythm is offered by Mark L. Taylor, "Polyrhythm in Worship: Caribbean Keys to an Effective Word of God," in Leonora Tubbs Tisdale, ed., *Making Room at the Table: An Invitation to Multicultural Worship* (Louisville: Westminster John Knox, 2001). Taylor cites Leopold Sedar Senghor on the subject of word and rhythm: "Only rhythm gives the word its effective fullness; it is the word of God, that is, the rhythmic word, that created the world" (108).

73. For the subject of sound in a phenomenological perspective, see Wolf-Eckart Failing and Hans-Günter Heimbrock, *Gelebte Religion wahrnehmen. Lebenswelt—Alltagskultur—Religionspraxis* (Stuttgart: Kohlhammer, 1998), 69–90; Hans-Günter Heimbrock, "Klang," in Gotthard Fermor and Harald Schroeter-Wittke, eds., *Kirchenmusik als religiöse Praxis—praktisch-theologisches Handbuch zur Kirchenmusik* (Leipzig: Evangelische Verlagsanstalt, 2005), 37–42. See also Webb, *The Divine Voice*, 33ff.

74. Reflections on the flow dimension of preaching are found in Manfred Josuttis, *Die Einführung in das Leben. Pastoraltheologie zwischen Phänomenologie und Spiritualität* (Gütersloh: Kaiser, 1996), 102–18; idem, "The Authority of the Word in the Liturgy: The Legacy of the Reformation," *Studia Liturgica* 22 (1992): 53–67.

75. Marcia McFee defines the concept of patterns of energy as follows: "'Patterns of energy' are recognized when a consistent force is repeated over time and . . . is identified as a 'dynamic' (characterized by variation of accent dependent on variation in force)" (McFee, *Primal Patterns*, 14).

76. See ibid., 2ff.

77. Taking the energy approach to homiletics seriously is of fundamental importance for the further development of an intercultural perspective. Primal pattern theory can be helpful for a perception of different energy milieus for preaching.

78. For the reception of Jürgen Habermas's theory of communicative action for a liturgical ethnography interested in the interpretation of ritual praxis, see Siobhán Garrigan, *Beyond Ritual: Sacramental Theology after Habermas* (Aldershot and Burlington: Ashgate, 2004); and Henk de Roest, *Communication Identity: Habermas' Perspectives of Discourse as a Support for Practical Theology* (Kampen: Kok, 1998).

79. See above, "In the Beginning: A Multitude of Voices," 2.

80. Frank M. Lütze, *Absicht und Wirkung der Predigt. Eine Untersuchung zur homiletischen Pragmatik* (Leipzig: Evangelische Verlagsanstalt, 2006), 15.

81. See John L. Austin, *How to Do Things with Words* (Cambridge, Mass.: Harvard University Press, 1962). German: *Zur Theorie der Sprechakte*, trans. Eike von Savigny, 2nd ed. with additional bibliography (Stuttgart: Reclam, 2002).

82. See John R. Searle, *Speech Acts: An Essay in the Philosophy of Language* (London: Cambridge University Press, 1969).

83. See Jürgen Habermas, "Vorbereitende Bemerkungen zu einer Theorie der kommunikativen Kompetenz," in idem and Niklas Luhmann, *Theorie der Gesellschaft oder Sozialtechnologie. Was leistet die Systemforschung?* (Frankfurt am Main: Suhrkamp, 1971), 101–41.

84. See Engemann, *Einführung in die Homiletik*, 330–44.

85. Illocutions can contain direct or indirect speech-acts. "Direct speech-acts are those that formally indicate—through verbs indicating action, through the mode of speech (optative, imperative, question, etc.), or corresponding particles (herewith, hopefully, please, etc.)—what their intention is. Indirect speech-acts are those that, in what they address, 'are up to' something other than what they present through the above indicators. They sound like advice, but are threats: 'I advise you not to take me for stupid.'" Ibid., 338.

86. See Karl Fritz Daiber, Hans-Werner Dannowski et al., *Predigen und Hören. Ergebnisse einer Gottesdienstbefragung*, part 2 (Munich: Kaiser, 1983), 124–86, esp. 184.

87. The utterance of words can be violent, or incite to violence. On the phenomenon of political and religious hate speech, see Judith Butler, *Excitable Speech: A Politics of the Performative* (New York: Routledge, 1997).

88. See also the analysis of unsuccessful speech-acts in preaching, especially the confusion between invitation and demand, in Peter Bukowski, *Predigt wahrnehmen. Homiletische Perspektiven* (Neukirchen-Vluyn: Neukirchener, 1990), 72ff.

89. For this reason, we also suggest the development of building blocks for a performative homiletics. On this see, e.g., Andrea Bieler, "Das bewegte Wort."

90. Preaching is performance. *Par fournir* in French means bringing something to full completion. Henning Luther has emphasized that the sermon only exists in the moment of its performance. He insists that the sermon lives "from its *realized* accomplishment before a group of hearers that is *present to* the process of production. . . . The reception of the speech is contemporaneous with its completed production" (Henning Luther, "Predigt als inszenierter Text. Überlegungen zur Kunst der Predigt," *Theologia Practica* 8 [1983]: 89–100, at 94).

91. Johannes Anderegg, *Sprache und Verwandlung* (Göttingen: Vandenhoeck & Ruprecht, 1985), 40. See also idem, "Über die Sprache des Alltags und Sprache im religiösen Bezug," *Zeitschrift für Theologie und Kirche* 95 (1988): 366–78.

92. On this, see also Rolf Zerfass, "Was heißt: miteinander reden? Homiletik und Rhetorik," in idem, *Grundkurs Predigt*, vol. 1: *Spruchpredigt*, 29–44.

93. In the last twenty years, there has been a debate about how helpful the classical study of communication is for the field of homiletics.

94. Alessandro Barrico, *Hegels Seele oder die Kühe von Wisconsin. Nachdenken über Musik* (Munich and Zürich: Piper, 1999), 40–41. See also Gert Otto, "Predigt als Sprache. Eine Zusammenfassung in sechs kommentierten Thesen," in Wilfried Engemann and Frank M. Lütze, eds., *Grundfragen der Predigt. Ein Studienbuch* (Leipzig: Evangelische Verlagsanstalt, 2006), 259–80, at 274–75.

95. Martin Nicol and Alexander Deeg speak of preaching as moved movement between the biblical text and the sermon: "Preaching is moved movement. The movement of the biblical word is continued in the move of the sermon. There is no distinction! Not: explication, scope, application. Not: movement, stop, impetus. Rather: the ball of the text rolls and gives impetus to the ball of the sermon. Tensions in the text become arcs of tension in the speech from the pulpit. The word of the Bible hands on its energy to the preacher's move" (Nicol and Deeg, *Im Wechselschritt zur Kanzel. Praxisbuch Dramaturgische Homiletik* [Göttingen: Vandenhoeck & Ruprecht, 2005], 21).

96. Linguistic-pragmatic and energy approaches are often discussed separately in homiletical debates. In our opinion, however, these approaches describe different ways of access to the performativity of the word that can certainly be set alongside one another so that they provide mutual enhancement.

97. See David Plüss, *Gottesdienst als Textinszenierung. Perspektiven einer performativen Ästhetik des Gottesdienstes* (Zürich: Theologischer, 2007).

98. Ibid., 92.

99. Ibid., 93.

100. Hans Ulrich Gumbrecht, "Produktion von Präsenz, durchsetzt mit Absenz. Über Musik, Libretto und Inszenierung," in Josef Früchtl and Jörg Zimmermann, eds., *Ästhetik der Inszenierung. Dimensionen eines künstlerischen, kulturellen und gesellschaftlichen Phänomens* (Frankfurt am Main: Suhrkamp, 2001), 63–76, at 76.

101. See Plüss, *Gottesdienst*, 97.

102. See ibid.

103. Ibid., 167.

104. Michael Meyer-Blanck, "Liturgische Rollen," in Hans-Christoph Schmidt-Lauber, Michael Meyer-Blanck, and Karl-Heinz Bieritz, eds., *Handbuch der Liturgie* (Göttingen: Vandenhoeck & Ruprecht, 2003), 778–86, at 780.

105. On this, see above, 79–83, 86–96.

106. For the concept of comprehension as discovery, introduced by Eberhard Jüngel, see above, 50–51, as well as Magdalene Frettlöh, *Gott Gewicht geben. Bausteine einer geschlechtergerechten Gotteslehre* (Neukirchen-Vluyn: Neukirchener, 2006), 15ff. Frettlöh develops the concepts of wondering knowledge and wounding encounter with reference to Karl Barth's reflections on theological existence, developed in his interpretation of the struggle at the Jabbok.

107. These two aspects (dramaturgy and presence) are also of central importance for Plüss's concept of dramatization, as shown above.

108. Meyer-Blanck, "Liturgische Rollen," 780.

109. Ibid., 781. See also Marcus A. Friedrich, *Liturgische Körper. Der Beitrag von Schauspieltheorien und –techniken für die Pastoralästhetik* (Stuttgart: Kohlhammer, 2001).

110. Erika Fischer-Lichte broadens the concept: "We speak of presence in performances especially in referring to the special mode of corporeal presence of the one presenting, but partly also in connection with atmospheres. In this sense presence means the specific projection of an actor produced by his or her mere corporeal presence in a space; hence it is not related to the dramatic figure (in case there is one), but emanates from the phenomenal body of the actor.

"One could describe this as a kind of transfer of energy from the actor to the audience, which makes it possible for the experience to possess an unusual intensity. The audience senses the power that emanates from the actor without feeling overwhelmed by that power" (Erika Fischer-Lichte, "Performativität und Ereignis," in idem, Christian Horn, Sandra Umathum, and Matthias Warstat, eds., *Performativität und Ereignis* (Tübingen: Francke, 2003), 11–37, at 30. Fischer-Lichte asserts that the actors can practice techniques of presence, but for the audience, that presence is a happening that grips them with the speed and power of lightning. In this sense, presence is always an event and is ultimately uncontrollable.

111. Meyer-Blanck, "Liturgische Rollen," 782.

112. Catherine Keller, in her theology of creation, formulates a radical critique of the idea of *creatio ex nihilo*, creation from nothing by the voice or word of God. Instead, she develops a theology of *creatio ex profundis*, of creation from the depths of the waters of chaos, which emphasizes the interdependence of all living things with God. See Catherine Keller, *Face of the Deep: A Theology of Becoming* (New York: Routledge, 2003).

113. The relevance of God's voice is underscored, from a Lutheran perspective, in view of faith, which arises from hearing the word preached. See the *fides ex auditu* in Romans 10:14-17 and Galatians 3:2.

114. Julio Cézar Adam, *Romaria da Terra. Brasiliens Landkämpfer auf der Suche nach Lebensräumen. Eine empirisch-liturgiewissenschaftliche Untersuchung* (Stuttgart: Kohlhammer, 2005).

115. Ibid., 14, 63–65, 68ff., 100–104.

BIBLIOGRAPHY

Adam, Julio Cézar. *Romaria da Terra. Brasiliens Landkämpfer auf der Suche nach Lebens-räumen. Eine empirisch-liturgiewissenschaftliche Untersuchung.* Stuttgart: Kohlhammer, 2005.

Ahrens, Theodor. *Gegebenheiten. Missionswissenschaftliche Studien.* Frankfurt am Main: Lembeck, 2005.

Albrecht, Horst. *Arbeiter und Symbol: Soziale Homiletik im Zeitalter des Fernsehens.* Munich: Kaiser, 1982.

Allen, Ronald J., Scott Black Johnston, and Barbara Shires Blaisdell. *Theology for Preaching: Authority, Truth and Knowledge of God in a Postmodern Ethos.* Nashville: Abingdon, 1997.

Anderegg, Johannes. *Sprache und Verwandlung.* Göttingen: Vandenhoeck & Ruprecht, 1985.

———. "Über die Sprache des Alltags und Sprache im religiösen Bezug." *Zeitschrift für Theologie und Kirche* 95 (1988): 366–78.

Arendt, Hannah. *Vita activa oder Vom tätigen Leben.* 8th ed. Munich: Piper, 1996.

Augst, Kristina. *Religion in der Lebenswelt junger Frauen aus sozialen Unterschichten.* Stuttgart: Kohlhammer, 2000.

Austin, John L. *How to Do Things with Words.* Cambridge, Mass.: Harvard University Press, 1962. German: *Zur Theorie der Sprechakte.* Translated by Eike von Savigny. 2nd ed. with additional bibliography. Stuttgart: Reclam, 2002.

Bail, Ulrike, et al., eds. *Bibel in gerechter Sprache.* 2nd ed. Gütersloh: Gütersloher, 2006.

Barié, Helmut. *Predigt und Arbeitswelt. Analyse und praktische Anregungen.* Stuttgart: Calwer, 1989.

Barrico, Alessandro. *Hegels Seele oder die Kühe von Wisconsin. Nachdenken über Musik.* Munich and Zürich: Piper, 1999.

Barth, Hans-Martin. "Rechtfertigung und Identität." *Pastoraltheologie* 86 (1997): 88–102.

Barth, Karl. "Das Wort Gottes als Aufgabe der Theologie," 156–78, in idem, *Das Wort Gottes und die Theologie. Gesammelte Vorträge.* Vol. 1. Munich: Kaiser, 1924. English: *The Word of God and the Word of Man.* Translated by Douglas Horton. London: Hodder and Stoughton, 1928.

———. "Der Christ als Zeuge." *Theologische Existenz* 12 (Munich, 1934). Reprint in *Theologische Fragen und Antworten. Gesammelte Vorträge.* Vol. 3, 185–96. 2nd ed. Zürich: Evangelischer, 1986.

————. "Evangelium und Gesetz." *Theologische Existenz* 13 (Munich, 1935). Reprint in Ernst Kinder and Klaus Haendler, eds. *Gesetz und Evangelium. Beiträge zur gegenwärtigen theologischen Diskussion*, 1–29. Darmstadt: Wissenschaftliche Buchgesellschaft, 1968.

————. *Homiletik. Wesen und Vorbereitung der Predigt*. 3rd ed. Zürich: EVZ-Verlag, 1986.

————. *Kirchliche Dogmatik*. Vol. I/1. *Die Lehre vom Wort Gottes. Prolegomena zur Kirchlichen Dogmatik, Erster Halbband*. 6th ed. Zollikon-Zürich: Evangelischer Verlag, 1952. English: *Church Dogmatics*. Edited by Geoffrey W. Bromiley and T. F. Torrance. Edinburgh: T & T Clark, 1975–.

————. *Kirchliche Dogmatik*. Vol. II/1. *Die Lehre von Gott. Erster Halbband*. 3rd ed. Zollikon-Zürich: Evangelischer, 1948.

————. *Kirchliche Dogmatik*. Vol. IV/2. *Die Lehre von der Versöhnung. Zweiter Teil*. Zollikon-Zürich: Evangelischer, 1955.

Barth, Ulrich, and Wilhelm Gräb, eds. *Gott im Selbstbewusstsein der Moderne. Zum neuzeitlichen Begriff der Religion*. Gütersloh: Gütersloher Verlagshaus Mohn, 1993.

Bataille, George. *Das theoretische Werk*. Vol. 1: *Die Aufhebung der Ökonomie*. Munich: Rogner & Bernhard, 1975.

Baumgarten, Otto. *Predigt-Probleme. Hauptfragen der heutigen Evangeliumsverkündigung*. Tübingen: Mohr, 1905.

Bayer, Oswald. "Was macht die Bibel zur Heiligen Schrift? Luthers Verständnis der Schriftautorität," 24–41. In Michael Krug, Ruth Lödel, and Johannes Rehm, eds. *Beim Wort nehmen. Die Schrift als Zentrum für kirchliches Reden und Gestalten. Friedrich Mildenberger zum 75. Geburtstag*. Stuttgart: Kohlhammer, 2004.

Beck, Ulrich. "Die uneindeutige Sozialstruktur. Was heißt Armut, was heißt Reichtum in der Selbstkultur?" In idem and Peter Sopp. *Individualisierung und Integration. Neue Konfliktlinien und neuer Integrationsmodus?* Opladen: Leske & Budrich, 1997.

————. *Risikogesellschaft. Auf dem Weg in eine andere Moderne*. Frankfurt am Main: Suhrkamp, 1986.

Becker-Schmidt, Regina. "Identitätslogik und Gewalt. Zum Verhältnis von Kritischer Theorie und Feminismus." *Beiträge zur Feministischen Theorie und Praxis* 12, no. 24 (1989): 51–64.

Biehl, Peter. *Symbole geben zu lernen. Einführung in die Symboldidaktik anhand der Symbole Hand, Haus, und Weg*. Neukirchen: Neukirchener, 1989.

Bieler, Andrea. *Die Sehnsucht nach dem verlorenen Himmel. Jüdische und christliche Reflexionen zu Gottesdienstreform und Predigtkultur im 19. Jahrhundert*. Stuttgart: Kohlhammer, 2003.

————. "'Wenn der ganze Haufen miteinander betet.' Über die Brüchigkeit und die Unverzichtbarkeit des liturgischen Wir." *Zeitschrift für Gottesdienst und Predigt* 3 (2001): 11–12.

————. "Das bewegte Wort. Auf dem Weg zu einer performativen Homiletik." *Pastoraltheologie* 7 (2006): 268–83.

————. "Das Denken der Zweigeschlechtlichkeit in der Praktischen Theologie." *Pastoraltheologie* 7 (1999): 274–88.

—. "Embodied Knowing: Understanding Religious Experience in Ritual," 39–60. In Hans Günter Heimbrock and Christopher Scholtz, eds. *Religion: Immediate Experience and the Mediacy of Research: Interdisciplinary Studies, Concepts and Methodology of Empirical Research in Religion*. Göttingen: Vandenhoeck & Ruprecht, 2007.

—. *Gottesdienst interkulturell. Predigen und Gottesdienst feiern im Zwischenraum*. Stuttgart: Kohlhammer, 2008.

—. "Ich habe Angst—Die Predigt vom Kreuz im narzißtischen Zeitalter," 132–49. In Benita Joswig and Claudia Janssen, eds. *Erinnern und Aufstehen. Antworten auf Kreuzestheologien*. Mainz: Matthias Grünewald, 2000.

—. "This is my Body—This is my Blood: Inventing Authority in Liturgical Discourse and Practice," 143–54. In *Yearbook of the European Society of Women in Theological Research*. Leuven: Peeters, 2005.

Beiler, Andrea, and Luise Schottroff. *Das Abendmahl. Essen, um zu leben*. Gütersloh: Gütersloher, 2007. English: *The Eucharist: Bodies, Bread, and Resurrection*. Translated by Linda M. Maloney. Minneapolis: Fortress Press, 2007.

Bizer, Christoph. "Die Schule hier—die Bibel dort. Gestaltpädagogische Elemente in der Religionspädagogik," 31–49. In idem, *Kirchgänge im Unterricht und anderswo. Zur Gestaltwerdung von Religion*. Göttingen: Vandenhoeck & Ruprecht, 1995.

—. "Liturgie und Didaktik." *Jahrbuch der Religionspädagogik*. Vol 5 (1988): 83–115.

—. "Verheißung als religionspädagogische Kategorie." *Wissenschaft und Praxis in Kirche und Gesellschaft PKG* 68, no. 9 (1979): 347–58.

Böhme, Gernot. *Atmosphäre. Essays zur neuen Ästhetik*. Frankfurt am Main: Suhrkamp, 1995.

Bohren, Rudolf. *Daß Gott schön werde. Praktische Theologie als theologische Ästhetik*. Munich: Kaiser, 1975.

—. *Predigtlehre*. 6th ed. Gütersloh: Kaiser, 1993.

Bornkamm, Karin, and Gerhard Ebeling, eds. *Martin Luther. Ausgewählte Schriften*. Vol. 1. Frankfurt am Main: Insel, 1982.

Boulton, Matthew. "Forsaking God: A Theological Argument for Christian Lamentation." *Scottish Journal of Theology* 55, no. 1 (2002): 58–78.

Brecht, Bertolt. "Ballade über die Frage: Wovon lebt der Mensch?" In idem, *Die Dreigroschenoper*. 40th ed. Frankfurt am Main: Suhrkamp, 1968.

Breckner, Ingrid, and Andrea Kirchmair, eds. *Innovative Handlungsansätze im Wohnbereich—Informationen über Projekte, Träger und Initiativen*. Dortmund: Dortmunder Vertrieb für Bau- und Planungsliteratur, 1995.

Brown, Malcolm, and Peter Sedgwick, eds. *Putting Theology to Work: A Theological Symposium on Unemployment and the Future of Work*. London: CCBI, 1998.

Bukowski, Peter. *Predigt wahrnehmen. Homiletische Perspektiven*. Neukirchen-Vluyn: Neukirchener, 1990.

Butler, Judith. *Hass spricht. Zur Politik des Performativen*. Frankfurt am Main: Suhrkamp, 2006. English original: *Excitable Speech: A Politics of the Performative*. New York: Routledge, 1997.

————. "Kontingente Grundlagen: Der Feminismus und die Frage der 'Postmoderne,'" 31–58. In Seyla Benhabib, Judith Butler, Drucilla Cornell, and Nancy Fraser. *Der Streit um die Differenz. Feminismus und Postmoderne in der Gegenwart.* Frankfurt am Main: Fischer, 1993.

Capps, Donald. *The Depleted Self: Sin in a Narcissistic Age.* Minneapolis: Fortress Press, 1993.

Childers, Jana. *Birthing the Sermon: Women Preachers on the Creative Process.* St. Louis: Chalice, 2001.

————. *Performing the Word: Preaching as Theatre.* Nashville: Abingdon, 1998.

Cornehl, Peter. *Der Evangelische Gottesdienst. Biblische Konturen und neuzeitliche Wirklichkeit.* Vol. 1. Stuttgart: Kohlhammer, 2006.

Cornehl, Peter, and Wolfgang Grünberg. "'Plädoyer für den Normalfall'—Chancen der Ortsgemeinde. Überlegungen im Anschluss an Ernst Lange," 119–34. In Sönke Abeldt and Walter Bauer, eds. *". . . was es bedeutet, verletzbarer Mensch zu sein." Erziehungswissenschaft im Gespräch mit Theologie, Philosophie und Gesellschaftstheorie. Helmut Peukert zum 65. Geburtstag.* Mainz: Matthias Grünewald, 2000.

Cornelius-Bundschuh, Jochen. *Die Kirche des Wortes. Zum evangelischen Predigt- und Gemeindeverständnis.* Göttingen: Vandenhoeck & Ruprecht, 2001.

Couture, Pamela. *Blessed Are the Poor? Women's Poverty, Family Policy and Practical Theology.* Nashville: Abingdon, in cooperation with the Churches' Center for Theology and Public Policy, Washington, D.C., 1991.

————. *Seeing Children, Seeing God: A Practical Theology of Children and Poverty.* Nashville: Abingdon, 2000.

Craddock, Fred B. *As One without Authority.* Rev. and with New Sermons. 4th ed. St. Louis: Chalice, 2001.

Cremer, August Hermann. *Die christliche Lehre von den Eigenschaften Gottes.* Gütersloh: Bertelsmann, 1897.

Crüsemann, Frank. "Gottes Fürsorge und menschliche Arbeit. Ökonomie und soziale Gerechtigkeit in biblischer Sicht," 43–63. In Rainer Kessler and Eva Loos, eds. *Eigentum: Freiheit und Fluch. Ökonomische und biblische Einwürfe.* Gütersloh: Kaiser, 2000.

Csikszentmihalyi, Mihaly. *Flow: Studies of Enjoyment.* Chicago: University of Chicago Press, 1974.

Daiber, Karl Fritz, et al. *Predigen und Hören. Ergebnisse einer Gottesdienstbefragung.* Part 2, 124–86. Munich: Kaiser, 1983.

Deeg, Alexander. *Predigt und Derascha. Homiletische Textlektüre im Dialog mit dem Judentum.* Göttingen: Vandenhoeck & Ruprecht, 2006.

Die Bekenntnisschriften der evangelisch-lutherischen Kirche. 12th ed. Göttingen: Vandenhoeck & Ruprecht, 1998.

Dierken, Jörg. *Selbstbewusstsein individueller Freiheit. Religionstheoretische Erkundungen in protestantischer Perspektive.* Tubingen: Mohr Siebeck, 2005.

Dinkel, Christoph. *Freiheitssphären—Vertrauensräume. Predigten.* Stuttgart: Betulius, 2005.

Drews, Paul. *Die Predigt im 19. Jahrhundert. Kritische Bemerkungen und Praktische Winke.* Gießen: J. Ricker, 1903.

Ebach, Jürgen. "Biblisch-ethische Überlegungen zur Armut," 203–16. In idem, . . . *und behutsam mitgehen mit deinem Gott. Theologische Reden 3.* Bochum: SWB, 1995.

Ebeling, Gerhard. "Die Bedeutung der historisch-kritischen Methode für die protestantische Theologie und Kirche." *Zeitschrift für Theologie und Kirche* 47 (1950): 1–46.

Engemann, Wilfried. *Einführung in die Homiletik: Theoretische Grundlagen, Methodische Ansätze, Analytische Zugänge.* Stuttgart: UTB; Tübingen: Francke, 2002.

———. "On Man's Re-Entry into his Future: The Sermon as a Creative Act," 25–49. In Gerrit Immink and Ciska Stark, eds. *Preaching: Creating Perspective.* Studia Homiletica 4. Utrecht: Societas Homiletica, 2002.

———. "Predigen und Zeichen setzen," 7–24. In Uta Pohl-Patalong and Frank Muchlinsky, eds. *Predigen im Plural.* Hamburg: EB-Verlag, 2001.

Failing, Wolf-Eckart, and Hans-Günter Heimbrock. *Gelebte Religion wahrnehmen. Lebenswelt—Alltagskultur—Religionspraxis.* Stuttgart: Kohlhammer, 1998.

Fichte, Johann Gottlieb. *Die Wissenschaftslehre. Zweite Vorlesung im Jahr 1804.* Philosophische Bibliothek 284. Hamburg: Meiner, 1986.

———. "Über den Grund des Glaubens an eine göttliche Weltregierung" (1798), 347–57. In I. H. Fichte, ed. *Johann Gottlieb Fichte Werke,* vol. 5. Berlin: Veit, 1845–46. Reprint, Berlin: de Gruyter, 1971.

Fischer-Lichte, Erika. "Performativität und Ereignis," 11–37. In idem, Christian Horn, Sandra Umathum, and Matthias Warstat, eds. *Performativität und Ereignis.* Tübingen: Francke, 2003.

Foucault, Michel. *Von der Subversion des Wissens.* Translated by Walter Seitter. Frankfurt am Main: Fischer, 1987.

Fowler, James W. *Becoming Adult, Becoming Christian: Adult Development and Christian Faith.* San Francisco: Harper & Row, 1984.

Frettlöh, Magdalene. *Gott Gewicht geben. Bausteine einer geschlechtergerechten Gotteslehre.* Neukirchen-Vluyn: Neukirchener, 2006.

Freud, Sigmund. "Der Traum," 67–192. In idem, *Vorlesungen zur Einführung in die Psychoanalyse* (1916–17). Frankfurt am Main: Fischer, 1980.

———. *Kulturtheoretische Schriften.* Frankfurt am Main: Fischer, 1974.

Friedrich, Marcus A. *Liturgische Körper. Der Beitrag von Schauspieltheorien und–techniken für die Pastoralästhetik.* Stuttgart: Kohlhammer, 2001.

Garrigan, Siobhán. *Beyond Ritual: Sacramental Theology after Habermas.* Aldershot and Burlington: Ashgate, 2004.

Geest, Hans van der. *Das Wort geschieht. Wege zur seelsorgerlichen Predigt.* Zürich: Theologischer, 1991.

———. "Von Himmel und Erde. Glaube an Gott aus einer individuellen Sicht." Unpublished text.

Glatzer, Wolfgang, and Werner Hübinger. "Lebenslagen und Armut," 31–55. In Diether Döring et al., eds. *Armut im Wohlstand.* Frankfurt am Main: Suhrkamp, 1990.

Gräb, Wilhelm. *Predigt als Mitteilung des Glaubens. Studien zu einer prinzipiellen Homiletik in praktischer Absicht.* Gütersloh: Gütersloher Verlagshaus Gerd Mohn, 1988.

———. *Religion als Deutung des Lebens. Perspektiven einer Praktischen Theologie gelebter Religion.* Gütersloh: Gütersloher, 2006.

Gräb-Schmidt, Elisabeth. "'Die Kirche ist kein Unternehmen!' Die Rede vom 'Unternehmen Kirche' in ekklesiologischer Sicht," 65–80. In Joachim Fetzer et al., eds. *Kirche in der Marktgesellschaft.* Gütersloh: Kaiser, Gütersloher, 1999.

Grau, Marion. *Of Divine Economy: Refinancing Redemption.* New York: T&T Clark, 2004.

Grözinger, Albrecht. *Toleranz und Leidenschaft. Über das Predigen in einer pluralistischen Gesellschaft.* Gütersloh: Gütersloher, 2004.

Groh-Samberg, Olaf, and Matthias Grundmann. "Soziale Ungleichheit im Kindes- und Jugendalter. Bundeszentrale für politische Bildung." *Aus Politik und Zeitgeschichte* 26 (2006).

Grünberg, Wolfgang. *Die Sprache der Stadt. Skizzen zur Großstadtkirche.* Leipzig: Evangelische Verlagsanstalt, 2004.

———. "Die Stadt—Laboratorium der Zukunft," 9–73. In Barbara Deml-Groth et al., eds. *Ernst Lange weiterdenken. Impulse für die Kirche des 21. Jahrhunderts.* Berlin: Wichern, 2007.

Gumbrecht, Hals Ulrich. "Produktion von Präsenz, durchsetzt mit Absenz. Über Musik, Libretto und Inszenierung," 63–76. In Josef Früchtl und Jörg Zimmermann, eds. *Ästhetik der Inszenierung. Dimensionen eines künstlerischen, kulturellen und gesellschaftlichen Phänomens.* Frankfurt am Main: Suhrkamp, 2001.

Gutmann, Hans-Martin. *Und erlöse uns von dem Bösen. Die Chance der Seelsorge in Zeiten der Krise.* Gütersloh: Gütersloher, 2005.

———. "Kreuz," 322–33. In Wilhelm Gräb and Birgit Weyel, eds. *Handbuch Praktische Theologie.* Gütersloh: Gütersloher, 2007.

———. "Symbol," 1139–44. In Friedrich Wilhelm Horn and Friederike Nüssel, eds. *Taschenlexikon Religion und Theologie.* 5th ed. Göttingen: Vandenhoeck & Ruprecht, 2008.

———. "Der gute und der schlechte Tausch. Das Heilige und das Geld—gegensätzliche ökonomische Beziehungen?" 162–225. In Jürgen Ebach et al., eds. *"Leget Anmut in das Geben." Zum Verhältnis von Theologie und Ökonomie.* Jabboq 1. Gütersloh: Kaiser, 2001.

———. "Die Wahrnehmung der Gegenwart," 94–107. In idem et al., eds. *Theologisches geschenkt. Festschrift für Manfred Josuttis.* Bovenden: Foedus, 1996.

———. *Ich bin's nicht. Die Praktische Theologie vor der Frage nach dem Subjekt des Glaubens.* Neukirchen-Vluyn: Neukirchener, 1999.

———. "Praktische Theologie im neuen Jahrhundert—nichts Neues?" 67–78. In Eberhard Hauschildt and Ulrich Schwab, eds. *Praktische Theologie für das 21. Jahrhundert.* Stuttgart: Kohlhammer, 2002.

———. *Symbole zwischen Macht und Spiel.* Göttingen: Vandenhoeck & Ruprecht, 1996.

————. *Über Liebe und Herrschaft. Luthers Verständnis von Intimität und Autorität im Kontext des Zivilisationsprozesses.* Göttingen: Vandenhoeck & Ruprecht, 1991.

————. "Warum leben?—Keine Frage! Bemerkungen aus theologischer Besorgnis," 34–44. In Regula Venske, ed. *Warum leben? Ein Lesebuch.* Munich: Scherz, 2001.

Habermas, Jürgen. "Vorbereitende Bemerkungen zu einer Theorie des kommunikativen Kompetenz," 101–41. In Jürgen Habermas and Niklas Luhmann. *Theorie der Gesellschaft oder Sozialtechnologie. Was leistet die Systemforschung?* Frankfurt am Main: Suhrkamp, 1971.

Härle, Wilfried. *Menschsein in Beziehungen. Studien zur Rechtfertigungslehre und Anthropologie.* Tübingen: Mohr Siebeck, 2005.

Hauschildt, Eberhard. "'Gesetz' und 'Evangelium'—eine homiletische Kategorie? Überlegungen zur wechselvollen Geschichte eines lutherischen Schemas der Predigtlehre." *Pastoraltheologie* 80 (1991): 262–87.

Heimbrock, Hans-Günter. "Klang," 37–42. In Gotthard Fermor and Harald Schroeter-Wittke, eds. *Kirchenmusik als religiöse Praxis—praktisch-theologisches Handbuch zur Kirchenmusik.* Leipzig: Evangelische Verlagsanstalt, 2005.

————. *Spuren Gottes wahrnehmen. Phänomenologisch inspirierte Predigten und Texte zum Gottesdienst.* Stuttgart: Kohlhammer, 2003.

Hilkert, Mary Catherine. *Naming Grace: Preaching and the Sacramental Imagination.* New York: Continuum, 1997.

Hirsch, Emanuel. "Gottes Offenbarung in Gesetz und Evangelium," 76–83. In idem, *Christliche Freiheit und politische Bindung.* Göttingen: Vandenhoeck & Ruprecht, 1934.

Hirsch-Hüffell, Thomas. *Gottesdienst verstehen und selbst gestalten.* Göttingen: Vandenhoeck & Ruprecht, 2002.

Hohl, Joachim. "Zum Symptomwandel neurotischer Störungen: Sozialhistorische und sozialpsychologische Aspekte," 103–24. In Heiner Keupp and Helga Bilden, eds., *Verunsicherungen. Das Subjekt im gesellschaftlichen Wandel.* Münchener Beiträge zur Sozialpsychologie, Münchener Universitätsschriften. Psychologie und Pädagogik. Göttingen: C. J. Hogrefe, 1989.

Hope, Glenda, and River Sims. "Tenderloin Way of the Cross, San Francisco, 2006." Unpublished liturgy.

Huber, Wolfgang, Johannes Friedrich, and Peter Steinacker, eds. *Kirche in der Vielfalt der Lebensbezüge. Die vierte EKD-Erhebung über Kirchenmitgliedschaft.* Gütersloh: Gütersloher, 2006.

Hudson, Mary Lin, and Mary Donovan Turner. *Saved from Silence: Finding Women's Voice in Preaching.* St. Louis: Chalice, 1999.

Huster, Ernst-Ulrich. *Neuer Reichtum und alte Armut.* Düsseldorf: Patmos, 1993.

Iser, Wolfgang. *Der Akt des Lesens. Theorie ästhetischer Wirkung.* 4th ed. Munich: Fink, 1994.

Joest, Wilfried. *Ontologie der Person bei Luther.* Göttingen: Vandenhoeck & Ruprecht, 1963.

————. *Dogmatik*. Vol. 2: *Der Weg Gottes mit den Menschen*. Göttingen: Vandenhoeck & Ruprecht, 1986.

Josuttis, Manfred. "Der Prediger in der Predigt—sündiger Mensch oder mündiger Zeuge?" 70–94. In idem, *Praxis des Evangeliums zwischen Politik und Religion. Grundprobleme der Praktischen Theologie*. 3rd ed. Munich: Kaiser, 1983.

————. "Die Bibel als Basis der Predigt," 385–93. In Andreas Baudis et al., eds. *Richte unsere Füße auf den Weg des Friedens. Helmut Gollwitzer zum 70. Geburtstag*. Munich: Kaiser, 1978.

————. "Die Predigt des Evangeliums nach Luther," 42–65. In idem, *Gesetz und Evangelium in der Predigtarbeit*. Homiletische Studien 2. Gütersloh: Kaiser, 1995.

————. *Die Einführung in das Leben. Pastoraltheologie zwischen Phänomenologie und Spiritualität*. Gütersloh: Kaiser, 1996.

————. "Offene Geheimnisse. Ein homiletischer Essay," 7–15. In idem, *Offene Geheimnisse. Predigten*. Gütersloh: Kaiser, Gütersloher, 1999.

————. "Seelsorge im energetischen Netzwerk der Ortsgemeinde," 117–26. In idem et al., eds. *Auf dem Weg zu einer seelsorgerlichen Kirche. Theologische Bausteine*. Göttingen: Vandenhoeck & Ruprecht, 2000.

————. "Seelsorge in der Gemeinde." *Pastoraltheologie* 90 (2001): 400–408.

————. *Segenskräfte. Potentiale einer energetischen Seelsorge*. Gütersloh: Kaiser, Gütersloher, 2000.

————. "The Authority of the Word in the Liturgy: The Legacy of the Reformation," *Studia Liturgica* 22 (1992): 53–67.

————. "Über den Predigteinfall" (1970), 70–86. In idem, *Rhetorik und Theologie in der Predigtarbeit*. Homiletische Studien 1. Munich: Kaiser, 1985.

————. "Von der Identität zur Konversion," 65–78. In idem, *Segenskräfte* (2000).

Jüngel, Eberhard. *Das Evangelium von der Rechtfertigung des Gottlosen als Zentrum des christlichen Glaubens*. 4th rev. ed. Tübingen: Mohr Siebeck, 2004.

————. "Metaphorische Wahrheit. Erwägungen zur theologischen Relevanz der Metapher als Beitrag zur Hermeneutik einer narrativen Theologie," 71–122. In idem and Paul Ricoeur, eds. *Metapher. Zur Hermeneutik religiöser Sprache*. Munich: Kaiser, 1974.

Kabel, Thomas. *Handbuch Liturgische Präsenz. Zur Praktischen Inszenierung des Gottesdienstes*. Vol. 1. Gütersloh: Gütersloher, 2002.

Karle, Isolde. *"Da ist nicht mehr Mann noch Frau . . ." Theologie jenseits der Geschlechterdifferenz*. Gütersloh: Gütersloher, 2006.

Kautzsch, Emil, ed. *Die Apokryphen und Pseudepigraphen des Alten Testaments*. Vol. 2. Tübingen: Mohr, 1900.

Keller, Catherine. *Face of the Deep: A Theology of Becoming*. New York: Routledge, 2003.

Kempin, Susanna. *Leben ohne Arbeit? Wege der Bewältigung im pastoralpsychologischen und theologischen Deutungshorizont*. Münster and Hamburg: Lit, 2001.

Kessler, Rainer. "Armut, Eigentum und Freiheit. Die Frage des Grundeigentums in der Endgestalt der Prophetenbücher," 64–88. In idem and Eva Loos, eds. *Eigentum: Freiheit und Fluch. Ökonomische und biblische Entwürfe*. Gütersloh: Kaiser, 2000.

Keupp, Heiner. "Auf der Suche nach der verlorenen Identität," 131–51. In idem, *Riskante Chancen. Das Subjekt zwischen Psychokultur und Selbstorganisation.* Sozialpsychologische Studien. Heidelberg: Asanger, 1988.

Klie, Thomas. "Wort—Ereignis—Raum. Kirchenpädagogische Überlegungen zur Predigt." *Praktische Theologie* 35 (2000): 251–63.

Kohlberg, Lawrence. *Zur kognitiven Entwicklung des Kindes.* Frankfurt am Main: Suhrkamp, 1974. Translation of *Collected Papers on Moral Development and Moral Education.* Cambridge, Mass.: Harvard University Press, 1973.

Koll, Julia. *Körper beten. Religiöse Praxis und Körpererleben.* Stuttgart: Kohlhammer, 2007.

Körtner, Ulrich H. J. *Theologie des Wortes Gottes. Positionen—Probleme—Perspektiven.* 72–93. Göttingen: Vandenhoeck & Ruprecht, 2001.

Kuhlmann, Helga. "Abschied von der Perfektion. Überlegungen zu einer 'frauengerechten' Rechtfertigungstheologie," 97–122. In Irene Dingel, ed. *Feministische Theologie und Gender-Forschung: Bilanz, Perspektiven, Akzente.* Leipzig: Evangelische Verlagsanstalt, 2003.

———. *Leib-Leben theologisch denken. Reflexionen zur theologischen Anthropologie.* Münster: Lit, 2004.

Lacan, Jacques. *Écrits.* Paris: Éditions du Seuil, 1966–71. German: *Schriften.* Vol. 1 (1966). Weinheim and Berlin: Quadriga, 1973. English: *Écrits: The First Complete Edition in English.* Translated by Bruce Fink in collaboration with Héloïse Fink and Russell Grigg. New York: Norton, 2006.

Landau, Elisabeth. *Psychologie der Kreativität.* Munich, et al.: Reinhardt, 1969.

Lange, Ernst. *Die verbesserliche Welt. Möglichkeiten christlicher Rede erprobt an der Geschichte des Propheten Jona.* Stuttgart: Kreuz, 1968.

———. "Zur Theorie und Praxis der Predigtarbeit," 9–51. In idem, *Predigen als Beruf.* Stuttgart and Berlin: Kreuz, 1976.

Lasch, Christopher. *The Culture of Narcissism: American Life in an Age of Diminishing Expectations.* New York: Warner, 1979.

Lauster, Jörg. *Gott und das Glück. Das Schicksal des guten Lebens im Christentum.* Gütersloh: Gütersloher, 2004.

Leonhard, Silke. *Leiblich lernen und lehren. Ein religionsdidaktischer Diskurs.* Stuttgart: Kohlhammer, 2006.

Lepenies, Wolf. *Soziologische Anthropologie. Materialien.* Munich: Hanser, 1971.

Lessing, Gotthold Ephraim. "Über den Beweis des Geistes und der Kraft," 9–14. In idem, *Werke*, vol. 8, *Theologiekritische Schriften.* Edited by Herbert G. Göpfert. Munich: Hanser, 1979.

Leutzsch, Martin. "Das biblische Zinsverbot," 107–44. In Rainer Kessler and Eva Loos, eds. *Eigentum: Freiheit und Fluch. Ökonomische und biblische Einwürfe.* Gütersloh: Kaiser, 2000.

Lévinas, Emmanuel. *Vier Talmud-Lesungen* (Orig.: *Quatre lectures talmudiques.* Paris, 1968). Frankfurt am Main: Verlag Neue Kritik, 2003.

Lorenzer, Alfred. *Das Konzil der Buchhalter. Die Zerstörung der Sinnlichkeit. Eine Religionskritik.* Frankfurt am Main: Europäische Verlagsanstalt, 1988.

Löw, Martina. *Raumsoziologie*. Frankfurt am Main: Suhrkamp, 2001.

Luther, Henning. "Ich ist ein Anderer." Zur Subjektfrage in der Praktischen Theologie," 62–87. In idem, *Religion und Alltag* (1992).

———. "Identität und Fragment. Praktisch-theologische Überlegungen zur Unabschließbarkeit von Bildungsprozessen," 160–82. In idem, *Religion und Alltag* (1992).

———. "Predigt als inszenierter Text. Überlegungen zur Kunst der Predigt." *Theologia Practica* 18 (1983): 89–100.

———. *Religion und Alltag. Bausteine zu einer Praktischen Theologie des Subjekts.* Stuttgart: Radius, 1992.

———. "Umstrittene Identität. Zum Leitbild der Bildung," 150–59. In idem, *Religion und Alltag* (1992).

Luther, Martin. All citations from *D. Martin Luthers Werke. Kritische Gesamtausgabe.* Weimar: Böhlau, 1883– (= *WA*). Idem, *Studienausgabe*, ed. Hans-Ulrich Delius. Leipzig: Evangelische Verlagsanstalt, 1979– (= *StA*).

Lütze, Frank M. *Absicht und Wirkung der Predigt. Eine Untersuchung zur homiletischen Pragmatik.* Leipzig: Evangelische Verlagsanstalt, 2006.

Martin, Gerhard Marcel, "Predigt als 'offenes Kunstwerk.'" *Evangelische Theologie* 44 (1984): 46–58.

———. *Sachbuch Bibliodrama. Praxis und Theorie.* Stuttgart: Kohlhammer, 1995.

Mauss, Marcel. *Soziologie und Anthropologie.* Vol. 2. Frankfurt am Main: Ullstein, 1978.

McClure, John S. *Otherwise Preaching: A Postmodern Ethic for Homiletics.* St. Louis: Chalice, 2001.

McFee, Marcia. *Primal Patterns: Ritual Dynamics, Ritual Resonance, Polyrhythmic Strategies and the Formation of Christian Disciples.* Unpublished dissertation, Graduate Theological Union, Berkeley, Calif., 2005.

McMickle, Marvin A. *Where Have All the Prophets Gone? Reclaiming Prophetic Preaching in America.* Cleveland: Pilgrim, 2006.

Mechiltha. Ein tannaitischer Midrasch zu Exodus. Erstmalig ins Deutsche übersetzt und erläutert von Jakob Winter und August Wünsche. Leipzig: Hinrichs, 1909.

Meeks, Wayne A. "The Image of the Androgyne: Some Uses of a Symbol in Earliest Christianity." *History of Religions* 13 (1974): 165–208.

Mette, Norbert, and Hermann Steinkamp, eds. *Anstiftung zur Solidarität. Praktische Beispiele der Sozialpastoral.* Mainz: Matthias Grünewald, 1997.

———. "Anstiftung zur Solidarität—zur not-wendenden Aufgabe der christlichen Gemeinde heute," 325–36. In idem, *Praktisch-theologische Erkundungen*, vol. 2. Berlin and Münster: Lit, 2007.

Meyer-Blanck, Michael. "Die Predigt in Raum und Ritual." *Praktische Theologie* 34 (1999): 163–73.

———. "Liturgische Rollen," 778–86. In Hans-Christoph Schmidt-Lauber, Michael Meyer-Blanck, and Karl-Heinz Bieritz, eds. *Handbuch der Liturgie.* Göttingen: Vandenhoeck & Ruprecht, 2003.

Moxter, Michael. *Kultur als Lebenswelt. Studien zum Problem einer Kulturtheologie.* Tübingen: Mohr Siebeck, 2000.

———. "Rechtfertigung und Anerkennung. Zur kulturellen Bedeutung der Unterscheidung zwischen Person und Werk," 20–42. In Hans Martin Dober and Dagmar Mensink, eds. *Die Lehre von der Rechtfertigung des Gottlosen im kulturellen Kontext der Gegenwart. Beiträge im Horizont des christlich-jüdischen Gesprächs.* Stuttgart: Akademie der Diözese Rottenburg-Stuttgart, et al., 2002.

Müller, Hans-Martin. *Homiletik. Eine evangelische Predigtlehre.* Berlin: de Gruyter, 1996.

Neumann, Ingrid. "Gestalttherapie und Predigtarbeit," 118–28. In Franz Kamphaus and Rolf Zerfaß, eds. *Ethische Predigt und Alltagsverhalten.* Munich: Kaiser, 1986.

Nicol, Martin. *Einander ins Bild setzen. Dramaturgische Homiletik.* Göttingen: Vandenhoeck & Ruprecht, 2002.

———. "To Make Things Happen. Homiletische Praxisimpulse aus den USA," 46–54. In Uta Pohl-Patalong and Frank Muchlinsky, eds. *Predigen im Plural. Homiletische Perspektiven.* Hamburg: EB-Verlag, 2001.

Nicol, Martin, and Alexander Deeg. *Im Wechselschritt zur Kanzel. Praxisbuch Dramaturgische Homiletik.* Göttingen: Vandenhoeck & Ruprecht, 2005.

Niebergall, Friedrich. *Die moderne Predigt: kulturgeschichtliche und theologische Grundlage, Geschichte und Ertrag.* Tübingen: Mohr, 1929.

———. *Wie predigen wir dem modernen Menschen?* 3 parts. Tübingen: Mohr, 1905–1921.

Okeke, Ossai. "The Message to the Poor." Unpublished sermon.

Otto, Gert. *Predigt als Rede. Über die Wechselwirkungen von Homiletik und Rhetorik.* Stuttgart: Kohlhammer, 1976.

———. "Predigt als Sprache. Eine Zusammenfassung in sechs kommentierten Thesen," 259–80. In Wilfried Engemann and Frank M. Lütze, eds. *Grundfragen der Predigt. Ein Studienbuch.* Leipzig: Evangelische Verlagsanstalt, 2006.

Ouaknin, Marc-Alain. *Das verbrannte Buch. Den Talmud lesen.* Weinheim: Quadriga, 1990. (French original: *Le livre brûlé: Lire le Talmud.* Paris: Lieu commun, 1986. English: *The Burnt Book: Reading the Talmud.* Translated by Llewellyn Brown. Princeton: Princeton University Press, 1995.)

Petersen, Silke. *Brot, Licht und Weinstock. Intertextuelle Analysen johanneischer Ich-bin-Worte.* Leiden: Brill, 2008.

Peterson, Eugene H. *The Message: The Bible in Contemporary Language.* Colorado Springs: NavPress, 2002.

Plüss, David. *Gottesdienst als Textinszenierung. Perspektiven einer performativen Ästhetik des Gottesdienstes.* Zürich: Theologischer, 2007.

Pohl-Patalong, Uta. *Bibliolog. Gemeinsam die Bibel entdecken im Gottesdienst—in der Gemeinde—in der Schule.* Stuttgart: Kohlhammer, 2005.

———. "Das schwarze Feuer achten, das weiße Feuer schützen. Inspirationen und Reflexionen zu einem Predigen mit der ganzen Gemeinde," 354–64. In Michael Krug, Ruth Lödel, and Johannes Rehm, eds. *Beim Wort nehmen—die Schrift als Zen-*

trum für kirchliches Reden und Gestalten. Friedrich Mildenberger zum 75. Geburtstag. Stuttgart: Kohlhammer, 2004.

———. *Ortsgemeinde und übergemeindliche Arbeit im Konflikt. Eine Analyse der Argumentationen und ein alternatives Modell.* Göttingen: Vandenhoeck & Ruprecht, 2003.

Raguse, Hartmut. *Der Raum des Textes. Elemente einer transdisziplinären theologischen Hermeneutik.* Stuttgart: Kohlhammer, 1994.

Resner, André, ed. *Just Preaching: Prophetic Voices for Economic Justice.* St. Louis: Chalice, 2003.

Ricoeur, Paul. *Die lebendige Metapher.* Munich: Zink, 1988. German translation of *La métaphore vive.* Paris: Seuil, 1975. English: *The Rule of Metaphor. Multidisciplinary Studies of the Creation of Meaning in Language.* Translated by Robert Czerny. Toronto: University of Toronto Press, 1981.

Roest, Henk de. *Communicative Identity. Habermas' Perspectives of Discourse as a Support for Practical Theology.* Kampen: Kok, 1998.

Roth, Michael, "Homo incurvatus in se ipsum—Der sich selbst verachtende Mensch. Narzissmustheorie und theologische Hamartiologie." *Praktische Theologie* 33 (1998): 14–33.

Rothschildt, Berthold. "Der neue Narzißmus—Theorie oder Ideologie?" 31–68. In *Die neuen Narzißmustheorien: Zurück ins Paradies,"* edited by Gabi Döhmann-Höh for the Psychoanaytisches Seminar Zürich. Frankfurt am Main: Syndikat, 1981; Hamburg: Europäische Verlagsanstalt, 1993.

Rudolph, Enno. "Metapher oder Symbol. Zum Streit um die schönste Form der Wahrheit. Anmerkungen zu einem möglichen Dialog zwischen Hans Blumenberg und Ernst Cassirer," 320–28. In Reinhold Bernhardt and Ulrike Link-Wieczorek, eds. *Metapher und Wirklichkeit. Die Logik der Bildhaftigkeit im Reden von Gott, Mensch und Natur. Dietrich Ritschl zum 70. Geburtstag.* Göttingen: Vandenhoeck & Ruprecht, 1999.

Ruster, Thomas. "Geld," 670–75. In Norbert Mette et al., eds. *Lexikon der Religionspädagogik.* Neukirchen-Vluyn: Neukirchener, 2001.

Schibilsky, Michael. *Alltagswelt und Sonntagskirche. Sozialethisch orientierte Gemeindearbeit im Industriegebiet.* Munich: Kaiser; Mainz: Matthias Grünewald, 1983.

Schleiermacher, Friedrich D. E. *Die praktische Theologie nach den Grundsätzen der evangelischen Kirche im Zusammenhange dargestellt.* Edited by Jacob Frerichs. In *Schleiermachers sämmtliche Werke*, Part 1, Vol. 13. Berlin: Reimer, 1850.

Schmid, Wilhelm. *Schönes Leben? Eine Einführung in die Lebenskunst.* Frankfurt am Main: Suhrkamp, 2000.

Schmidt, Clayton, and Jana Childers, eds. *Performance in Preaching: Bringing the Sermon to Life.* Grand Rapids: Baker Academic, 2008.

Schmitz, Hermann. *System der Philosophie.* Vol. 1: *Die Gegenwart.* Bonn: Bouvier, 1964.

Schneiders, Sandra M. *The Revelatory Text: Interpreting the New Testament as Sacred Scripture.* New ed. Collegeville, Minn.: Liturgical, 1999.

Schoberth, Ingrid. "Aufmerksamkeit für die Spur des Anderen: zum Alltag der Seelsorge," 264–74. In Heinz-Dieter Neef, ed. *Theologie und Gemeinde: Beiträge zu Bibel, Gottesdienst, Predigt und Seelsorge.* Stuttgart: Calwer, 2006.

Schottroff, Luise. *Die Gleichnisse Jesu.* Gütersloh: Gütersloher, 2005. English: *The Parables of Jesus.* Translated by Linda M. Maloney. Minneapolis: Fortress Press, 2006.

———. "Die Schreckensherrschaft der Sünde und die Befreiung durch Christus nach dem Römerbrief des Paulus," 57–72. In idem, *Befreiungserfahrungen. Studien zur Sozialgeschichte des Neuen Testaments.* Munich: Kaiser, 1990.

Schramm, Tim. *Die Bibel ins Leben ziehen. Bewährte "alte" und faszinierende "neue" Methoden lebendiger Bibelarbeit.* Stuttgart: Kohlhammer, 2003.

———. "Schwarzes und weißes Feuer," 231–39. In Friedemann Green et al., eds. *Um der Hoffnung willen. Praktische Theologie mit Leidenschaft. FS für Wolfgang Grünberg.* Hamburg: EB-Verlag, 2000.

Schroeter-Wittke, Harald. "Übergang statt Untergang. Victor Turners Bedeutung für eine kulturtheologische Praxistheorie." *Theologische Literaturzeitung* 128 (2003): 575–88.

———. *Unterhaltung. Praktisch-theologische Exkursionen zum homiletischen und kulturellen Bibelgebrauch im 19. und 20. Jahrhundert anhand der Figur Elia.* Frankfurt am Main: Peter Lang, 2000.

Schweizer, Alexander. *Homiletik der evangelisch-protestantischen Kirche systematisch dargestellt.* Leipzig: Weidmann, 1848.

Searle, John R. *Speech Acts: An Essay in the Philosophy of Language.* London: Cambridge University Press, 1969.

Sennett, Richard. *The Fall of Public Man.* New York: Knopf, 1977.

Seters, Arthur van. "To What Do Preachers Appeal?" 99–118. In idem, *Preaching and Ethics.* St. Louis: Chalice, 2004.

Sidorow, Waldemar. *Gemeinden geben Raum für andere am Beispiel von Aids-Betroffenen in Hamburg und Obdachlosen in Berlin.* Schenefeld: EB-Verlag, 2005.

Sölle, Dorothee. *Mystik und Widerstand. "Du stilles Geschrei."* 5th ed. Hamburg: Hoffmann und Campe, 1999. English: *The Silent Cry: Mysticism and Resistance.* Translated by Barbara and Martin Rumscheidt. Minneapolis: Fortress Press, 2001.

Steffensky, Fulbert. *Der alltägliche Charme des Glaubens.* Würzburg: Echter, 2002.

———. *Schwarzbrot-Spiritualität.* Stuttgart: Radius, 2005.

Stegemann, Eckehard W., and Wolfgang Stegemann. *Urchristliche Sozialgeschichte: die Anfänge im Judentum und die Christusgemeinden in der mediterranen Welt.* Stuttgart: Kohlhammer, 1997. English: *The Jesus Movement: A Social History of its First Century.* Trans. O. C. Dean Jr. Minneapolis: Fortress Press, 1999.

Suchocki, Marjorie Hewitt. *In God's Presence: Theological Reflections on Prayer.* St. Louis: Chalice, 1996.

Tamez, Elsa. *The Amnesty of Grace: Justification by Faith from a Latin American Perspective.* Translated by Sharon H. Ringe. Nashville: Abingdon, 1993.

Taylor, Mark L. "Polyrhythm in Worship: Caribbean Keys to an Effective Word of God 108-128." In Leonora Tubbs Tisdale, ed. *Making Room at the Table: An Invitation to Multicultural Worship.* Louisville: Westminster John Knox, 2001.

Thurneysen, Eduard. "Die Aufgabe der Predigt" (1921), 105–19. In Gerd Hummel, ed. *Aufgabe der Predigt.* Darmstadt: Wissenschaftliche Buchgesellschaft, 1971.

Tietz, Christiane. *Freiheit zu sich selbst. Entfaltung eines christlichen Begriffs der Selbstannahme.* Göttingen: Vandenhoeck & Ruprecht, 2005.

Tillich, Paul. "Das religiöse Symbol" (1928). In *Gesammelte Werke 5.* Stuttgart: Evangelisches Verlagswerk, 1959.

Tobler, Sybille. *Arbeitslose beraten unter Perspektiven der Hoffnung. Lösungsorientierte Kurzberatung in beruflichen Übergangsprozessen.* Stuttgart: Kohlhammer, 2004.

Tolbert, Mary Ann. "Reading the Bible with Authority: Feminist Interrogation of the Canon," 141–62. In Harold C. Washington, Susan Lochrie Graham, and Pamela Thimmes, eds. *Escaping Eden: New Feminist Perspectives on the Bible.* Sheffield: Sheffield Academic Press, 1998.

Türcke, Christoph. *Kassensturz. Zur Lage der Theologie.* Frankfurt am Main: Fischer, 1992.

Turner, Mary Donovan. "Disrupting a Ruptured World," 131–40. In Jana Childers, ed. *Purposes of Preaching.* St. Louis: Chalice, 2004.

Turner, Victor. *From Ritual to Theatre: The Human Seriousness of Play.* New York: Performing Arts Journal Publications, 1982.

Ulanov, Ann Belford. *Finding Space: Winnicott, God, and Psychic Reality.* Louisville: Westminster John Knox, 2001.

Webb, Stephen H. *The Divine Voice: Christian Proclamation and the Theology of Sound.* Grand Rapids: Brazos, 2004.

Wheelwright, Philip. "Semantik und Ontologie," 106–19. In *Theorie der Metapher,* ed. Anselm Haverkamp. 2nd ed. Darmstadt: Wissenschaftliche Buchgesellschaft, 1996.

Winnicott, Donald W. *Reifungsprozesse und fördernde Umwelt. Studien zur Theorie der emotionalen Entwicklung.* Munich: Kindler, 1974. German translation of: *The Maturational Processes and the Facilitating Environment: Studies in the Theory of Emotional Development.* New York: International Universities Press, 1965.

Wolf-Withöft, Susanne. *Predigen lernen. Homiletische Konturen einer praktisch-theologischen Spieltheorie.* Stuttgart: Kohlhammer, 2002.

Woydack, Tobias. *Der räumliche Gott. Was sind Kirchengebäude theologisch?* Hamburg: Schenefeld EB-Verlag, 2005.

Zerfass, Rolf. *Grundkurs Predigt.* Vol. 1, *Spruchpredigt.* 2nd ed. Düsseldorf: Patmos, 1989.

INDEX

Related titles from Fortress Press

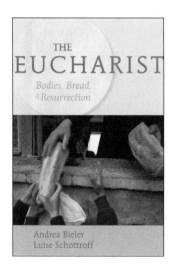

The Eucharist
Bodies, Bread, and Resurrection
Andrea Bieler and Luise Schottroff
Paperback, 256 pages
978-0-8006-3867-2

Trauma Recalled
Liturgy, Distruption, and Theology
Dirk Lange
Hardcover, 220 pages
978-0-8006-6462-6

Related titles from Fortress Press

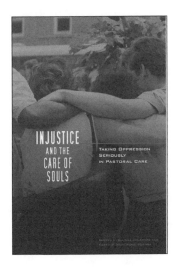

Injustice and the Care of Souls
Taking Oppression Seriously
in Pastoral Care
Sheryl A. Kujawa-Holbrook and
Karen B. Montagno
Paperback, 352 pages
978-0-8006-6235-6

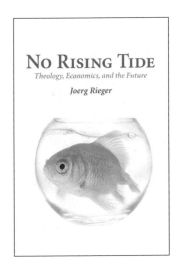

No Rising Tide
Theology, Economics, and the Future
Joerg Rieger
Paperback, 208 pages
978-0-8006-6459-6

Related titles from Fortress Press

Kairos Preaching
Speaking Gospel to the Situation
David Schnasa Jacobsen and Robert Allen
      Kelly
Paperback, 176 pages
978-0-8006-6250-9

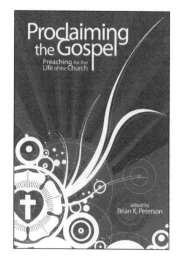

Proclaiming the Gospel
Preaching for the Life of the Church
Brian K. Peterson
Paperback, 208 pages
978-0-8006-6331-5